United States Coast Guard
Leaders and Missions,
1790 to the Present

ALSO BY THOMAS P. OSTROM

*The United States Coast Guard and
National Defense: A History from
World War I to the Present* (McFarland, 2012)

*The United States Coast Guard in
World War II: A History of Domestic and
Overseas Actions* (McFarland, 2009)

United States Coast Guard Leaders and Missions, 1790 to the Present

THOMAS P. OSTROM *and*
JOHN J. GALLUZZO

Foreword by
W. RUSS WEBSTER

McFarland & Company, Inc., Publishers
Jefferson, North Carolina

LIBRARY OF CONGRESS CATALOGUING-IN-PUBLICATION DATA

Ostrom, Thomas P.
  United States Coast Guard leaders and missions, 1790 to the present / Thomas P. Ostrom and John J. Galluzzo ; foreword by W. Russ Webster.
      p. cm.
  Includes bibliographical references and index.

  ISBN 978-0-7864-9526-9 (softcover : acid free paper) ∞
  ISBN 978-1-4766-1805-0 (ebook)

  1. United States. Coast Guard—History. 2. United States. Coast Guard—Officers—Biography. 3. Lifesaving—United States—History. 4. United States—History, Naval. I. Galluzzo, John. II. Title.
  VG53.O874 2015
  363.28'60973—dc23   2015003626

BRITISH LIBRARY CATALOGUING DATA ARE AVAILABLE

© 2015 Thomas P. Ostrom and John J. Galluzzo. All rights reserved

No part of this book may be reproduced or transmitted in any form or by any means, electronic or mechanical, including photocopying or recording, or by any information storage and retrieval system, without permission in writing from the publisher.

On the cover: United States Coast Guard Legend-class cutter *Bertholf* (United States Coast Guard)

Printed in the United States of America

McFarland & Company, Inc., Publishers
  Box 611, Jefferson, North Carolina 28640
  www.mcfarlandpub.com

Table of Contents

Acknowledgments vii
Foreword by Captain W. Russ Webster 1
Preface 3
Introduction 5

    1. U.S. Revenue Marine and U.S. Revenue Cutter Service (1790–1915) 7
    2. U.S. Lighthouse Service (1789–1939) 16
    3. U.S. Life-Saving Service (1878–1915) 26
    4. Revenue Marine Chiefs (1843–1889) 39
    5. Revenue Cutter Service Chiefs and Commandants (1889–1915) 51
    6. The U.S. Coast Guard Is Born (1911–1919) 61
    7. Rum Runners and Depression (1919–1936) 71
    8. The Coast Guard in the World War II Era (1936–1946) 82
    9. The Post-War and Cold War Eras (1946–1962) 96
    10. Vietnam, DOT, "Bender's Blues" and Fisheries Patrols (1962–1982) 107
    11. Militarization, Middle East, Interdiction and Ecology (1982–1994) 121
    12. Maritime Outreach, Asset Innovation and War on Terror (1994–2002) 129

13. U.S. Navy and Coast Guard Articulation and
    Homeland Security (2002–2006)   137

14. Deep Water Project and Natural Disasters
    (2006–2010)   144

15. International Outreach, Security Cutters and Arctic
    Expansion (2010–)   153

Epilogue: 2015 and Beyond   176

Appendix: Commandants of the Coast Guard and Chiefs of the Revenue Marine Bureau   191

Chapter Notes   183

Bibliography   195

Index   203

Acknowledgments

Thomas P. Ostrom

Writing books and speaking publicly require that the author and speaker be motivated by the subject matter and supported and encouraged by publishers, editors, listeners, readers, friends and role models. I have been fortunate on all those fronts.

My wife, Mary Patricia Lamal Ostrom, has been generous in her support, encouragement, and schedule flexibility. Her brother James C. Lamal has encouraged my writing and motivated me with his own historical interests. Jim travelled with Mary and me to Washington, D.C., for my research and presentations at the U.S. Navy Memorial.

U.S. Navy Memorial Foundation curator Mark T. Weber kindly invited me to make presentations on Coast Guard and naval history. The curator showed me Coast Guard displays at the Navy Memorial and shared his impressive knowledge of Coast Guard history and personnel, and his experience with the U.S. Coast Guard on the Great Lakes. I appreciated the courtesy and support of Mr. Weber and his staff.

Dr. David F. Winkler, author, writer, and director of programs and development at the Naval Historical Foundation in Washington, D.C., has inspired me with his own publications, and invitations to do naval book reviews. Commander Winkler (United States Navy Reserve) granted us the privilege of visiting the Washington Navy Yard, U.S. Navy Museum, and Naval Foundation and History Center in the summer of 2012, where we enjoyed the hospitality of the staff.

My cousin and fellow Wisconsin native, Lt. Col. George R. Ostrom, U.S. Air Force (Ret.), and his wife, Jackie, joined us in Washington, D.C., and inspired us with their support, congeniality, and professional careers that included Pentagon assignments and national security responsibilities.

Lt. Col. Ostrom later worked in the defense industry and educated me with his good humor and anecdotes about military leadership and human relations in the military hierarchy.

Robert Fuhrman, executive director of the Richard I. Bong Veterans Historical Center and lecturer on naval and military history, has invited me to speak about Coast Guard history on several occasions at that magnificent museum in Superior, Wisconsin. Fuhrman and his staff have extended their courtesy and support work diligently to preserve the heritage of Wisconsin native Maj. Richard I. Bong, the famed World War II Pacific Theater ace.

Bong Historical Center staff member Robert Hoyt contributed his enthusiasm and knowledge to a lecture I gave on the U.S. Coast Guard and National Defense. Petty Officer Hoyt served in the U.S. Navy Reserve in Duluth, Minnesota, and with the U.S. Navy in Vietnam. PO3 Hoyt was aware then of Coast Guard activities in Vietnam. Hoyt completed Survival School training, served on Navy ships, rode on PBRs (Patrol Boat, River) and Swift Boats in riverine regions, transferred to a Coast Guard cutter, and resided in volatile Saigon.

Major Scott E. Markle, U.S. Air Force (Ret.), Hoyt's staff colleague at the Bong Museum, also encouraged and supported me in the Bong presentation. Maj. Markle served on active duty and in leadership roles at Air Force bases in the United States, with NATO in Europe, in Croatia and Bosnia, South Korea, Australia, and South America, and stateside in Texas, Florida and South Dakota, and with the North American Aerospace Defense Command (NORAD) in Duluth, Minnesota.

Bob Hughes, a fellow graduate of Superior East High School, informed former U.S. Coast Guard Reserve (USCGR) Lt. Robert L. Raaflaub about the lecture session. Mr. Hughes, a retired grain elevator and cargo vessel inspector, is familiar with maritime commerce. Lt. Raaflaub earned his commission at U.S. Coast Guard Training Center, Yorktown, Virginia, and went on to serve at Search and Rescue (SAR) Support Center, New York City. Lt. Raaflaub's duties during his 1960s active duty tour included Atlantic Ocean station weather and SAR duty on the USCGC *Mackinac* (W-377) and AMVER (Automated Mutual Assistance Vessel Rescue) watches ashore.

Following his Coast Guard career Raaflaub worked in the commercial maritime shipping industry. With that background, the former USCG officer enriched my class with his considerable knowledge about Coast Guard cutters, history, and missions, including World War II and Vietnam.

Douglas Cederholm, a member of the U.S. Coast Guard Auxiliary in District 8, has served in several leadership capacities, earned awards, instructed boating safety classes, and has served as a Coast Guard Auxiliary liaison to the Minnesota state legislature. Doug's enthusiasm, friendship, and devotion to the auxiliary have been inspirational, and taught me about that important facet of Coast Guard history.

John Galluzzo, author, editor, lecturer, and director of the U.S. Life-Saving Service Heritage Association in Hull, Massachusetts, has inspired and encouraged me. Mr. Galluzzo contributed to this book as advisor and co-author, and to my previous book on the Coast Guard in World War II. It has been my privilege to write articles for the U.S. Life-Saving Service Heritage Association journal, *Wreck and Rescue*, and to collaborate with John and learn so much from him. John's collaboration with Coast Guard personnel at U.S. Coast Guard Headquarters and associate Coast Guard historian Scott Price provided quality contributions to the book.

Lt. Jim Dolbow (USCGR) has inspired me with his career as a writer, author, active duty officer, and congressional military legislative assistant. Lt. Dolbow studied at the U.S. Naval War College and is the author of the 10th edition of *The Coast Guardsman's Manual*. Lt. Dolbow wrote a positive review of my book on the U.S. Coast Guard and national defense, a further inspiration for this author to keep on writing.

The encouragement of U.S. Coast Guard Historian Dr. Robert Browning, Jr., has been much appreciated, as have the resources of the Coast Guard Historian's Office at U.S. Coast Guard Headquarters in Washington, D.C, where assistant historian Chris Havern found and forwarded to me several primary source documents, as did diligent archive specialist Chris Killillay at the National Archives in Washington, D.C.

Senior Chief Craig Trefney, USCGR (Ret.), and Chief Machinist Technician Tina M. Claflin (USCG) were present at the U.S. Navy Memorial Foundation presentation, and inspired me with their achievements and professionalism. MECS Trefney, a Michigan native, served in Arlington (Virginia), Philadelphia (Pennsylvania) and with a boat crew in Delaware. Maritime law enforcement was Senior Chief Trefney's specialty. He contributed his knowledge of Coast Guard operations and personnel to my presentation.

MKC Tina Claflin, a native of Rhinelander, Wisconsin, also stationed in Arlington, served as the USCG women afloat coordinator. Chief Claflin is a student of military leadership and the role and achievements of women in the service. Claflin served at sea and in search and rescue and law enforcement missions. Chief Claflin was lead petty officer on the U.S. Coast Guard Academy training sailing ship *Eagle*.

I conversed with Rear Adm. Edward Walker, Jr., USN (Ret.) at the U.S. Navy Memorial. The Naval Academy graduate served ashore and at sea, in the USN Supply Corps, in a variety of assignments in the naval hierarchy, on the board of the memorial foundation; and in consulting and administrative capacities in a variety of institutions and organizations. Rear Adm. Walker was kind enough to send me an August 2012 letter in which he alluded to the important working relationship between the Coast Guard and Navy, and its significance as a "study of cooperation and overcoming institutional barriers."

I met another naval notable at the foundation. After my presentation a well-dressed gentleman approached me and expressed appreciation, in careful and eloquent English, of my presentation about the Coast Guard in national defense at home and overseas. The gentleman was Cmdr. Andrey V. Grechikho (Russian Federation Navy), the assistant naval attaché at the Russian Embassy in Washington, D.C. The U.S. Coast Guard has maintained a historic presence in the North Pacific, and has cooperated with the Russian navy in border and maritime sovereignty and security, search and rescue, and in the enforcement of fishing regulations.

In May 2013 I received a telephone call from Edward Andrusko out of Boulder, Colorado. Mr. Andrusko expressed interest in my book, *The U.S. Coast Guard in World War II*, because he served in combat in the Pacific Theater with the United States Marine Corps. Andrusko was seriously wounded, returned to the United States, and went on to study history and literature, write articles and short stories, paint illustrations, and write *Love and War Beneath the Southern Cross*, the riveting story of his military career. Mr. Andrusko shared his background with me in a spirited conversation during which he revealed his knowledge and appreciation of the contributions of the U.S. Coast Guard in the Pacific War.

Dave Allen, military historian, computer engineer, writer, war games aficionado, and president of the Scott Hosier Veterans History Center, has inspired me with his knowledge and military family background. A supporter of my lectures and writing and a contributor of sources and Coast Guard material, he has encouraged me with his congeniality, enthusiasm, eclectic scholarship, and efforts to preserve the stories of military service. Inspirational, as well, is the ever-supportive co-founder and program director of the Scott Hosier Veterans Round Table and veteran and emergency services museum Executive Director Thomas Hosier.

I have been enriched by the experiences noted above, and by discussions, supplemental information, and corrections offered by readers. Such is the stuff that motivates writers to continue learning from and doing research and writing.

John L. Galluzzo

I would like to thank the many Coast Guard officers and enlisted personnel with whom I have worked or otherwise shared historical discoveries and conversations during my two decades of service to the Coast Guard history community, including Admiral James M. Loy, USCG (Ret.), Admiral Robert J. Papp, USCG (Ret.), VADM Jim Hull, USCG (Ret), CDR Gary Thomas USCG (Ret.), Capt. W. Russell Webster, USCG (Ret.), and the many service personnel, active or retired, who have contributed to the work of the Foundation for Coast Guard History, the United States Life-Saving Service Heritage Association, the United States Lighthouse Society and the many other Coast Guard history nonprofit organizations in existence today. On the civilian side, I would like to profusely thank Robert Browning, Scott Price and Bill Thiesen from the Coast Guard Historian's Office, and fellow historians Dennis L. Noble, Richard M. Boonisar, Maurice Gibbs, Tim Dring, USNR (Ret.), Fred Stomehouse, Jeff Shook, Bob Trapani and Jeff Gales, just the vanguards of a list of names far too long to count.

Foreword
by Captain W. Russ Webster

Maritime historians, aficionados of military leaders and service heritage, and current and future leaders of military service alike will relish Tom Ostrom and John Galluzzo's treatment of the challenges and strength of character of the Coast Guard commandants from Commodore Bertholf to Admiral Papp. Few readers are ever exposed to the continuum of leadership hurdles throughout the Coast Guard's history: the establishment of an amalgam of the Lifesaving Service and Revenue Cutter Service immediately prior to World War I; participation in every armed conflict; warding off multiple attempts to assimilate the Coast Guard into the Navy; and modern day operational successes after natural disasters. The authors deftly analyze the personal background of the Coast Guard's Commandants, their affiliations, characters, and circumstances and interconnectedness with the Navy, their presidents, and in some cases, previous commandants. The result is a high quality product appropriate for educators and students of leadership and service heritage, mariners of all types and the general interest reader.

Historian Tom Ostrom, a leading expert in the history of the service, and John Galluzo, also a prolific maritime author, begin with an analysis of Ellsworth Bertholf, the first U.S. Revenue Cutter Service (USRCS, a predecessor organization of the Coast Guard) officer to attend the Naval War College in Newport, Rhode Island, when Navy Captain Alfred Thayer Mahan was on the faculty. At the same time Mahan argued, in *The Influence of Sea Power Upon History* (1890), that the Navy should have an expanded global presence to contest foreign navies, Bertholf concluded the USRCS would then assume responsibility for the control and defense of U.S. coastal waters. As the last leader of the USRCS, he warded off the challenges of President William Howard Taft's politcos until the tragic sinking of the SS *Titanic* proved that the Navy had insufficient resources to support a maritime safety mission. As the first modern era commandant of the Coast Guard, he was selected over 22 more senior officers and presided over the 1915 establishment of his service and later assimilation under U.S. Navy control during the war, and again fought to preserve the identity of his service at great political expense.

From the Coast Guard's inception as it transitioned from "heroes of the surf" under Bertholf's guiding hand to policing rumrunners, to its involvement in military conflict in World War II, Vietnam, and the Persian Gulf, to its domestic achievements in the aftermath of Hurricane Katrina, and within the newly formed Department of Homeland Security and in response to the Deepwater Horizon oil spill under Admiral Thad Allen's leadership, readers will be regaled with vignettes that will entertain and satisfy.

As a former Coast Guard field and operational commander, serving with and for several of the modern day commandants chronicled in this book, and as an acknowledged historian of our shared service heritage, I have witnessed firsthand some of the nuanced observations of leadership in this book.

Captain W. Russ Webster, U.S. Coast Guard (Retired), is former commander, Group Woods Hole, Massachusetts (1998–2001), and a maritime historian and author.

Preface

The authors have shared a history of collaboration in writing articles and books on the U.S. Coast Guard. John Galluzzo has edited and written articles for *Wreck and Rescue*, the journal of the U.S. Life-Saving Service Heritage Association, and published other maritime articles, book reviews, and Coast Guard history books.

Tom Ostrom, a retired college history instructor, was a member of the U.S. Coast Guard Reserve, has written articles for *Wreck and Rescue*, reviewed naval history books, and published books about the Coast Guard on the Great Lakes, in World War II, and in national defense and drug interdiction.

Galluzzo brings his expertise on the U.S. Life-Saving Service and the U.S. Revenue Marine and Revenue Cutter Service and the joining of those agencies to form the U.S. Coast Guard in 1915, and on the U.S. Lighthouse Service that the Coast Guard absorbed in 1939. Galluzzo has been actively involved with the historic preservation of Coast Guard lighthouse and lifeboat stations.

The history of the Coast Guard dates back to 1790, when U.S. Treasury Secretary Alexander Hamilton formed "the system of cutters" that constituted the first federal navy. Hamilton assigned Revenue Cutter crews to enforce tariff and customs laws. The Revenue Marine established the precedent of search and rescue and coastal and river scientific surveys, a mission that survives in contemporary Coast Guard oceanographic expeditions.

The national defense mission of the U.S. Revenue Cutter Service began early when the Service teamed up with the U.S. Navy to protect American sovereignty against the naval encroachments of France (1800) and Britain (War of 1812). The USRCS and later the Coast Guard participated in the nation's wars and coordinated their missions with the other U.S.

Armed Forces at home and overseas. The missions have included wars against pirates, the Civil War, Spanish-American War, World War I, World War II, Korea, Vietnam, the 2001 ("9/11") terror attacks on the U.S., and the Middle East conflicts. These national defense missions are covered in our book, as are Coast Guard responses to natural disasters and environmental pollution. Our book considers and analyzes the responses to those and other events that illustrate the consummate leadership skills required of senior enlisted, commissioned, and civilian Coast Guard personnel.

U.S. Coast Guard personnel have suffered fatalities at home and abroad in life-saving, aids to navigation, contraband and immigration interdiction, and national defense missions. Our book will show how the missions have historically expanded through policy and mission modifications, budget cuts, agency and departmental transfers, and attempts by budget conscious members of Congress to abolish the Coast Guard, or, in the name of false efficiencies, to combine the U.S. Coast Guard with the U.S. Navy, or transfer its responsibilities to other federal and state institutions, agencies and departments.

The authors consider how domestic maritime law enforcement, port security, aids to navigation, and national defense missions forged the technological evolution of land, sea, personnel and eventually aircraft assets as the service expanded its presence from U.S. interior and coastal waters to Antarctica, the Bering Sea and Alaska, and the Pacific and Atlantic oceans. We will explain how the Coast Guard has assumed and expanded its legislatively mandated tasks with the utilization of the well trained and highly motivated civilian, reserve, and active duty male and female personnel of "Team Coast Guard."

The authors have been inspired by Coast Guard history, and have attempted in this book to explain how the personnel of the multi-mission service have acquired and demonstrated the leadership skills that enabled the USRCS and USCG to meet their responsibilities and enhance their legacy and motto: "Semper Paratus: Always Ready."

The primary and secondary sources used by the authors include material from our previous writings, research, and public presentations; material and illustrations from the National Archives and the Library of Congress; and files from the exemplary staff at the Coast Guard Historian's Office in Washington, D.C. The bibliography chronicles the outstanding contributions of the authors, writers, and speakers we have learned so much from.

We hope the historical journey offered in this book contributes to the preservation of the history and legacy of the United States Coast Guard, and cultivates an appreciation of the contributions of the service in its life-saving, maritime safety, law enforcement, and national defense missions.

Introduction

The origin of the U.S. Revenue Marine under Treasury Secretary Alexander Hamilton in 1790 is the Coast Guard's starting point. The Coast Guard missions of aids to navigation (ATON); law enforcement; resource preservation; search and rescue (SAR); fishing, immigration, and narcotics enforcement; ship, boat, and bridge safety instruction and inspection; and national defense have contributed significantly to the economic, environmental, humanitarian, and national security responsibilities of the United States government.

As one of the military services of the United States, the Coast Guard has cooperated in missions at home and overseas with the U.S. Navy, U.S. Marine Corps, U.S. Army, and U.S. Air Force, as well as with civilian and foreign commercial shipping agencies and the navies and coast guards of other nations. Key events in Coast Guard history include participation in all of the nation's wars at home and overseas, including the War of 1812, Civil War, World Wars I and II, Korea, Vietnam, and War on Terror; port security, joint missions with other federal agencies and departments in drug and immigration enforcement, and national defense at home and overseas.

New missions and an expanded geographic presence have been part of the Coast Guard legacy, as has the absorption of ancillary agencies, the U.S. Revenue Marine, Revenue Cutter Service, U.S. Life-Saving Service, U.S. Lighthouse Service, and the transfer of the Coast Guard from the Treasury Department to the Department of Transportation (1967) and the Department of Homeland Security (2003).

In the World War II period, the civilian U.S. Coast Guard Auxiliary was formed, as were the Coast Guard Reserve and Coast Guard Women's Reserve, the latter known as SPARS, a name created from the Coast Guard motto, "Semper Paratus: Always Ready."

From the brief history noted above, one can appreciate the innovative skills and contributions offered by the Coast Guard leaders who guided the service through the multiplier effects of mission expansion, personnel training, asset acquisition, and technological innovation.

The leaders' titles evolved from secretary, director, chief, superintendent, captain and captain-commandant to commandant, with ranks of captain and admiral. These top administrators served under cabinet secretaries and answered to Congress and the president. The commandants and treasury secretaries have been honored by having Coast Guard cutters named after them, as have distinguished service members.

Famed Coast Guard leaders include Alexander Fraser of the U.S. Revenue Marine; Sumner Kimball of the U.S. Life-Saving Service; Ellsworth Bertholf, the famed polar explorer-rescuer who directed the transition of the Revenue Cutter Service into the Coast Guard (1915) and through World War I; Frederick Billard, who led a controversial Prohibition mission; Russell R. Waesche, the extraordinary World War II commandant; Paul Yost, who led naval forces in Vietnam, enhanced the militarization of the service, and responded to a historic oil spill; Edwin Roland and Willard Smith, who supervised the Coast Guard in Vietnam; James Loy, at the helm during the 11 September 2001 terrorist attacks upon the United States; Thomas Collins, who led the service through significant budget and mission transitions; Thad Allen, commandant during Hurricane Katrina and the Gulf of Mexico oil spill; and Admiral Robert J. Papp, captain of the U.S. Coast Guard Academy's famed sailing ship *Eagle*, who readied the service for its changing global responsibilities and expanded polar-Arctic presence.

The reader shall hopefully acquire a better understanding and appreciation of the contributions of the commandants to the essential missions of the Coast Guard, and the legacy of the service motto: "Semper Paratus."

1

U.S. Revenue Marine and U.S. Revenue Cutter Service (1790–1915)

The United States Coast Guard (USCG) acquired its name in 1915 when the federal government, in the name of efficiency, combined the United States Life Saving Service (USLSS) with the United States Revenue Marine, by then called the U.S. Revenue Cutter Service (USRCS), into the new United States Coast Guard.

The U.S. Revenue Marine originated in 1790 during the presidential administration of George Washington. The 4 August 1790 founding of the Revenue Marine is considered the birthdate of the United States Coast Guard.

Congress passed the legislation that founded and funded the U.S. Revenue Marine (USRM) and placed the naval service under the control of its first civilian leader, U.S. Treasury Secretary Alexander Hamilton.

The U.S. Revenue Marine was the first federal navy. The United States Navy (USN) traces its origins to the colonial Revolutionary War, as does its naval military arm, the United States Marine Corps (USMC). During the Revolutionary War (1775–1783) and into the post–British era, the Euro-Americans exhibited their fear of centralized national authority and monarchies by founding and administering a confederate (states rights oriented) government, and abolished the standing colonial army, navy, and marines in favor of maintaining civilian state militias and navies.

The problematic confederacy was soon replaced by a centralized federal government structure under the United States Constitution and the Washington administration in 1789. The first United States navy was the Revenue Marine, tasked with coastal surveys and exploration, saving life and property at sea, defending United States territorial waters, enforcing customs (tariff) and smuggling laws, and collecting the customs duties from international trade and shipping to fund the federal government.

The federal United States Navy evolved between 1794 and 1798. The year of chronological preference is dependent upon the historical priority list of significant congressional legislation, shipbuilding, training, and launching events. But without question, the USN was combat ready and water-borne when it partnered with the USRM in the Quasi-War with France in 1799–1800 and in the War of 1812–1814 against Britain in what some historians have termed America's "Second War of Independence."

The Navy and USRCS/USCG have performed joint missions at home and overseas throughout their respective naval histories. On several occasions, U.S. presidents have invoked federal authority to place the Coast Guard directly under U.S. Navy control, as happened during the American involvements in World War I (1917–1918) and World War II (1941–1945). In its long history, the USCG has served under and been transferred to the Departments of Treasury (1790), Transportation (1967), and Homeland Security (2003).[1]

To tell the Coast Guard story, attention must be paid to Coast Guard predecessor agencies; civilian and military leadership from 1790 to the present; and the missions, assets, and personnel which functioned under those leaders who were variously referred to as chiefs, directors, captains, captain-commandants, and commandants.

The U.S. Revenue Marine was created by Congress in 1790 and placed under the jurisdiction of the U.S. Treasury Department and its first secretary, Alexander Hamilton. Civilian and commissioned Revenue Marine Bureau (RMB) chiefs directed the Revenue Marine between 1843 and 1889. Listed by the first year of their terms, the chiefs included Captain Alexander V. Fraser (USRM), 1843, and Capt. Richard Evans (USRM), 1848. In 1849 the bureau was abolished and the Revenue Marine was placed under the U.S. Customs Commissioner until 1869, when the bureau was reestablished.

Then the following Revenue Marine Bureau chiefs directed the USRM/USRCS: N. Broughton Devereux (1869); Sumner I. Kimball (1871); Ezra Clark (1878); and Peter Bonnett (1885). The chiefs, captains, captain-commandants, and commandants of the Revenue Cutter Service and Coast Guard, the first two still called "chiefs," date from 1889 to the present.[2]

The service that the chiefs headed has a compelling history. On 4 August 1790, Congress authorized the Revenue Marine/Cutter Service to enforce tariff, trade and other maritime laws, and stop the smuggling trade that avoided duty payments. In 1832, U.S. Treasury Secretary Louis McLane

1. Revenue Marine and Revenue Cutter Service (1790–1915)

ordered the revenue cutters to emphasize life-saving and conduct cruises in Atlantic storm seasons to aid mariners in distress.

The Revenue Marine was the only federal armed naval service until U.S. Navy operations commenced in 1798. The USRM was officially named the U.S. Revenue Cutter Service in 1894. Revenue cutter captains took their orders and assignments from local port customs collectors. Revenue cutter crews seized contraband vessels and goods, boarded vessels in port, and inspected export cargoes to police revenue law violations.

In a letter of instruction to revenue cutter captains, Treasury Secretary Alexander Hamilton directed them to remember, "Their countrymen are freemen ... impatient ... of a domineering spirit." The cutter commanders were instructed "to overcome difficulties ... by a cool and temperate perseverance in their duty (and) by address and moderation, rather than by vehemence or violence."[3]

The U.S. Revenue Cutter *Massachusetts* and USRC *Pickering* were among the first ten cutters constructed for the USRM. In the Quasi-War with France (1798–1801), the Navy and Revenue Marine captured or assisted in the capture of 20 French vessels. The USRC *Pickering* is credited with USN-USRC involvement in the capture ten ships.

The Revenue Marine was tasked with intercepting slave ships illegally transporting contraband humans into the United States after 1794. Interdiction efforts resulted in the freeing or release of the slaves. The unpopular Embargo Act of 1807 outlawed European trade with the United States in the British and French war. The USRM was tasked with enforcing the embargo until the repeal of the act in 1807.[4]

Before the service's leaders are considered, a brief history of a few of the famed Revenue Marine cutters will be

Alexander Hamilton is generally credited with creating the concept of the fleet of revenue cutters, which evolved into the modern-day Coast Guard (Library of Congress).

discussed to provide a picture of ships, missions, seafaring exploits, seamanship, naval engineering, the maritime domain, historical significance and contributions.

The boats and ships of the USRCS were called "cutters," a term of origin in British naval history which referred to a sail-powered vessel with one or more sails, masts, jibs and support yards. The British cutters served the Royal Customs Service, hence the phrase "revenue cutters." The U.S. Treasury Department called its fledgling vessels revenue cutters. Today the Coast Guard refers to any of its watercraft over 65 feet in length as cutters.[5]

The first cutter in the "system of cutters" was the USRC (or RC) *Massachusetts*, a small (60 foot) vessel steered by a stern (rear) tiller (not a wheel or helm), with low freeboard and draft, and lightly armed. The *Massachusetts* was launched in 1791 but sold about 14 months later.

The 58-foot USRC *Pickering* was a two-masted cutter that served the USRM in the Quasi-War with France. The USRC *Harriet Lane* was a 180-foot sail and steam powered paddle wheel steamer. Dual powered vessels in the period of transition from sail to steam were called auxiliary vessels and were more maneuverable in shoal and deep water than strictly sail powered vessels. Captain John Faunce was the first commanding officer of the *Harriet Lane*, the cutter that fired the first Union naval shot of the Civil War in 1861 at Fort Sumter, South Carolina.

The 163-foot, three masted iron-hulled steamer

Captain John Faunce, on the cutter *Harriet Lane*, fired the first naval shots of the American Civil War, outside Charleston Harbor (Library of Congress).

1. *Revenue Marine and Revenue Cutter Service* (1790–1915) 11

The cutter *Seminole*, constructed in 1900, was in many ways representative of the grand era of the Revenue Cutter Service, built during the transitional age when seagoing ships sported both stacks and masts (United States Coast Guard).

USRC *Grant* entered the RC service in 1871, and sailed the Atlantic and Pacific coasts and the Bering Sea on vessel rescue, seal and salmon rookeries and fisheries enforcement and rescue missions. The 192-foot sail and paddle wheel steamer USRC *Fessenden* cruised on the Great Lakes after 1883, performing duties and participating in civic and historical ceremonies, including the 1901 commemoration of Commodore Oliver H. Perry (USN) and his defeat of the British navy on Lake Erie in the War of 1812.[6]

The 165-foot USRC *Commodore Perry* served on Lake Erie after 1884, and sailed around Cape Horn at the southern tip of South America in 1894. The 198-foot sailing steamer USRC *Bear* operated in the Arctic and Bering Sea in a plethora of missions dating from the late nineteenth century and into World War II, where the cutter served on the Greenland Patrol in the North Atlantic. The *Bear* had a reinforced hull to sustain its voyages in the icy seas of the polar regions. The 149-foot USRC *Winona* sailed in the Gulf of Mexico and protected the southern coast of the United States in the Spanish-American War (1898).[7] The 219-foot sailing barque and steam powered USRC *McCulloch* served with the squadron of Commodore

George Dewey (USN) at Manila Bay in the Philippines in the Spanish-American War. As a U.S. Navy auxiliary vessel, the combat cutter had a torpedo tube in the bow and was equipped with four three-inch deck guns.[8]

Alexander Hamilton is generally credited with conceiving and administering the operation of the revenue cutter service. But naval historians Truman R. Strobridge and Bernard C. Nalty offered a different perspective on the origins of the revenue marine cutter system in a March 1976 *Proceedings* article published by the U.S. Naval Institute. The historians discussed documentary evidence discovered in 1962 at the Philadelphia Customs House. The document suggests that Hamilton may have had a cognitive predecessor: Colonel Sharp Delaney, a Revolutionary War combat veteran who was appointed as the first Philadelphia customs collector in 1789.[9]

Two months after Col. Delaney assumed the office of customs collector, a letter was sent to him by Secretary Hamilton asking whether the customs officer might favor employing revenue cutters, and inquiring about Delaney's advice on the number of cutters required and their armament, operation, and estimated expenses. Colonel Delaney, absent because of illness, did not immediately read and respond to Hamilton's letter. Delaney belatedly responded that such a cutter system was necessary to interdict the smuggling in the Philadelphia coastal and riverine region. In his letter to Hamilton, Col. Delaney affirmed that he had already "procured a barge with sails ... and kept her plying [between area ports] strictly obliging all [ship] masters" to show their manifests to boarding officers and inspectors.

Delaney's letter was mailed from Philadelphia on 31 October 1789. Treasury Secretary Hamilton did not respond to it until 19 May 1790, about one month after Congress received a request for the creation of a revenue marine with a ten-boat fleet. Strobridge and Nalty wrote that Col. Delaney encouraged Hamilton to send vessels to him, and informed the secretary that he had confiscated a contraband vessel, added the smuggler's craft to his flotilla, and that Hamilton subsequently acknowledged Col. Delaney's success in collecting federal duties and carrying out revenue marine missions.

Strobridge and Nalty affirmed that Philadelphia Customs Collector Fred C. Peters discovered the Delaney-Hamilton correspondence, and his colleague, Thomas Hornsby, wrote the historical monograph that led to subsequent periodical articles. The two historians made a valid case for acknowledging Col. Delaney's contribution to the genesis and missions of the U.S. Revenue Marine.[10]

Nonetheless, the brilliance, background, and achievements of Treasury Secretary Alexander Hamilton can hardly be overemphasized. The West Indies native migrated to the colonies and influenced the American independence movement with his pamphlets, speeches, and combat role in the Revolutionary War against the United Kingdom (1775–1783), and made contributions as a member of the Confederate Congress and at the Constitutional Convention (1787). The Constitutional Convention paved the way for the creation of the United States Constitution and the federal government. Also of historical significance were Hamilton's advisory role to President George Washington and administrative and policy achievements after Hamilton's appointment to the U.S. Treasury in 1789. Hamilton's reports on public credit, revenue generation, establishment of the U.S. Revenue Marine system of cutters, creation of a central bank and federal mint, and report on manufacturing[11] were instrumental in stabilizing and operating the fledgling federal government, and providing the philosophical, political, and bureaucratic frame work that facilitated the growth and prosperity of the United States.

Hamilton's substantive political and philosophical disputes with Thomas Jefferson, President Washington's secretary of state, led to the partisan Hamiltonian Federalist and the Jeffersonian Democratic-Republican political parties, out of which evolved the Republican and Democrat parties.

American historians Larry Schweikart and Michael Allen described the military side of Hamilton, who argued "that the new government would thrive once 'the power of the sword' (a standing army) was established, opening the door for his detractors to label him a militarist and monarchist, whereas in reality he was a pragmatist."[12]

The USRM filled some of the early American military and naval gaps between 1790 and 1915. The Revenue Marine carried out domestic and national defense missions on interior, coastal, and international waters. After the Quasi-War with France, the United States fought what some historians call the "Second War of Independence" (1812–1814) against Britain on the Great Lakes, Chesapeake Bay, Lake Champlain, and off the ocean coasts. The United States fought the United Kingdom on land, lakes, rivers, oceans, and in Canada. The war was caused by the refusal of the United Kingdom to leave U.S. territories after the Revolutionary War, British impressment (capture) of American seamen off American merchant ships, and the British blockade and capture of U.S. merchant vessels.

Under the command of the U.S. Navy, the USRC *Jefferson* captured a British warship in June 1812. In August, British frigates captured the 6-gun revenue cutters *Commodore Barry* and the 14-gun *James Madison* and its 65-man crew. In June 1813, a night boarding party from a British warship captured the anchored USRC *Surveyor* (Capt. William Travis) on the York River. Three British sailors were killed and five Americans wounded. The British commander returned the surrendered sword of Captain Travis out of respect for the defensive actions and courage of the cutter men.

In October 1814, the revenue cutter *Eagle* (Capt. Frederick Lee) was outgunned and then beached on Long Island, New York. The Revenue Marine crew labored to remove the cutter guns and fought back from the top of a bluff, firing upon the HMS *Dispatch*. After exhausting their own ammunition, the brave cutter crew used British cannon balls that had been fired at them. Eventually the British navy prevailed and captured the cutter and crew.[13]

After the War of 1812, the Revenue Marine engaged in counter-piracy operations (the United States Coast Guard and the U.S. Navy again conducted anti-piracy missions off the East African coast in the early 21st century). The 19th century piracy wars were conducted in the Gulf of Mexico and Caribbean Sea. In 1819, the U.S. Revenue Cutters *Louisiana* and *Alabama* fought pirates on the open seas. In 1820, the *Alabama* captured four pirate vessels off the northeast coast of South America. In a joint operation of the U.S. Navy, the U.S. Revenue Marine, and Royal (British) Navy, the USRC *Alabama*, USS *Peacock*, and HMS *Speedwell* captured five pirate ships.[14]

Revenue Marine cutters, under U.S. Navy command in the Mexican-American War (1846–1848), engaged in amphibious and shoal water operations.[15] Fifteen years after the Mexican-American War, the USRM, again in partnership with the USN, was engaged in the Civil War (1861–1865) against the naval and army forces of the Confederate States of America (CSA). The CSA navy vessels were identified as CSS (Confederate States Ships). The U.S. naval vessels were identified as USN (USS) and USRM vessels, although some cutters were directly transferred to the U.S. Navy.

The USRC *Harriet Lane* fired the first naval shots of the Civil War at Charleston Harbor, South Carolina, on 12 April 1861, and later operated with a U.S. Navy squadron in the capture of two Southern forts, Clark and Hatteras. The USRC *E.A. Stevens* joined two small gunboats and the USS *Galena* and USS *Monitor* in a brief attack from the James River against Richmond, Virginia, the Confederate capital. The USRC *Miami* transported President Abraham Lincoln into a combat area in May of 1862, and then supported the U.S. Navy in putting U.S. troops ashore at Ocean View, Virginia.

President Lincoln ordered the treasury secretary to use Revenue Marine cutters to assist the Navy, protect U.S. commerce, and engage CSA military and naval forces. Upon Lincoln's assassination on 15 April 1865, revenue cutters searched for suspected enemy agents who tried to escape by sea.[16]

By the time of the Spanish-American War (1898), the U.S. Revenue Marine was commonly referred to as the U.S. Revenue Cutter Service in official government documents. In that war, the USRCS engaged in joint missions with the U.S. Navy in Havana Harbor and Cardenas against Spanish military forces in colonial Cuba. Off the Cardenas coast, the USRC *Hudson* (Lt. Frank Newcomb) towed the damaged torpedo boat USS *Winslow* to safety under Spanish naval and coastal gunfire. Captain Newcomb received a congressional gold medal for his competence and courage in combat. In the Battle of Manila Bay in the Spanish Philippines, the USRC *McCulloch* fought in the U.S. Navy fleet headed by Adm. George Dewey.[17]

As a cost and mission efficiency measure, President Woodrow Wilson signed into law the Act to Create the United States Coast Guard on January 28, 1915. The act combined the Revenue Cutter Service with the U.S. Life-Saving Service. In 1939, the United States Lighthouse Service was placed under the United States Coast Guard, as was the Navigation and Steamboat Inspection Service in 1942[18] during World War II.

The history and functions of the Life-Saving Service and Lighthouse Service will be more fully discussed in subsequent chapters, as will the Revenue Marine chiefs, captains, and captain-commandants of the predecessor agencies of the United States Coast Guard and the commandants of the Coast Guard. For purposes of terminology and history, and the format of this book, the leaders of the U.S. Revenue Marine Bureau, whether civilian or military, will be considered in the list of historic "commandants."

Some historians of the Coast Guard consider Captain Alexander V. Fraser, chief of the Revenue Marine Bureau from 1843 to 1848, a captain-commandant, the first "commandant" of the Coast Guard. Other historians apply the "commandant" title to subsequent dates in the early 20th century. With that in mind, it must be stated that terminological and chronological controversies exist within the various explanations of historical Coast Guard ranks and titles. Among the Coast Guard predecessors that the chiefs and captain-commandants administered were the U.S. Lighthouse Service and the U.S. Life-Saving Service, the histories of which will be subsequently considered.

2

U.S. Lighthouse Service (1789–1939)

The United States Lighthouse Service (USLHS) was one of the autonomous predecessor agencies transferred to the jurisdiction of the United States Coast Guard (USCG), this one in 1939, two years before the United States entered World War II. The United States was officially neutral before 1941, but not in sympathy or policy, as the Axis Powers (Germany, Italy, and Japan) waged war in Europe, North Africa, and Asia and the Pacific from the late 1930s to 1945.

The Lighthouse Service dated from British colonial times (1716) in North America when it built and then administered aids to navigation like lighthouses and buoys in British America and then the United States. The U.S. Lighthouse Service was under the Treasury Department of Secretary Alexander Hamilton in the administration of President George Washington, and later under the U.S. Department of Commerce, given the significance of navigation aids in maritime commerce.

Truman R. Strobridge, a historian at U.S. Coast Guard Headquarters in Washington, D.C., researched and wrote the extensive *Chronology of Aids to Navigation and the United States Lighthouse Service: 1716–1939*. The USLHS dates back to the agency's authorization by the first United States Congress in 1789.[1]

Strobridge chronicled USLHS activities, missions, and technology in each decade of the agency's existence, from the inception of the service in the British colonies to the transfer of the U.S. Lighthouse Service into the United States Coast Guard. Strobridge covered the historical period from 1716 to 1939.

Eighteenth century milestones from 1716 to 1797 included the establishment of the first American lighthouse in Boston Harbor, Massachu-

2. U.S. Lighthouse Service (1789–1939)

setts, on Little Brewster Island (1716); the placement of a cannon on the island to sound off in foggy weather, and the building of beacons and lighthouses in New England, New Orleans, Louisiana, Tybee Island, Georgia, and Charleston, South Carolina.

Buoys were placed in Pennsylvania waters and on the Delaware River and other New England sites. In 1789, an act of Congress created the "Lighthouse Establishment" and mandated the construction, support and maintenance of lighthouses, buoys, piers, and beacons, with expenses paid out of federal revenues. Lighthouses were built along the shores of North Carolina and Long Island, New York.[2]

Mariners in the 19th century (1802–1899) witnessed the testing of porpoise and whale oils as lighthouse lamp illuminants; parabolic reflectors and other magnifiers to diffuse and reflect lighting farther out to sea; the building of lighthouses on the Great Lakes; fog bells; a floating lightship on Chesapeake Bay near Norfolk, Virginia; the use of the advanced spherical lenses and prisms invented by French physicist Augustin Fresnel; a lightship off the New Jersey coast; experimentation with natural gas and kerosene illumination; the 1836 attack by Seminole Indians on a Florida lighthouse; and a Great Lakes floating lightship stationed between Lakes Huron and Michigan.

U.S. Navy officers were assigned to inspect lighthouse operations, facilities, and construction, tasks also assigned to U.S. Army engineers. Other 19th century achievements were the compilation of a Light List publication which identified the location of lighthouses, beacons, buoys, floating lights and lightships for official and mariner use, and changes in the shape, coloring and construction of various kinds of buoys.

There were interrelated duties and exchanges of functions and administration between lighthouse keepers (later called supervisors) and U.S. Customs collectors; investigations of lighthouses damaged and personnel swept away in storms; the use of bell buoys and steam fog whistles; the electrification of lights and stations; the dispersal of lighthouse tenders (called ships, later cutters and buoy tenders); interconnections with the U.S. Revenue Cutter Service; and logistical and tactical operations to maintain, abandon, and recapture lighthouse stations during the ebb and flow of the Civil War.

Other developments included dispersal of navigation aids on inland rivers and waterways; lighted gas and electric buoys and beacons; uniform standardization for male and female lighthouse keepers; pension plans and civil service protection for light station crews; gradual personnel access to the U.S. Public Health Service; enhanced connectivity between isolated stations by improved road and electric line assets; expansion of light stations and tenders along the Pacific Coast; and the transfer of some lighthouse tenders to the U.S. Navy in the Spanish-American War (1898).

Light station crews were assigned greater responsibility for life saving, and for monitoring wrecks and other obstructions to navigation. Electronic technology advances gradually allowed wireless radio communication between ship, shore, lightship, and lighthouse stations.[3]

The decades of further evolution of the Lighthouse Service was chronicled by historian Truman R. Strobridge from 1900 to 1939. More than 10 U.S. Lighthouse districts were consolidated and modified to correspond with U.S. Army Corps of Engineers departments. Lighthouses, lights, buoys, boats and ships were updated with more advanced electrical systems, radio communications, gas and chemical power sources, and infrastructural technology. Better roads and electrical lines connected the more rural and isolated light stations and governmental units.

Light stations and tenders were built, modified, and situated across the continent on the Great Lakes, major inland waterways and rivers, into U.S. territories, on the Gulf of Mexico and Caribbean Sea, the U.S. Navy base at Guantanamo Bay, Cuba; the Pacific Coast; islands of the Pacific (Hawaii, Midway, Guam); and maritime, insular, and peninsular Alaska.[4]

Lighthouse Service personnel gradually achieved better pension, health, disability, and civil service benefits, and access to the medical care of the U.S. Public Health Service during their active duty and retirement years. The fleet of lighthouse supply and transportation ships (tenders) and lightships was expanded in number and strategic locations, as was access to seaplane and land based aircraft for transportation and inspection purposes. But as technology, communications, and personnel training advanced, the number of USLHS personnel on land, sea, and internal waterways diminished.[5]

Strobridge cited numerous innovations to 20th century aids to navigation. The taller can and nun buoys were introduced and stood higher out of the water for better mariner observation. After 1900, radio communication systems were established on lightships and at other light stations, and acetylene gas generated from calcium carbide was used at lighthouses. In 1903, Congress transferred the Lighthouse Service from the Treasury Department to the newly created Commerce Department. In 1908, sailing lightships were decommissioned, six tenders were assigned to Pacific Coast stations, and three lightships, identified with numbers and not names, steamed from New York to San Francisco in 4 months.

Between 1911 and 1917, the year the United States entered World War I, a more effective vapor oil lamp was used at light stations, as were signal lights rotated by electric motors to emit flashing light powered by

2. U.S. Lighthouse Service (1789–1939)

rechargeable storage batteries. More efficient methods were utilized to transfer supplies from ship to shore at isolated stations in Alaska, safer gas lights were installed at isolated Great Lakes winter stations, naval funds were appropriated to mobilize the Lighthouse Service for the coming war, and plans were made for the possible transfer of USLHS assets to the U.S. Navy and the War Department.

Motor powered boats were assigned to Great Lakes stations. Lighthouse tenders, lightships, and light stations, with a total of more than 1,000 personnel and 50 vessels, were transferred to the War Department and U.S. Navy. Lighthouse assets were used to mark vessel sites after German U-boat sinkings, for hauling practice targets, and placing and removing submarine nets at harbor and channel entrances during and after the Great War.

Between 1920 and 1930, hydroplanes (float or sea planes) were used by USLHS inspectors and superintendents to supervise districts. Radio fog signals and bell and gong buoys were distributed to light stations. Weather reports were broadcast by radio from light ships and shore stations. In 1928, the USLHS developed and used the first automatic direction-finding radio beacon, and adapted the signal system on Lake Michigan to prevent vessel collisions. In May 1934, Lightship No. 117 was struck by a steamship off Nantucket Shoals Station, Massachusetts, with the loss of seven sailors.

Nun buoys were constructed and used at Great Lakes stations during the brutal winters. The damage by flowing ice to more than 80 experimental buoys was minimal. Lighted whistle buoys were built with aluminum alloy superstructures to increase buoy height and visibility with less weight.

In 1937, radio-telephones were first used by the Lighthouse Service at Sault Ste. Marie, Michigan, for broadcasting emergency information and weather reports to mariners. This method of communications supplemented the telephone communications technology then available at lighthouses. In February 1938, the Lighthouse Service Radio Laboratory was moved from the Detroit, Michigan, depot to Baltimore, Maryland, into a building constructed especially for the expert engineers and technicians that administered this critical technology.

Although Japan had initiated war in China in the early 1930s, and Italy in North Africa before 1939, and Germany in Europe that year, historians generally cite 1939 as the beginning of World War II (1939–1945). The United States officially entered the war after the Imperial Japanese Navy attacked the U.S. military base at Pearl Harbor, Hawaii, on 7 December 1941.

The year 1939 was critical for the United States because preparations for war commenced. The year is also significant for the U.S. Lighthouse

Service and the United States Coast Guard. In 1939 the USLHS was transferred into the USCG.

On 30 June 1939, the USLHS had 4,119 full-time and 1,156 part-time personnel. Of the 5,355 total, there were 1,170 light keepers and their assistants, 56 light attendants, and nearly 2,000 officers and crewmembers on lightships and tenders. There were several hundred bureau officers, district superintendents, technicians, and engineers; and more than 500 clerks, messengers, custodians, laborers, depot keepers, watchmen, field employees, and skilled construction and repair workers. U.S. Lighthouse Service assets in 1939 included 65 steam propelled diesel powered tenders, the majority of which were variously equipped with radio-telephones, radio direction finders, or radio-telegraphs. The total number of aids to navigation of all types and categories as of 30 June 1939 was 29,606.[6]

As of 1 July 1939, under President Franklin D. Roosevelt's Reorganization Plan No. 11, the USLHS was transferred into the U.S. Coast Guard. And, as of 7 July 1939, as historian Truman Strobridge quoted his source, "The Lighthouse Bureau went out of existence, and its personnel moved themselves and their equipment to Coast Guard Headquarters from the Commerce Department. Thus did lighthouses return to Treasury, the department they had been part of for so long."[7]

Strobridge ended his history by citing a Commerce Department document dated 7 August 1939: "Suitable observance of the one hundred and fiftieth anniversary of the Lighthouse Service was called for by a joint resolution of Congress, signed by the President on May 15, which was known as Public Resolution No. 16. By this resolution the week of August 7, 1939, was designated lighthouse week."[8]

The Michigan Lighthouse Conservancy illuminated the USLHS legacy in its publication "The United States Lighthouse Service: A Brief Administrative History."[9] The conservancy history stated that each colonial government constructed and operated the essential lighthouses. Twelve existed and that number expanded during the pre–Republic confederacy period of the newly independent former colonies until, in 1789, President Washington signed legislation which created the Lighthouse Establishment under the Treasury Department and placed lighthouses and lights and buoys under federal control. In 1792, Treasury Secretary Alexander Hamilton turned the lighthouses over to the commissioner of revenue. Hamilton's successor, Secretary Albert Gallatin, regained control of the Lighthouse Establishment for his two terms of office, after which the commissioner of revenue assumed control until 1820.[10]

U.S. Treasury auditor Stephen Pleasonton was assigned control of the lighthouses under the authority of the revenue commissioner. Collectors of customs administered local lighthouses. Pleasonton administered the U.S. Lighthouse Establishment from 1820 to 1852, during which time the infrastructure expanded to 42 lightships and 331 lighthouses. Slow to innovate and adopt new technologies, Pleasonton was forced by the U.S. Congress to adopt the advanced and complex lens invented by French physicist Augustin Fresnel. Commercial shipping interests and maritime leaders consistently complained about Pleasonton's leadership, until aids to navigation administration was mandated to the U.S. Light House Board (1852–1910) composed of military officers and civilian scientists. Board members gathered data, surveyed ship captains, and offered solutions to the troubled aids to navigation system in the United States.[11]

To facilitate the work of the U.S. Lighthouse Board, a commissioned U.S. Army engineer was appointed to each of the nation's 12 districts to supervise the construction, technologies, and maintenance of the assets of the U.S. Lighthouse Establishment. The U.S. Army Corps of Engineers assumed greater responsibilities over the U.S. lighthouse infrastructure. A "Light List" of facility and asset locations was published and disseminated to maritime interests and entities, as were changes in navigational aids printed and distributed in the "Notice to Mariners."

Lighthouse operations, training, and appointments were closely monitored. The Civil Service Reform Acts and applications between 1871 and 1896 made the Lighthouse Establishment personnel more professional, and hiring and placement less political.

A variety of lighthouse construction methods and composites were created. Iron buoys were utilized, as were fog whistles, bell and gong buoys, and sound signals powered by steam engines. A gas lighted buoy was illuminated in 1882. In 1886, the Statue of Liberty in New York City Harbor was lighted by electricity. The gradual process of the electrification of lighthouses commenced in 1900.[12]

A plethora of activities, missions, and events occurred under Bureau of Lighthouse in the nearly three decades between 1910 and 1939, the year the USLHS was absorbed by the United States Coast Guard.

By 1910, according to the historical research of the Michigan Lighthouse Conservancy, there existed nearly 12,000 aids to navigation. In 1910, the Bureau of Lighthouses under the U.S. Commerce Department replaced the U.S. Lighthouse Board. The new bureau was commonly referred to as the U.S. Lighthouse Service. Civilians replaced many of the military officers, and district inspectors were titled superintendents. Civilians called "lamp lighters" and "lamp attendants" tended many of the aids to navigation along interior rivers.

George R. Putnam was selected by President William Howard Taft

President William Howard Taft appointed George R. Putnam to run the Bureau of Lighthouses in 1910. In the center of this photograph taken on January 17, 1929, from left to right, are: Secretary of Commerce William Fairfield Whiting, President Coolidge and George R. Putnam (Library of Congress).

to head the bureau. Putnam acquired the title of commissioner of lighthouses. During his 25-year tutelage, Putnam oversaw an expansion of aids to navigation and electronic innovations. The number of aids increased from about 11,700 to more than 24,000 on Putnam's watch. Most of those were small lights and buoys. Among Putnam's administrative achievements were his implementation of lighthouse personnel retirement legislation and the use of the radio beacon as a navigation aid. Electronic advances and automated technologies reduced the number of bureau employees at light stations. In 1934, an unmanned lightship was successfully run by remote radio signals that controlled the ship's lights, radio beacon, and fog signal. A battery powered buoy that replaced acetylene gas proved successful in 1935.

By the 1930s, most lighthouses were the beneficiaries of extended electric power line and transportation networks that contributed to a

In the long view of history, the days of Coast Guardsmen posted at lighthouses, represented here by a Coastie at Truro, Massachusetts' Highland Lighthouse, will be viewed as a short experiment indeed (United States Coast Guard).

reduction of lighthouse station employees. Technological innovations led to automated light stations by the 1960s. Lighthouses then gradually[13] became superfluous; many were demolished or sold to historical societies for preservation and recreational use.

H.D. King, a career Lighthouse Service employee and district superintendent, succeeded Commissioner Putnam in 1935, and served until the

The Nantucket Lightship was one of America's aids to navigation among a fleet of lightships predominantly named for the shoals, reefs and ledges from which they warned mariners away. The lightship era lasted well into the Coast Guard years (United States Coast Guard).

Bureau of Lighthouses was placed under U.S. Coast Guard jurisdiction in 1939. Lighthouse Service personnel then had to choose between accepting a Coast Guard military rank or maintaining civilian status. About half the employees chose the military option.

After World War II erupted, the United States geared up for national defense. The U.S. Coast Guard domestic Beach Patrol was formed. Beach Patrols consisted of civilian auxiliary, enlisted reserve, and regular personnel. The Beach Patrols covered the nation's ocean coasts by boat, on horseback, and with foot patrol personnel aided by trained canines.

The patrols rescued victims of U-boat sinkings, retrieved bodies of drowned civilians and mariners, supported search and rescue operations, and prevented enemy shore incursions by espionage and sabotage teams. The Coast Guard partnered with former U.S. Lighthouse Service stations, boats, and personnel. The light and lifeboat stations were used as lookout posts and centers of radio and telephone communications.

Short-range navigation aids (SHORAN) and long-range navigation aids (LORAN) were placed in lifeboat and light stations. Large navigational buoys (LNBs) replaced lightships in the 1970s.

By 1990, all U.S. lighthouses except the famous Boston (Massachusetts) Harbor Island Lighthouse were completely electronically operated. By the 1980s, special Aids to Navigation Teams (ANTS) inspected, maintained, and repaired lighthouses across the nation, and have monitored the remaining USCG light stations to the present day.

Modeled after airport lights, "aero-beacons" and solar power have replaced the magnificent and historic Fresnel lighthouse lenses.[14] The well-trained crews of the former U.S. Life-Saving Service and the U.S. Lighthouse Service used their training and courage to contribute significantly to the Coast Guard mission in World War II.

3

U.S. Life-Saving Service (1878–1915)

The United States Life-Saving Service (1848–1915) was a predecessor agency of the United States Coast Guard. The U.S. Life-Saving Service (USLSS) contributed a history of volunteer and professional service and courageous personnel. The USLSS worked with the U.S. Lighthouse Service and the U.S. Revenue Marine, later called the U.S. Revenue Cutter Service. The USLSS was formally integrated into the U.S. Revenue Cutter Service to form the United States Coast Guard in 1915.

Historians offer different dates as the origin of the federal life-saving service, depending on definitions of terms. Some historians use 14 August 1848, the date when Congress appropriated funds for civilian volunteers to use for equipment and station structures located in known shipwreck locations off the New Jersey, Massachusetts, and New York coasts. The Massachusetts Humane Society received funding because that civilian organization was a historic leader in the life-saving business. The U.S. Revenue Marine initially administered the life-saving and lifeboat stations.

Others historians use 18 June 1878, the year the U.S. Life-Saving Service was established as a separate agency under Treasury Department control, and headed by General Superintendent Sumner I. Kimball, who had previously headed the Revenue Marine Bureau. Full-time trained crews, not volunteers, eventually ran the life saving and lifeboat stations. Dennis L. Noble, the distinguished maritime and Coast Guard historian, uses the 1878 date of origin in his books and articles.

The legacy of the USLSS, and its exemplary leader Sumner I. Kimball, is commemorated in modern times. The crew of the U.S. Coast Guard Aids to Navigation Team in Duluth, Minnesota, was honored for its work on February 9, 2011. The Duluth Aids to Navigation Team (ANT) received

3. U.S. Life-Saving Service (1879–1915)

the Sumner I. Kimball Readiness Award for exceptional performance during a weeklong assessment of Aids to Navigation operations, drills, written tests, training assessments, and equipment inspections.

Chief Petty Officer Justin Olson, in charge of the Duluth ANT, said many of the personnel had not been aware of the existence of the award, or its legacy, until the award was granted. Olson explained that the ANT was simply performing its mission when inspectors concluded the team achieved the necessary 90 percent plus assessment evaluation.

Sumner I. Kimball, the first general superintendent of the U.S. Life-Saving Service, was appointed to the post by the U.S. Congress in 1878 in recognition of his successful efforts to organize and upgrade the crews of the coastal life-saving boat stations. Kimball's system led to the small boat and aids to navigation stations exemplified by the Duluth Aids to Navigation Team.[1]

The U.S. Life-Saving Service Heritage Association is dedicated to the preservation of the history and the artifacts of the U.S. Coast Guard and its predecessor agencies, the U.S. Lighthouse Service, U.S. Revenue Cutter Service, and the U.S. Life-Saving Service. In 2012, the association president was Frederick Stonehouse, maritime history professor, author, and director of the Marquette (Michigan) Maritime Museum. The executive director was John Galluzzo. The officers and directors included maritime historians, authors, artifact owners, active and retired members of the U.S. Navy and U.S. Coast Guard, museum directors, and staff.[2]

The history of the U.S. Life-Saving Service can be traced from agency and federal documents, and other scattered records that evolved from the missions the USLSS carried out at operational sites on the Great Lakes and ocean coasts. Its history can be studied from artifacts, lighthouse and lifesaving stations, surfboats, lightships, lighthouse tenders, equipment, and maritime museum exhibits. Fascinating glimpses of missions, operations, and personnel can be gained from photographs, maps, hats, caps, full uniforms, work clothing, cork life vests, coat buttons, walking sticks, lanterns, wading boots, oars, badges, wagons, lines, line-throwing Lyle guns, lanterns and flares. The horses that pulled the large and heavy beach wagons survive only in photographs.

Dr. Dennis L. Noble, in his book *A Legacy: The United States Life-Saving Service*,[3] said the primary mission of the USLSS was to assist mariners and passengers "in peril upon the seas," a mission performed by the predecessor agencies of, and including, the United States Coast Guard.[4]

Lighthouse keepers assisted people in peril near their stations. The U.S. Revenue Cutter Service assisted mariners at sea. The Steamboat Inspection Service originated in 1838 and performed inspections to reduce the chance of steam engine disasters. The Steamboat Inspection Service merged with the USCG in 1942, during World War II. The USLSS passed on its methods of operation to the USCG, including the skills of small boat coxswains in heavy surf. Small boats powered by oar and sail rescued mariners in distress from wrecked sailing ships close to shore and farther out to sea, where vessels sank in storms, or broke apart on rocks and in shoal waters close to the harbors where the lifeboat stations and lighthouses were located.

The first life-saving crews were volunteers with the Massachusetts Humane Society in the 1830s. The service gradually spread throughout coastal New England to New York, and then into the Atlantic, Great Lakes, and Gulf Coast states. In 1848, William A. Newell, a member of Congress from New Jersey, acquired $10,000 in federal funding to provide rockets, cannons, surfboats, and volunteer crews to engage in shore to sea rescue operations. But the quality of crews, services, and equipment varied greatly. Gradually, increased federal appropriations and guidelines, including the hiring of full time station keepers (or superintendents), improved the quality of crews, facilities, mission response times, and successful rescues.

The Civil War (1861–1865) interrupted coastal operations until 1870, when coastal storms produced maritime carnage, destruction and casualties that caused a national outcry. The positive result was the 1871 appointment of Sumner Increase Kimball, a New England lawyer, to the position of chief of the Revenue Marine Division in the U.S.

The Life-Saving Service knew only one true leader throughout its existence, General Superintendent Sumner Increase Kimball (United States Coast Guard).

Treasury Department. Kimball ordered Captain John Faunce (U.S. Revenue Marine) to inspect the training, operations, and equipment of the lifesaving system and assess the quality and training of crews and keepers.[5]

Using Capt. Faunce's thorough report, Kimball acquired more federal funds to build facilities, train crews, acquire equipment, regularize operations, codify regulations, establish physical requirements, and weed out incompetence and political favoritism. Life-saving stations were then extended along the Atlantic, Great Lakes, Gulf, and Pacific coasts, and north to Alaska.

In 1878, the stations and personnel were firmly federalized into the U.S. Treasury Department and officially identified as the U.S. Life-Saving Service. Life-saving stations, equip-

While they provided leadership on the local level only, the keepers of the United States Life-Saving Service stations, like Joshua James, provided national inspiration (United States Coast Guard).

ment, boats, and other elements of infrastructure were better designed, built, expanded, and distributed. Facilities included buildings for offices, for berthing and feeding crews, boathouses, piers, and watchtowers. By the 1890s, architect A. B. Bibb designed the stations to look like summer homes and resorts. Kimball monitored budgets, logbooks, training, supplies, and inspection reports. Kimball's chain of command included inspectors, assistants, keepers, and captains and lieutenants of the U.S. Revenue Marine. The Revenue Marine was designated the U.S. Revenue Cutter Service in the late 19th century.

In the process of overseeing the saving of 186,000 lives from disaster at sea, Sumner Kimball also oversaw the first African Americans in the Life-Saving Service, at Pea Island, North Carolina. This undated photograph shows Keeper Richard Etheridge on the far left, with an unidentified group of surfmen (United States Coast Guard).

The life-saving crews trained intensely to become skilled in the use of self-bailing, self-righting surf boats which weighed up to four tons; line-throwing Lyle guns; flares and lanterns on beach patrols; horses and huge wagons to pull the surf boats through sand when not close to the wooden slide that emanated from the boat houses down to the beaches and into shoal waters; the rescue car attached to the line connecting ship to shore; and the more useful and manageable breeches buoy with a canvas ring and pants to accommodate the rescued mariner or passenger. The breeches buoy (or chair) slid along a ship-to-shore pulley system pulled by the shore side life-saving crewmen.[6]

Beach carts and wagons carried the necessary equipment across the variably grassy, sandy undulating, and flat beaches. Sometimes the surfmen (called "storm warriors" and "surf soldiers") hauled their equipment in wagons to the scene. At other times, horses did the hauling. After 1900, gasoline fueled tractors did the job. The oar-powered (human rowed) lifeboats occasionally used sail power, and eventually, gasoline engines. But, with the advent of gasoline, diesel and steam powered engines, ships could stay farther off shore and be better controlled in winds, heavy seas, and narrow harbor entrances, guided by increasingly sophisticated lighthouses, light stations, buoys, and other aids to navigation.

The gradual demise of commercial sailing ships would eventually put the USLSS out of business. The advent of sail and motorized recreational boating would require the lifesavers of the Coast Guard (after 1915) to adapt to motorized boat and ship technology, and the utilization of land and sea aircraft.

District superintendents chose the station keepers. Inspectors and keepers (called "captain" by their crews) often came from commercial mariner and fishing backgrounds. Revenue Marine Service officers inspected stations, crews and boats. The Marine Hospital Service (the future U.S. Public Health Service) provided physical and health examinations and treatment. By 1889, USLSS personnel were wearing clothing that replicated naval uniforms.

Station drills, cleaning, equipment maintenance, first aid training, and coordinated foot beach patrols which linked stations were the order of weekdays and Saturdays. Sunday was generally an off day, except in emergencies. Beach patrol duty was demanding and sometimes dangerous, given the variable topography, weather conditions, and seasonal change that USLSS crewmembers experienced across the vast North America geographic realm.

The well-organized training regimen led to an exemplary USLSS record of saving thousands of lives and warning untold numbers of sail-powered ships away from shores, shoal waters, and rocks. Surfmen and keepers were the recipients of life-saving medals and commendations. Many lifesavers gave up their own lives in the line of duty.

After decades of trying to secure retirement, health, injury, and disability benefits for the increasingly aging station keepers and surfmen of the USLSS, Sumner Kimball supported the pragmatic plan to merge the U.S. Life-Saving Service into the militarized U.S. Revenue Cutter Service to form the U.S. Coast Guard in 1915. Kimball and his USLSS cohorts were provided retirement plans, and the United States Coast Guard continued the life-saving and search and rescue legacy of its predecessor.

The U.S. Coast Guard has continued to serve and protect mariners in distress by building upon the training and life-saving procedures of the United States Life-Saving Service. The Coast Guard has utilized the advancing technology of motorized lifeboats, and propeller, helicopter, and jet aircraft. Life-saving boat and cutter crews and rescue swimmers are trained in the most rigorous conditions to save life and property in varied and dangerous maritime realms.[7]

As maritime historian Dennis L. Noble aptly concluded, "Building upon the strong foundation established by the U.S. Life-Saving Service, the Coast Guard has become the recognized expert in search and rescue over the water [and] the leading agency for those 'in peril upon the seas.'"[8]

Much has been written about U.S. Life-Saving Service stations, boats, and crews on the Atlantic, Gulf, and Pacific coasts. A rich USLSS heritage can also be found on the coastal reaches of the Great Lakes, appropriately designated the "Inland Seas." The extremes of hot summers, frigid subarctic temperatures, swirling rains, deep snow, heavy seas, and isolation posed particular challenges for the intrepid mariners, passengers, and USLSS crewmembers that dared operate in that vast hydrographic realm.

The Inland Seas consists of Lakes Ontario, Erie, Huron, Michigan and Superior. The USLSS came to the Great Lakes in 1876. The U.S. Lighthouse Service, also a life-saving bureau, came to the Great Lakes earlier. The Lighthouse Board Report of 1862 recorded detailed information about Great Lakes lighthouses and the numbers and dates of the earliest stations: Lake Ontario, 7 (1820); Lake Erie, 12 (1820); Lake Huron, 10 (1825); Lake Michigan, 26 (1829); and Lake Superior, 15 (1847).

In 1854, Great Lakes ship disasters prompted Congress to increase appropriations to fund positions of district supervisors and life-saving station keepers. Paid crews came later. Lifeboats were provided in that year for Lakes Superior, Michigan, Ontario and Erie. Ship disasters in the winter of 1870–1871 forced Congress to appropriate more funding to train paid crews and equip stations with upgraded gear and boats.

In 1876–1877, Superintendent Sumner Kimball reported that Lakes Ontario and Erie contained nine USLSS stations; Huron and Superior hosted nine stations; and Lake Michigan supported 12 stations. Maritime historian Frederick Stonehouse consulted federal *Annual Reports* records and discovered the Duluth (Minnesota) Life-Saving Station on Lake Superior was operational on Minnesota Point on 1 June 1895. In 1908, Station Duluth possessed a 34-foot motor launch powered by a 25-horsepower engine, and a 6-horsepower 22-foot surfboat. But the crews favored rowboats on rescues and wrecks located less than 400 yards from shore, rather than going through the process of fueling and starting gasoline engines.

In the 1870s, more than 24 vessels sank on Lake Superior, with the loss of 84 mariners. November gales in 1872 destroyed the Duluth port that had been built on the windward side of Minnesota Point. Waves topped the breakwater and reached a grain elevator. Duluth construction experts then rebuilt the Twin Ports of Duluth (Minnesota) and Superior (Wisconsin) behind the natural shield formed by Minnesota Point.[9]

The Duluth station, at the southwestern end of the largest fresh water lake in the world, contributed to architectural history in its Lake Superior setting. The USLSS station was designed by architect George R. Tolman in 1893 and completed in 1894. The rectangular lookout tower and separated buildings for crews, boats, and equipment was attractive, sturdy, and functional. The style was emulated on the other Great Lakes and on the East Coast. Of the 279 USLSS stations in the United States in 1914, about 10 percent of the sites housed Duluth-type structures.

Lighthouse and Life-Saving Service keepers and crews faced isolation, winter storms, stinging summer insects, and ice caves that threatened beach patrols. Seasonal layoffs in the dead of winter forced crews and their families to fend for themselves. Station keepers had absolute disciplinary authority over crews, as ship captains did. Hiring and firing was instant. Cowardice and failure to go out into the stormy surf meant instant discipline and dismissal. Gale-force winds, surf and ice accounted for injuries and fatalities to USLSS crews and keepers. The captains and crews of the service and transportation ships called lighthouse tenders faced enormous waves, ice, and winds while bringing supplies and crews to and from isolated life-saving and lighthouse stations.

An 1880 Lake Michigan storm killed more than 100 people and sank as many ships. Maritime statisticians have claimed that 10,000 vessels and 30,000 people have been lost in Great Lakes storms and wrecks throughout the history of the Inland Seas. USLSS crews at the 61 Great Lakes stations saved more than 50,000 people with the loss of 40 surfmen.

In 2004, members of Congress paid tribute to the U.S. Life-Saving Service and Coast Guard stations and crews for the significant role the services played in life saving and protecting and facilitating maritime commerce, and saving property, and for the loss of life suffered by the rescuers.

The 1975 loss of the 729-foot lake freighter SS *Edmund Fitzgerald* and its entire crew in a Lake Superior November gale is a historic reminder of the power of the lakes. Winds clocked at 95 miles per hour and 35-foot waves sank the giant freighter. The *Fitzgerald* tragedy enshrines for all time the threat the Inland Seas have always posed to ships, mariners, passengers, and the life-savers of the U.S. Lighthouse Service, U.S. Life-Saving Service, U.S. Revenue Cutter Service, and the United States Coast Guard.[10]

Considerable lifeboat station history occurred at what became U.S. Coast Guard Station Duluth. U.S. Lighthouse Service and U.S. Life-Saving

Service history at the Duluth station on the southwestern shore of Lake Superior was surveyed in Thomas P. Ostrom's book, *The United States Coast Guard on the Great Lakes: A History*. Photographs and documentary sources were acquired for the *Great Lakes* book from the Maritime Collection in the Jim Dan Hill Library at the University of Wisconsin–Superior.[11]

The Twin Ports of Duluth, Minnesota, and Superior, Wisconsin, have contributed significantly to maritime commerce, shipbuilding, and national defense. The Twin Ports are a significant international port today. The U.S. Coast Guard and its predecessor agencies have been an integral part of that history.

The Duluth Coast Guard Station has utilized a variety of boats and cutters in its historical and contemporary operations. After World War II, the 41-foot and 45-foot wooden-hull utility boats were used for the general Coast Guard missions such as law enforcement, port security, and search and rescue. The sturdy 36-foot motor lifeboat served from the 1930s through the 1970s, and later. U.S. Coast Guard Station Duluth used motor lifeboat 36527 until it was donated to the Coast Guard Station Maritime Museum in Michigan.

The history of the U.S. Lighthouse Service is memorialized on the Minnesota's North Shore of Lake Superior where Split Rock Lighthouse was built in 1910. In that year, the Duluth Life Saving Station crew was active, as was the Duluth U.S. Life-Saving Service Station in 1915, when the USLSS merged with the U.S. Revenue Cutter Service to form the United States Coast Guard.

In 1907, a durable U.S. Life Boat House, prominently labeled, was situated on the Duluth shoreline with a crew ready to row out into the often-dangerous waves and storms of Lake Superior. As late as 1985, a motorized Coast Guard lifeboat was plying the quiet waters of Superior Bay at Superior, Wisconsin. And north of Ashland, Wisconsin, near the beautiful Apostle Islands, the crew at U.S. Coast Guard Station Bayfield stood ready in 2004 to sail into the variable seas and weather of Lake Superior on search and rescue missions, just as the crews of life stations and lighthouses did in earlier times.

The rescue boats of the USLSS and USCG have evolved since the 19th century from wooden, hull and oar and man-powered craft to fiberglass, steel and aluminum, and rigid hull inflatable boats, from 36 and 44-foot motor lifeboats to 47-foot surf and sea craft to the versatile 25-foot aluminum enclosed rigid-hull Defender Class boats. The historic legacy continues. The small boat stations of today's Coast Guard replicate the traditions, lessons, skills, and missions of the United States Life-Saving

Service.[12] The well-trained crews of modern Coast Guard boats would have been challenged by the Lake Superior storms the USLSS faced with their man-powered rowboats and extensive oars.

When the 200th anniversary of the United States Coast Guard was commemorated in 1990, the Coast Guard and its predecessor agencies had been in Duluth for approximately 100 years. The Steam Boat Inspection Service was operating in the city just after the Civil War, in the 1870s. The U.S. Lighthouse Service operated a light in southeastern Lake Superior on Whitefish Point as early as 1847, and in Duluth at Minnesota Point in 1857.

In 1873, the USLSS began to use the large, self-righting, pulling (rowing) and sailing lifeboats and surfboats. The boats were modeled after the life-saving craft of the British volunteer Royal National Lifeboat Institution. The modified lifeboats were useful at the Great Lakes stations where endangered mariners and passengers might be miles from stations, accessible beaches and roads, and surfmen challenged by scattered winter ice and snow.[13]

Revenue cutters sailed the late 19th century Great Lakes. The USRC *Fessenden* was a sleek, white, two-masted, iron-hulled auxiliary paddle wheel steamer. The revenue cutter was launched in 1883 in Buffalo, New York, on Lake Erie and sailed for the USRCS until 1903. The *Fessenden* was the last side-wheel steamer in the USRCS. The 190-foot cutter patrolled Lakes Erie, Huron, and Michigan.[14]

The location of the U.S. Live-Saving Service Station and Lifeboat Station at Duluth dates to 1866, the year after the Civil War ended. The land for the station was donated by the City of Duluth on 19 June 1866. The land plot of Franklyn Square was located on Minnesota Point, which extends into Lake Superior. The warranty deed was provided by the City of Duluth on 29 July 1890, but not officially recorded until 1894. The 1890 date is stated in city records as the "Date of Conveyance." The station was completed in 1894 and categorized in architectural style as "Station Type: Duluth." Donald McKenzie was appointed the first Duluth USLSS keeper in 1898. Federal records indicate he was at his post in 1915 when the USLSS was transferred to the new United States Coast Guard.

The *Annual Report* of the Life-Saving Service for fiscal year ending 30 June 1894 listed the Establishment of Stations. The report noted that the Duluth Station was receiving equipment and was "manned and put into operation." In 1894 the Duluth station was listed in the Tenth Life-Saving District. Later it was listed in the Ninth District.[15]

In fiscal year 1895, the *Annual Report* of the USLSS described the Duluth Life-Saving Station as coming to the aid of the cargo schooner

Sam Flint under the command of Captain Sevens. The sail-powered vessel was carrying copper ore from Duluth to New York when it was stranded one mile northeast of Duluth. The cargo was valued then at $10,000 and the schooner at $12,000. Personnel from the Duluth Station and a tugboat saved the vessel and all persons aboard.

One steam vessel collided with another boat and sank about one mile from the Duluth Station in September 1895. One crewman was not recovered. In the same month, another steamer was damaged in Duluth Harbor and the 20-man crew was saved.

The *Annual Report* of 1896 recorded 11 rescues the Duluth crew made on sailboats, small boats, and steam vessels. In July 1896, a 77-ton steamer was towed into safe waters. Seven smaller boats were assisted in 1897. Eighteen rescues of sailboats, sloops, and yachts occurred in 1898. The sinking of the steamer *Record* in Duluth Harbor in June 1898 cost three lives. In 1899, the Duluth Station performed 13 rescues, including assistance to a 2,476-ton steamer one mile from the station with no loss of life. In 1900, fourteen vessels were assisted by Duluth Life-Saving crews, including a steamer with a coal cargo valued at $10,000 in a vessel worth ten times as much. From 1910 to 1915, ten rescues and assistance cases were recorded.[16]

In 1897, Keeper Donald McKenzie's Duluth Station crewmember role call included John McLeod, Charles Foss, George Emerson, John Creighton, Angus Gillis, Billy McKay, Henry Casey, and John Woods. In 1947, John Woods was the surviving member of the U.S. Life-Saving Service, Lighthouse Service, and Coast Guard in Duluth. Woods had retired in 1940 after a 42-year career in lighthouses, lifeboats, and on beach patrol in the hot, humid summers and the fog, snow and cold of the Minnesota winters.[17]

Maritime writer Konnie LeMay described "one fatal drama" in the 1905 Lake Superior storm that was "played out before an estimated 19,000 horrified witnesses in Duluth ... and 24 stranded men on a vessel just beyond reach of help and hope.... Nine of the crew had drowned or were frozen or battered to death in the storm branded forever with the name of their stout ship: the *Mataafa* Blow." During that storm 11 cargo carriers were beached, split in pieces, or seriously damaged in a maritime line stretching from the site of a future lighthouse built after the storm (Split Rock Lighthouse) to Park Point in Duluth. The Duluth USLSS crew ventured out into the frigid, storm-tossed waves in their massive, strong, but vulnerable, open oar-powered lifeboat to save the surviving mariners from two of the grounded vessels.

The *Mataafa* was a gigantic 430-foot steam powered ore carrier under the command of Captain Richard Humble, who miraculously survived to later explain the 12 hours of sailing jeopardy along the North Shore of Lake Superior in the failed attempt to get safely into port. Sixty to eighty mile per hour winds, heavy seas, and blinding snow prohibited visual navigation from the bridge. The *Mataafa* ran aground outside the Duluth Canal and was broken apart by wind and waves 230 yards from shore. Several attempts by the USLSS crew to shoot a lifeline and breeches buoy to pull survivors to shore in the dark of night failed in the freezing winds and waves. The following day the courageous Duluth USLSS crew managed to save 15 survivors in two rowing trips. And the day after that, the LSS members went out onto Lake Superior again to recover nine frozen corpses.[18]

In 1915, under the jurisdiction of the newly formed United States Coast Guard, the Duluth Life-Saving Station became the Duluth Lifeboat Station. Radio voice communications were soon installed along with an electronic repair shop, light station, and office facility.[19]

Before we leave the U.S. Life-Saving Service, two unique USLSS stations must be considered. From 1880 until its decommissioning after World War II in 1947, the Pea Island Life-Saving Station on the hazardous Outer Banks of North Carolina "was crewed entirely by blacks," Dennis Noble described, and the maritime historian asked, "How could a unit in the nineteenth-century South have such a composition?"[20]

Noble answered his own query with a vivid description of the courage and success the African American crew displayed in the 30 November 1879 rescue of the crew of the British bark *M&S Henderson* in heavy seas. Station Keeper Richard Etheridge got high praise from Noble, who described the exemplary courage and leadership which motivated 1st Lt. Charles F. Shoemaker (USRCS) to successfully recommend that Captain Etheridge permanently lead his black colleagues at the station.

The community around Pea Island evidently came to appreciate the bravery and competence of the life-saving professionals in that hazardous maritime region. Captain Etheridge and his crew vindicated the faith Lt. Shoemaker and the Pea Island area community had in them in subsequent rescues, and particularly in the hurricane on 11 October 1896. On that dark night, with swirling winds and surf, the Pea Island Station surfmen rescued the crew of the commercial schooner *E. S. Newman*. Among the rescued survivors were the wife and child of the grateful schooner captain.[21]

The second unusual life-saving station crew complement Noble described was in Evanston, Illinois, on the western shore of Lake Michigan. The Evanston Life-Saving Station site was on the Northwestern University

Campus. The surfmen were generally students. The university life-savers each earned a Gold Life Saving Medal for rescuing the crew of the steamer *Calumet* in a storm on icy waters in November of 1890.[22]

The survey of the U.S. Lighthouse Service, U.S. Revenue Marine, and U.S. Revenue Cutter Service, and the U.S. Life-Saving Service in this and previous chapters provides the background to better understand the missions of the agencies and their interrelationships with the chiefs, captains, captain-commandants, and commandants of the USRCS and United States Coast Guard.

4

Revenue Marine Chiefs (1843–1889)

The commandant of the United States Coast Guard is the highest-ranking member of that unit of the United States Armed Forces. The commandant is the only four-star admiral in the Coast Guard, appointed to a four-year term by the president of the United States and confirmed by the U.S. Senate. The flag commands of admirals who assist the commandant include the vice commandant, vice admirals, assistant commandants, and rear admirals who are commanders of special departments, or serve as area and district commanders.

The chiefs of the four other U.S. Armed Forces are members of the Joint Chiefs of Staff. Although the Coast Guard is included as the fifth member of the U.S. Armed Forces—with liaison officers in the Pentagon, missions correlated with the U.S. Department of Defense, joint overseas missions with the U.S. Navy, and historic placement under the Navy in time of war—the commandant is not a member of the Joint Chiefs of Staff.

The U.S. Revenue Marine and U.S. Revenue Cutter Service had been under the U.S. Treasury Department since 1790. The U.S. Coast Guard, so-named in 1915, remained under the Treasury Department until it was assigned to the U.S. Department of Transportation in 1967 and the U.S. Department of Homeland Security in 2003. Coast Guard missions in civilian law enforcement and maritime safety remove it from exclusive military jurisdiction. Nonetheless, the Coast Guard commandant receives the same supplemental salary as a member of Joint Chiefs and sits with the Joint Chiefs during presidential State of the Union speeches.

Titles of the commissioned leaders of the U.S. Revenue Marine, U.S. Revenue Cutter Service (1790–1915) and the early U.S. Coast Guard (1915 to present) have varied. The top commanders historically have been called chiefs, captain-commandants, and commandants. To make the commandant title even more confusing, official histories designate Capt. Leonard G. Shepard, chief of the Revenue Marine Division (1889–1895), as the first titled commandant, although Shepard did not officially receive the captain-commandant title.

In 1908, Captain Worth G. Ross became the first Revenue Cutter Service officer to be officially titled captain-commandant in his appointed term of 1905–1911. The top Coast Guard commander who led the service during the transition from the Revenue Cutter Service to the newly formed U.S. Coast Guard in 1915 was Commodore Ellsworth Bertholf (1911–1919). Captain-Commandant Bertholf led the Coast Guard into and through World War I of 1914–1918, which the United States belatedly entered in 1917.

Secretary of the Treasury John C. Spencer, shown here, appointed Alexander V. Fraser the first "commandant" of the Revenue Marine in 1843 (Library of Congress).

With that description of chief, captain-commandant, and commandant titles, we can begin the history of the first two commissioned chiefs of the Revenue Marine Bureau: Captain Alexander Fraser, 1843 to 1848, and Captain Richard Evans in his 1848–1849 term.[1]

Historians of the U.S. Coast Guard place Alexander V. Fraser first on the list of chiefs of the Revenue Marine. Fraser was born in New York in 1804 and died in 1868, three years after the Civil War ended. Fraser studied nautical and commercial mathematics in New York City, and sailed as a first mate in the commercial East India trade.

Commissioned by President Andrew Jackson into the U.S. Revenue Marine in 1832, 2nd Lt. Alexander Fraser put his skills as a master mariner to use aboard the U.S. Revenue Cutter (USRC) *Alert* on patrol in Charleston Harbor, South Carolina. The U.S. Revenue Marine was ordered by President Jackson to enforce federal tariff laws that some Southern states had declared nullified. Lt. Fraser and his crew boarded commercial vessels and forced them to discharge cargoes on shore until federal duties were paid. The "Nullification Crisis" was eventually resolved, but the sectional economic and political issues of the 1830s would fester until the eruption of the Civil War (1861–1865) between the United States of America and the seceded Confederate States of America. Fraser was promoted to first lieutenant in 1838, and in 1842 Captain Fraser assumed command of the USRC *Ewing*.

U.S. Treasury Secretary John C. Spencer bestowed another promotion upon Capt. Fraser, and appointed him the first "commandant" of the Revenue Marine Bureau in 1843. Captain Fraser's innovative leadership led to merit promotions for service members and the modernization of the cutter fleet from wooden hulls and sails to iron and steam powered vessels. Marine engineers were added to the ranks, slaves were no longer used as laborers aboard cutters, pay and working conditions for enlisted personnel were improved, and the drinking of alcohol on board cutters was forbidden.[2]

Captain Fraser regularly inspected the lighthouses of the U.S. Lighthouse Service and other light stations, aids to navigation, and U.S. Life-Saving Stations. Ahead of his time, Capt. Fraser advocated merging the Life-Saving Service and Lighthouse Service with the Revenue Cutter Service, but local customs collectors controlled the stations and resisted.[3] Fraser's agency integration plans would have to wait until 1915, when the Life-Saving Service was merged with the Revenue Cutter Service to form the

Secretary of the Treasury George S. Boutwell oversaw that department through the important first years after the purchase of Alaska and the reorganization of the United States Life-Saving Service (Library of Congress).

U.S. Coast Guard; the Lighthouse Service merged with the Coast Guard in 1939.

When his term as commandant ended, Capt. Fraser took command of the USRC *Lawrence* and sailed the vessel from the Atlantic Ocean around Cape Horn in South America, and north in the Pacific Ocean to San Francisco, California, in what has been described as an epic voyage.[4]

Captain Fraser was dismissed from the service because of political and logistical quarrels with U.S. Treasury officials. Fraser went into the marine insurance business in New York, and then failed in his attempt to get reinstated into the Revenue Cutter Service during the Civil War.

Prior to leaving the Revenue Marine, Fraser displayed his innovative propensities by assisting in the development of the side-wheel steamer USRC *Harriet Lane* that gained fame in Civil War naval combat.[5]

The historians H.R. Kaplan and Lt. Cmdr. James F. Hunt (USCG) described the many positive contributions Captain Fraser made to the Revenue Cutter Service in promotion by merit, officer training methods, successful maritime and law enforcement missions, the suppression of mutiny on commercial vessels in San Francisco Harbor, advocacy of the transition from wooden sailing cutters to iron, steam-powered, paddle wheel cutters, and the placement of more cutters in New York Harbor. Kaplan and Hunt concluded Fraser's aggressive style and successes incurred the animosity of the assistant secretary of the treasury and led to the shortsighted political dismissal of Capt. Fraser from the service.[6]

Worth G. Ross accepted the title "captain-commandant" of the U.S. Revenue Cutter Service in 1908 (United States Coast Guard).

The naval historian Robert Erwin Johnson, who served on the Coast

Guard cutter *Haida* in the north Pacific during World War II, offered perceptive assessments of Capt. Alexander V. Fraser. Johnson described the animosity some superior officers displayed toward the reform-minded, innovative captain-commandant; malfunctions of the iron steam-powered cutters that Fraser had sponsored; resentful customs collectors who wanted jurisdiction over revenue cutters stationed and sailing out of their ports returned to them; and Treasury Department officials who favored transferring the problematic Revenue Cutter Service over to the United States Navy.

Professor Johnson credited Treasury Secretary John C. Spencer with a serious commitment to the service, and the wisdom to appoint Captain-Commandant Fraser to that post. But the transfer of 11 revenue cutters to support the U.S. Navy in the Gulf during the Mexican-American War (1846–1848) undermined Fraser's mission objectives.[7]

Historian Howard V.L. Bloomfield described the disputes over naval technology that caused conflicts between Fraser and other Revenue Cutter officers and Treasury Department officials. Treasury Secretary Spencer, a former secretary of war, assisted Captain-Commandant Fraser in making Revenue Cutter officers and enlisted personnel more military in bearing, discipline, and training. Revenue Cutter armament was improved and made similar to U.S. Navy standards and operations. That transformation enhanced effectiveness and morale, and respect for the service and Revenue Marine personnel.

But Captain-Commandant Fraser ran afoul of some of his colleagues and Treasury Department officials because of his insistence on transforming wooden-hull sail-powered cutters into iron-hull, paddle-wheel, steam-powered vessels. Fraser's critics pointed out cutter mechanical breakdowns, the danger of malfunctioning steam engines, and the vulnerability of hulking steam powered paddle-wheels prominently positioned on the sides of hulls to enemy rifle and cannon fire.

So, for a brief period of time, cutters returned to sails without the advantage of a steady power source when chasing sail-powered smugglers and contraband craft. Later, steam powered screw propellers that churned beneath the surface of the water were used, but initially mechanical breakdowns increased resistance to that innovative power source. Nonetheless, auxiliary commercial vessels and naval warships would use both sail and steam power during the Civil War and after. The dual power source increased ship-handling precision, and sail (wind) power conserved stores of coal on vessels during long oceanic voyages.

The internecine quarrels between the Revenue Cutter Service and the Treasury Department resulted in Fraser being relieved of his command

and placed in charge of the USRC *Lawrence*,[8] during which time Capt. Fraser further distinguished himself in feats of seamanship and officer training methods.

In his classic 1949 history of the United States Coast Guard, Captain Stephen H. Evans (USCG) surveyed the years 1790–1915 in considerable detail. Evans chronicled the increased role the U.S. Revenue Marine played in search and rescue missions in the Atlantic during heavy winter seas. In 1832, Treasury Secretary Louis McLane ordered the Revenue Marine to increase search and rescue patrols in the Atlantic, the success of which caused Congress to pass the act of 1837 that authorized the United States president to order revenue vessels "adapted to the purpose, to cruise upon the coast in the severe portion of the season ... to afford such aid to distressed navigators as circumstances and necessities require."[9]

The increased measure of Revenue Marine search and rescue activities was warranted because of the growing merchant trade and increased maritime traffic in and out of ports along the Atlantic coast, especially New York City. Foreign and domestic shipping consisted of sailing vessels like commercial schooners, whalers, clippers, and passenger vessels. The winds, storms and fog off the East Coast put ships in peril at sea and in coastal rocky shoal waters.

The U.S. Revenue Service, U.S. Life-Saving Service, and U.S. Lighthouse Service were especially busy during the stormy winter months, and increasingly coordinated their life and property saving missions. Hence the expanded role of the Revenue Cutter Service in its inspection and supply responsibilities with the lighthouse and life-saving services. First Lieutenant Alexander V. Fraser's contributions to search and rescue out of New York Harbor earned him the acclaim of the marine insurance industry and promotion to captain.[10]

With the expanded role, significance, and congressional scrutiny over expenditures, Treasury Secretary John C. Spencer concluded the service required the most competent marine bureau chief possible. Spencer's confidence in Lt. Fraser was expressed in his April 12, 1843, letter to him appointing the accomplished mariner to the position of chief of the Revenue Marine Bureau: "I have detailed you [Fraser] for duty in the Department ... under the supervision of the Secretary of the Treasury.... Your duties [will include] the charge and investigation of all estimates for the Revenue Service for disbursements made by Collectors for Revenue [and] the construction and equipment of new vessels and repair or other disposition of the old ones ... the charge of appointments in the Service ... assignments of officers to their stations ... disposition of the vessels ... force to be employed in them ... and the arrangement for their cruising

... the investigation of all charges of neglect of duty or other misconduct [and] preparation of all letters touching on these details."[11]

In forwarding the commandant's annual report of January 9, 1844, to Congress, Secretary Spencer included his positive assessment of Capt. Fraser: "Economy in expenditures and efficiency in service have been greatly promoted. The officers and men feel that the service has been elevated, and a corresponding zeal in the discharge of their duty has been strikingly exhibited."[12] With such influence and authority of command, it was inevitable that Captain-Commandant Fraser would receive the accolades and animosity of members of the Revenue Marine, disgruntled Treasury officials and customs collectors. The rivalries would cost Fraser his command of the Revenue Cutter Service, and subsequent transfer to the USRC *Lawrence*.

Captain Richard Evans succeeded Captain-Commandant Alexander Fraser. Captain Evans occupied the post of chief of the Revenue Marine Bureau (RMB) for just one year (1848–1849). Then in 1849, the RMB was abolished and the service came under the control of the commissioner of U.S. Customs until the RMB was re-established in 1869.

The morale, missions, and efficiency declined in the antebellum and Civil War years under the control of U.S. Customs. Customs collectors were not trained mariners and neglected the reforms Captain-Commandant Fraser established. The revenue cutters returned to the sectional and regional control of the customs collectors in the homeports of the vessels. The cutters were used to entertain officials and prominent civilians.

The Lighthouse and Life-Saving Services were decentralized, although the newly created Lighthouse Board, under the treasury secretary, was graced with competent scientists and U.S. Army and Navy officers, of whom several would become celebrated in U.S. military history. The notables included Adm. George Dewey (U.S. Navy) of later Spanish-American War (1898) fame; Major General George Meade (U.S. Army), later famous as commander of federal forces in the Civil War (1861–1865); and future Confederate States Navy commander and high seas raider Adm. Raphael Semmes.

In the antebellum and Civil War periods, the influence of Captain-Commandant Alexander Fraser was exhibited in the construction and missions of the 180-foot side-wheel auxiliary (sail and steam) USRC *Harriet Lane*. Under the able command of Capt. John Faunce, the *Harriet Lane* served with distinction on a U.S. Navy diplomatic and combat mission to Latin American waters and fired the first naval shot at Fort Sumter, South Carolina, in the outbreak of the Civil War.

The USRC *Miami* cruised down the Potomac River on a rainy night in May 1862. On board were Secretary of the Treasury Salmon P. Chase, General Egbert L. Viele (U.S. Army), Secretary of War Edwin M. Stanton, and President Abraham Lincoln. Their secret reconnaissance mission led them ashore in Confederate territory at Norfolk, Virginia, to investigate why the Union army had stalled, ostensibly because of the offshore shoal water barrier that prevented naval amphibious support. The revenue cutter *Miami* brought Lincoln to shore. Stanton ordered a successful attack on Confederate forces the following day.[13]

Professor Robert Erwin Johnson summarized the tenure of Captain-Commandant Fraser's successor succinctly: "[Fraser] left his successor a promising beginning, which came to naught when [Captain] Evans was transferred in 1849, after only a year in Washington."[14]

N. Broughton Devereux directed the Revenue Marine Bureau after it was re-established in 1869. Revenue Marine Chief Devereux carried out the reforms of the attentive Treasury Secretary George Boutwell from 1869 to 1871.[15]

With the United States' purchase of Alaska in 1867, U.S Revenue cutters and crews acquired the responsibility of patrolling and policing Alaska's maritime and coastal waters. Congress and the Treasury Department realized the significance of the Revenue Marine as the maritime service carried out the law enforcement, national defense, search and rescue, aids to navigation, and resource missions in the vast Arctic and polar realms. Treasury Secretary Boutwell was up to the challenge of reorganizing the Revenue Marine to have the capability to carry out the new missions.

Chief Devereux administered changes that included combining the operations of the Revenue Marine, Marine Hospital Service, Steam Boat Inspection Service, and Life-Saving Service. The inestimable Capt. John Faunce was brought on board to facilitate the reconstruction of the division. Several other capable Revenue Marine officers and a civilian assisted Faunce.

The reform commission changed the administrative structure of the Revenue Marine; modified the design, armament, and technology of cutters; and acquired motor powered vessels with sails. Devereux and Boutwell re-established some of the policies of Capt. Alexander Fraser concerning officer promotions based on merit and professional competence, not politics.

Secretary Boutwell assigned the revenue chief to administer the cutter fleet and life-saving stations. Boutwell departed from the practice of appointing a commissioned officer to head the department, and instead named a civilian chief: Sumner I. Kimball. Kimball was a competent federal bureaucrat, college graduate, and chief clerk of the U.S. Treasury. Kimball assumed his duties in 1871, and would head the new Revenue Marine Division and Life-Saving Service until 1878. Chief Kimball invariably referred to the division as a bureau.[16]

Sumner Kimball resurrected Captain Fraser's ideas. Although iron hulls were the wave of the future, budget conditions forced Kimball to build new wooden hull cutters. Kimball ended the practice of using cutters as the private yachts of customs collectors, and centralized the administration of the U.S. Revenue Marine in Washington, D.C.

President Ulysses S. Grant's treasury secretary, George S. Boutwell, supported Kimball's reforms and, as Captain-Commandant Fraser had requested, brought the Life-Saving Service into the Revenue Marine Bureau.

Kimball relieved incompetent officers from duty, cut hundreds of enlisted and commissioned personnel from the ranks for budget and professional reasons, and initiated a physical fitness regimen for officers and enlisted personnel that included climbing aloft into the towering masts and rigging that supported the sails of the wind-powered cutters.

Officers were restricted to two year duty assignments in any one port to sever political ties and broaden the knowledge of cutter officers about the coastal, lake, and river systems. Kimball failed to convince a budget conscious Congress that cutter men in the Treasury Department deserved a retirement pension like their U.S. Navy counterparts. Pensions were awarded to Navy personnel who served in combat. Revenue Cutter Service personnel served in combat only when assigned to the Navy in wartime. Sumner Kimball's insistence that winter patrols on storm-tossed ocean waters were as dangerous as Navy combat duty fell on deaf congressional ears.

Captain-Commandant Alexander V. Fraser had insisted on rigorous professional training on board seagoing cutters for officers. Kimball applied the Fraser concept in ways that led to the founding of the U.S. Coast Guard Academy in New London, Connecticut. Kimball established the U.S. Revenue Cutter Service School of Instruction. Revenue Marine officers were trained aboard the revenue schooner *Dobbin*. The school ship plied New England waters with crews of experienced cutter men who taught seamanship to carefully selected cadets.[17]

Sumner Increase Kimball lacked seagoing experience, but was familiar with the dangers of the sea and storms and shipwrecks because of his life in New England generally, and on Cape Cod, Massachusetts, in particular. Kimball's experience as state legislator, attorney, U.S. Treasury auditor, and chief clerk provided him with the intellectual and administrative background to study the issues and effectively administer the U.S.

Revenue Marine and Life-Saving Service. By 1878, Kimball "enjoyed the credit of having raised the Revenue Cutter Service from a condition of disreputable inefficiency to one of very high repute."[18]

After his appointment in 1871 as chief of the Revenue Marine Division, Sumner Kimball contributed significantly to the life-saving missions of the U.S. Revenue Marine/Revenue Cutter Service, and the Life-Saving Service. Within the next decade the Life-Saving Service administered 189 stations strategically distributed on the Atlantic, Gulf, and Pacific coasts, and Great Lakes. In 1878, Congress abided by Kimball's suggestion and established the U.S. Life-Saving Service (USLSS). In that year, Kimball was appointed the general superintendent of the Life-Saving Service and served with distinction until it was combined with the Revenue Cutter Service to form the United States Coast Guard in 1915.[19]

The historical file on Kimball's successors at the Revenue Marine Bureau is sparse. Kimball was immediately succeeded by Ezra Clark, whom Capt. Stephen H. Evans (USCG) described as supporting Kimball's policy plan and who "commented very favorably upon the success of the 1877 scheme."[20] Sumner I. Kimball had administered the cutters and life-saving stations from 1871 to 1878, until Ezra W. Clark became chief of the Revenue Marine. But even after 1878, Revenue Cutter officers performed Life-Saving Service duties, and Kimball continued to rely on Revenue Cutter Service officers for inspection and construction duties in the U.S. Life-Saving Service.[21]

Sumner Kimball was generally considered an exemplary chief. Ezra Clark or anyone else would have had difficulty measuring up to the Kimball standard. Revenue Marine Division (or Bureau) Chief Clark was assisted by civilians: Assistant Chief C.S. Trevitt in Washington, D.C., C.E. Emery, the consulting engineer located in New York, and several headquarters clerks in 1878. Some analysts believe the Clark team did not contribute significantly to cutter development, but did wisely continue the positive tradition of maintaining a federal headquarters in Washington, D.C. Revenue cutters achieved an admirable record of maritime service. The legacy of the service was greatly enhanced by the renewed tradition of appointing commissioned officers to the commandant position after 1889,[22] beginning with Captain Leonard G. Shepard.

In the meantime, the sparse and undistinguished record of Revenue Bureau Chief Peter Bonnett must be briefly considered. Contemporary *New York Times* articles contributed brief and problematic assessments of Chief Bonnett. Peter Bonnett will be discussed within the context of secretaries of the Treasury, and his successor, Captain Leonard G. Shepard.

4. Revenue Marine Chiefs (1843–1889)   49

On 17 December 1889, the *New York Times* reported that Capt. L.G. Shepard (Revenue Marine Service), commander of the steam-powered Revenue cutter *Rush* out of San Francisco, was ordered to Washington, D.C., by the treasury secretary for appointment as chief of the Revenue Marine Division. Captain Shepard was to succeed the civilian Revenue Marine Chief Peter Bonnett, who resigned after serving from 1885 to 1889. The appointment of Capt. Shepard, according to the *Times*, "was the conclusion of a long fight for the restoration of Ezra Clark."[23] Treasury Secretary William Windom (1881, 1889–1891) was persuaded to bypass Ezra Clark because of strong opposition from Revenue Marine officers who described Clark's "mismanagement, whims, irritability, and lack of adaptability to his surroundings."[24]

The *Times* described Capt. Shepard's Revenue Marine career and credentials positively and chronicled his command of the USRC *Rush*; previous command of the RC *Chase*, a cadet training vessel out of New Bedford, Massachusetts; and Shepard's cutter patrols along the North American Coast and Gulf of Mexico, and in Pacific, Atlantic, and European waters.[25]

John Sherman served as U.S. representative and U.S. senator from Ohio, and U.S. secretary of state in a career that stretched from before the Civil War to the end of the 19th century (1855–1898). Sherman's term as treasury secretary (1855–1898) and his legislative and executive branch experience gave him personal interest and significant influence over the U.S. Revenue Marine Bureau, the U.S. Revenue Cutter Service, and mission and leadership issues.

A *New York Times* letter to the editor from a U.S. Revenue Marine (USRM) spokesperson dated 14 September 1890 alluded to Sherman's influence. Reference was made to the 26 August 1890 substitute bill by then Senator Sherman "in place of the bill to transfer the Revenue Cutter Service from the Treasury Department to the Navy Department."[26]

The letter writer described the machinations of certain political leaders, their motives for supporting or opposing the transfer bill, and alleged attempts to divide the loyalties of the officers of the U.S. Revenue Service, some of whom favored, and others opposed, the proposed transfer of the cutter service to the U.S. Navy.

The anonymous USRM spokesperson alluded to former Revenue Marine chief Ezra W. Clark (1878–1885) and described Clark as an incompetent administrator during Treasury Secretary Sherman's term. The writer then described Clark's successor, Peter Bonnett (1885–1889), Bonnett's resignation, and Senator Sherman's attempts to get Clark reappointed as Revenue Marine Bureau chief. The writer concluded Sherman's failure to have Clark reinstated was the reason Sherman opposed the transfer bill, and asserted that Sherman's proposed criteria for dismissing future USRM chiefs would increase political control of the USRM Bureau and facilitate the convenient reappointment of Clark.[27]

From the context of the letter to the editor, the USRM spokesperson appeared to favor the transfer to the Navy, perhaps for enhanced prestige, benefits, mission expansion, and political influence. There would be other attempts by various interest groups to transfer the service to the U.S. Navy. The defeat of those measures occurred because courageous and articulate commandants would argue that mission autonomy, skilled and experienced personnel, responsibilities, and budget considerations would make such a transfer problematic, counterproductive, and unwise.

John Griffin Carlisle was U.S. Treasury secretary from 1893 to 1897. President Grover Cleveland appointed the former Kentucky congressman because of Carlisle's expertise on revenue, tariff, and free trade issues.[28] Secretary Carlisle and Revenue Chief Peter Bonnett (1885–1889) were cited in the 10 June 1894 edition of the *New York Times* in an uncomplimentary article datelined Washington, D.C. Carlisle was described as having inserted a request in a legislative bill out of the House Appropriations Committee to appoint a 1st lieutenant or captain to the position of Revenue Marine chief. The provision passed the House and was sent to the Senate Committee on Appropriations.

The *Times* contended former Revenue Marine chief Peter Bonnett was visiting with lawmakers to convince them to remove the Carlisle provision in order to allow a civilian chief, namely himself, to be reappointed to the post. Bonnett was also reported to have visited committee rooms to convince lawmakers that he be appointed to replace Sumner I. Kimball as head of the U.S. Life-Saving Service. The *Times* advised Secretary Carlisle to make committee members "understand that Mr. Bonnett does not represent him in his [Bonnett's] busy-bodying errands in the committee room."[29]

5

Revenue Cutter Service Chiefs and Commandants (1889–1915)

The leaders of the U.S. Revenue Marine and Revenue Cutter Service from 1843 to 1889 were generally referred to as chiefs of the Revenue Marine Bureau (or Division). Two of the early chiefs who served prior to 1889 and were commissioned officers were discussed Chapter 4: Captain Alexander Fraser, who served from 1843 to 1848; and Capt. Richard Evans, who served in 1848–1849.

In 1849, the Revenue Marine Bureau was dissolved, and the Revenue Marine was placed under the control of the U.S. Customs Commissioner until the Revenue Marine Bureau was re-established in 1869. From 1869 to 1889, four civilian chiefs, covered in previous chapters, administered the Revenue Marine: N. Broughton Devereux (1869–1871); Sumner I. Kimball (1871–1878); Ezra Clark (1878–1885); and Peter Bonnett (1885–1889).

In historical perspective, the official Coast Guard list of the leaders of the service refers to the Revenue Marine chiefs as "commandants" of the U.S. Coast Guard, even though the official term "Coast Guard" did not occur until the U.S. Revenue Cutter Service and the U.S. Life-Saving Service merged into the "U.S. Coast Guard" in 1915.

In 1911, Captain-Commandant Ellsworth P. Bertholf was the chief of the U.S. Revenue Cutter Service. In 1915, Bertholf became the commandant of the Coast Guard. Between 1889 and 1911, Coast Guard historians cite Capt. Leonard G. Shepard, Capt. Charles F. Shoemaker, and Capt. Worth G. Ross in the official historic list of "Commandants" of the Coast Guard, even though Shepard and Shoemaker were called chiefs of the Revenue Marine Division, and Capt. Ross was called "captain-commandant," a title officially created in 1903. Captain Alexander Fraser (Revenue Marine Bureau chief, 1843–1848) was sometimes referred to as "captain-commandant" but not officially granted the command title.

The term "commandant" will be used to refer to the leaders of the Revenue Cutter Service between 1889 and 1911 in this chapter. The 1911–1919 tenure of Captain-Commandant Ellsworth Bertholf will be considered in Chapter 6.

Captain Leonard G. Shepard was appointed chief of the Revenue Marine Service on 28 December 1889, and chief of the Revenue Cutter Service on 31 July 1894. Captain Shepard is cited in the official Coast Guard historical chronology under the category of "Commandants" and served as the chief of the Revenue Marine Division from 1889 to 1895.

Captain Shepard was concerned about atrophy in the Revenue Cutter Service officer corps. The aging commissioned officer corps was composed of leaders up to and over the age of 80 in high command positions, blocked opportunities for junior officers to advance. Shepard established a medical board that examined and forced officers unfit for duty out of the service. That process opened opportunities for younger officers to advance in rank and responsibility, and was a catalyst for the construction of new cutters. Captain Shepard died from pneumonia in March 1895 before completing his term of office.[1]

Treasury Secretary William Windom was determined to solve the problems of corruption and incompetence that plagued the Revenue Marine. Windom sought to remedy the situation by choosing as chief, a cutter captain experienced and knowledgeable about maritime law and safety at sea, with high personal standards for himself and the commissioned officer establishment. Accordingly, Windom ordered Captain Shepard to Washington, D.C., and named him chief of the division on 14 December 1889.[2] Captain Shepard was the first "commandant" of the Revenue Cutter Service and therefore the first commandant in U.S. Coast Guard history.

Captain Shepard advised the treasury secretary and Congress on the needs of the service to carry out its mission responsibilities. On cutters, Shepard reported that modern vessels were essential for efficiency and the capability of meeting the increasing demands of maritime safety, law enforcement, and commerce on the Great Lakes, Atlantic, Gulf, and Pacific coasts, and Alaska and to intercept escalating opium smuggling. He advocated a retirement system that rewarded and secured the lives of veteran cutter men, and championed expanded promotion opportunities for younger officers.

Shepard enhanced the professionalism, training, opportunities, and benefits of enlisted personnel, endorsed the building of steel hulled ships,

5. Revenue Cutter Service Chiefs and Commandants (1889–1915)

and encouraged the training and appointment of engineering officers to manage increasingly sophisticated cutter technology. Shepard established the position of commander of the Bering Sea Fleet, and coined the descriptive phrase that defined the Revenue Cutter Service maritime mission as "the maritime constabulary of the nation."[3]

Historian Howard Bloomfield noted that the *Army and Navy Journal* (1889) commended Treasury Secretary Windom's appointment of Captain Shepard as Revenue Marine chief because Shepard was "an experienced nautical, military leader" well qualified to head "one of the most useful government services."[4]

Captain Leonard G. Shepard served as chief of the Revenue Marine Division from 1889 to 1895 (United States Coast Guard).

Shepard convinced Congress to build up-to-date steam powered cutters instead of just repairing old ones. This led to the building of the fast 15-knot USRC *Windom*. Captain Shepard pushed for retirement pay for cutter officers and stationed the training cutter USRC *Chase*, the ship Shepard had commanded, at Arundel Cove in Baltimore to serve again as the School of Instruction vessel.

The *Chase* was now commanded by Capt. Oscar Hamlet, whose executive officer was Arctic Overland Expedition hero and future commandant Lt. E.P. Bertholf. The school ship *Chase* was resurrected by Shepard to serve as the training vessel for cadets in part to avoid, in historian Bloomfield's words, "having to depend on Naval Academy overflow for officers (given Shepard's belief that they would come) from the bottom of the barrel." Commandant Shepard's new 200-foot cutters "filled their crews with pride."[5]

Revenue Marine chiefs oversaw men like Captain Michael Healy, ruggedly suited to patrol the Alaskan frontier, but occasionally straddling the line between military discipline and impropriety (United States Coast Guard).

Truman Strobridge was a federal government archivist and worked for the U.S. Army National Archives, U.S. Marine Corps, and Joint Chiefs of Staff, and served as the official U.S. Coast Guard historian in the late 1970s. Dennis L. Noble (Ph.D.) retired from the Coast Guard in 1978 as a senior chief in marine science technology with mission experience on Bering Sea patrols and in the Arctic. Strobridge and Noble chronicled the careers of several Revenue Marine chiefs and commandants and Revenue Cutter Service missions in their book *Alaska and the U.S. Revenue Cutter Service* (1867–1915).[6]

Stonebridge and Noble described the strengths and weaknesses of Captain Michael Healy, the commander of the famed Arctic sail-steamer USRC *Bear*. Reports of Healy's heroism and alleged drunkenness and cruelty in disciplining enlisted cutter men came to the attention of Captain Shepard in the latter's capacity as chief of the Revenue Marine Division (1889–1895).

Captain Healy received a letter from Capt. Shepard, who was made aware of Healy's drinking episodes and threatened to remove him from command of the *Bear* if incidents continued. Healy responded with apologies and promised to modify his behavior. Healy subsequently showed his concern for the plight of the native population of the Eskimo/Inuit people

5. Revenue Cutter Service Chiefs and Commandants (1889–1915)

by interdicting supplies of alcohol to them, and working to ameliorate the near starvation of native populations by facilitating the transportation of reindeer herds to needy villages.[7]

Irving H. King served as professor of history and department head at the U.S. Coast Guard Academy in New London, Connecticut. King authored several naval history books, including *The Coast Guard Expands, 1865–1915: New Roles, New Frontiers*. In his book, King credited Captain Leonard G. Shepard with improving the training of Revenue Marine officers, laying the groundwork for the granting of retirement pensions first to officers and later enlisted personnel, and elevating the quality and reliability of the Revenue Cutter Service with the building of iron-hulled, technologically advanced, oceangoing cutters. To maintain the cutter fleet, Captain Shepard hired naval construction experts, appointed a Revenue Cutter officer as superintendent of construction and repair, and placed John W. Collins, a former U.S. Navy engineer, as engineer-in-chief.[8]

As chief of the Revenue Marine Division, Charles Shoemaker fostered the change of the cutter fleet from sail to steam (United States Coast Guard).

Charles F. Shoemaker was born in Iowa on 27 March 1841, the son of a U.S. Army veteran. In 1858, Shoemaker received admission as a cadet to the United States Naval Academy. After two years, Shoemaker entered the U.S. Revenue Cutter Service as a third lieutenant and was assigned to the USRC *Lewis Cass* out of Mobile, Alabama. When Capt. James J. Morrison turned the *Cass* over to the secessionist Confederate States of America, Lt. Shoemaker led the loyal enlisted and commissioned officer crew on a long trek across the South into United States territory.

After serving on several cutters, Shoemaker resigned his commission in 1864. In 1868, Lt. Shoemaker rejoined the U.S. Revenue Cutter Service and was stationed in New York City as an inspector in the Life-Saving Service. In 1878, Lt. Shoemaker was sent to Washington, D.C., and then went back to sea on the USRC *Seward* (1882). Shoemaker returned to the Life-Saving Service (1885) and was appointed inspector over several districts. In 1891 and 1893, Shoemaker served as commander of the USRC *Washington* and USRC *Hudson*. In March 1895, U.S. Treasury Secretary John G. Carlisle appointed Capt. Shepard to the post of chief of the Revenue Cutter Service.[9]

Between the years of his appointment as Revenue chief and the Spanish-American War (1898), Captain Shoemaker modernized and increased the cutter fleet with steel hull construction, compartmentalized watertight bulkheads, and advanced steam generators and engines. In 1905, at the age of 64, Capt. Shoemaker faced mandatory retirement, but was subsequently granted captain-commandant rank in 1908.[10]

On Shoemaker's watch, the last cutters rigged for sail came on station to cope with smugglers, law enforcement, and life-saving in an age of greater numbers of large pleasure and commercial steam vessels. The new steam cutters were over 200 feet long and propelled by single-screw power sources that could cruise at high speeds on oceangoing missions, and would prove themselves in the coming Spanish-American War (1898), and World War I (1914–1918).

The new revenue cutters included the *Onondaga, Algonquin, Gresham, Manning, and McCulloch*.[11] The military status of the U.S. Revenue Cutter Service was proven and enhanced by the contribution of revenue cutters in joint missions with the U.S. Navy in the Spanish-American War. Revenue Marine Chief Shoemaker consulted with Asst. Secretary of War and future president Theodore Roosevelt. Revenue cutters and crews performed gallantly in combat roles in the Caribbean and Gulf of Mexico, and in the Pacific in the Philippine Islands.[12]

In addition to skillfully administering the service in war and peace, Capt. Shoemaker concerned himself with improving the education and professionalism of cadets and commissioned officers. Shoemaker established winter quarters and classrooms at the School of Instruction. In 1903, the curriculum and training period was increased from two to three years. Later, the cadet program at the future U.S. Coast Guard Academy would be increased to four years.[13]

Shoemaker leased an area on Curtis Bay at Baltimore in Arundel Cove, where a ship (cutter) repair and boat-building yard was established.[14] Revenue Marine cutters were assigned and used by the federal government to do charting and mapping, and to support civilian and military agencies in the Arctic and other peripheral regions.

In 1902, for example, LeRoy Pelletier wrote to Capt. Shoemaker to explain that a newspaper syndicate was sponsoring his proposed polar mission. Pelletier listed his objectives, proposed a team of "hardened Arctic travelers," and outlined the needed provisions and equipment, including dog sled teams. The explorers planned to journey from Point Barrow, Alaska, to the North Pole, and then to Greenland. Pelletier requested passage on a revenue cutter. Permission was granted by Captain-Commandant Shoemaker.[15]

Between 1895 and 1904, Captain-Commandant Shoemaker was involved in publically embarrassing incidents, allegations, and court-martial proceedings that involved explorer and ice navigator Capt. Michael A. Healy. Captain Healy was the courageous commander of the revenue cutter *Bear* in Alaskan, Bering Sea, and Arctic waters. The resulting San Francisco hearings, and testimony for and against Healy by crewmembers and revenue cutter officers from the *Bear* and other vessels, made for salacious newspaper stories and negative publicity for the U.S. Revenue Cutter Service.

Captain-Commandant Shoemaker submitted Revenue Service records to support varied testimony. The service leaders and the secretary of the treasury responded to charges of Healy's alleged drunkenness, cruelty, mental breakdowns, institutional commitment, recovery, reassignment to a cutter command, forced retirement, and then Healy's death by heart failure in 1904. In 1998, the United States Coast Guard honored the controversial commander by launching a polar icebreaker, the U.S. Coast Guard cutter *Michael A. Healy*.[16]

Shoemaker's long career is worth reviewing to better understand his professional achievements and leadership skills. Shoemaker initially began his naval career with an appointment to the U.S. Naval Academy. After serving two years as a cadet midshipman, Shoemaker transferred to the Revenue Cutter Service and earned a commission in 1860.

Third Lt. Shoemaker was assigned to the USRC *Lewis Cass*, home-ported in Mobile, Alabama. As previously mentioned, Captain James J. Morrison, the commanding officer of the *Cass*, joined the secessionist cause and transferred the cutter to Confederate officials in 1861. Lt. Shoemaker and the other Union crewmembers chose to travel overland back into United States territory. During the Civil War (1861–1865), Shoemaker served on cutter escort missions off the East Coast, guard duty in the port of New York City, resigned his commission to go into business, and subsequently rejoined the service in 1868. Shoemaker then inspected Life-

Saving Stations and commanded two different cutters. This compelling professional background motivated Treasury Secretary Carlisle to appoint Shoemaker to head the U.S. Revenue Cutter Service in 1895.[17]

Captain Shoemaker's success in adding modern vessels to the cutter fleet improved the missions and morale of service members. The USRC *Manning* was one of the finest additions and would be heralded for its advanced technology and World War I mission successes. Sturdy steel frames and hull plates, copper covered wooden planks, a triple expansion engine, and single screw (propeller) drove the sleek sail-rigged, steam-powered 205-foot *Manning* at speeds exceeding 17 knots.[18]

Captain Shoemaker's successor, Capt. Worth G. Ross, was commandant when the evolution of radio significantly changed naval and merchant marine seafaring, and the U.S. Navy and U.S. Revenue Cutter fleets. The Navy constructed its first radio transmitting and receiving shore station in 1905. References to radio usage in the revenue cutter regulations that Commandant Ross dispatched in 1907 affirmed the operation of the wireless telegraph (radio) system in the fleet.

Captain Ross initiated the cadet-engineering program at the School of Instruction to train seagoing commissioned officers in the maintenance and operation of the increasingly technical cutter machinery. Professor Chester E. Dimick was appointed to the School of Instruction as a mathematics instructor in 1906. Dimick served as instructor and cadet mentor with distinction. In 1907, under Ross's watch, the USRC *Chase* was decommissioned and replaced by the auxiliary (steam and sail) training vessel USRC *Itasca*, and he added seagoing engineering training to the School of Instruction curriculum.[19]

Captain-Commandant Worth G. Ross assumed command of the Revenue Cutter Service in April 1905. Ross had entered the Revenue Cutter Service School of Instruction as a cadet in 1877 in the first graduating class. Ross was executive officer on the USRC *Woodbury*, served on the USS *Harvard*, and received a bronze medal from Congress for his actions off Santiago, Cuba, in the Spanish-American War. Four years later Ross earned the rank of captain.

Captain-Commandant Ross found a permanent location for the Revenue Cutter School of Instruction and improved the curriculum. The School of Instruction was constructed at Curtis Bay, Maryland. Congress later approved the transfer of the school to the former U.S. Army installation at Fort Trumbull in Connecticut. Fifty cadets and the faculty began the training program at Fort Trumbull in 1910. In subsequent decades, the School of Instruction would evolve into the U.S. Coast Guard Academy.

5. Revenue Cutter Service Chiefs and Commandants (1889–1915) 59

Captain-Commandant Worth G. Ross retired in 1911. Captain-Commandant Ellsworth Bertholf, the famous revenue cutter commander, Arctic explorer, and rescuer, would succeed Commandant Ross.[20]

The service assisted U.S. Customs inspectors in enforcing regulations. It enforced fishing and seal hunting statutes, immigration laws, and assisted and provided transportation for U.S. marshals and other government officials. Captain-Commandant Ross communicated regularly with the Bureau of Immigration, then under the Department of Commerce and Labor.

Captain Ross, acting under orders from the Treasury Department, directed the commanding officer of the USRC *Thetis* to transport aliens in the custody of an Alaskan district attorney to regional customs officials. The USRC *Perry* transported 17 Japanese seal hunters and a U.S. marshal from Unalaska to Valdez, Alaska.[21]

Captain-Commandant Ross responded to a 1907 transmitted request from a polar exploration team that supplies be transported to Flaxman Island off the Alaskan coast. Captain Ross notified interested representatives that Revenue Marine cutters rarely sailed much beyond Point Barrow on the North coast of Alaska, but he would consider the matter in the spring of 1908. Then Captain Ross granted permission for the commanding officer of the USRC *Thetis* "to transfer a reasonable amount of supplies as far north and east as he may be able to go next summer."[22]

Captain-Commandant Ross directed the operations of the USRC *Winona* to prevent the spread of a yellow fever epidemic in the Gulf of Mexico region (1905), and supervised six U.S. Revenue cutters in rescue missions off San Francisco in the earthquake of 1906.

Commandant Ross took charge of and sailed with the cutter fleet in its quarantine of fisherman and vessels at New Orleans, Louisiana, and out of Gulf Port, Mississippi, in coordination with the policies and activities of the Marine Hospital Service and U.S. Public Health Service.[23]

The Revenue Cutter Service School of Instruction offered a rigorous academic program ashore, and challenging sea training on the school ship. Ross had occasion to describe the curriculum at the School of Instruction and the voyage at sea on the USRC *Chase*. The cadets engaged in physical exercise, shipboard labor, climbing aloft into the towering rigging, and rigorous classes in the two-year curriculum of "Mathematics, History, English, Law, Composition, Rhetoric, Philosophy, Steam Engineering, Astronomy, International and Revenue Law," constitutional history, government, customs regulations, commerce, navigation, and ship's documents.[24]

In May 1911, Commandant Ross retired from the U.S. Revenue Cutter

Service and was succeeded by Commodore Ellsworth P. Bertholf. Then, with the amalgamation of the U.S. Revenue Cutter Service and the U.S. Life-Saving Service in 1915, the United States Coast Guard was born. Commandant Bertholf was immediately appointed to head that new sea service[25] in the name of efficiency and economy in the administration of President Woodrow Wilson.

6

The U.S. Coast Guard Is Born (1911–1919)

Captain-Commandant Ellsworth Bertholf headed both the U.S. Revenue Cutter Service and then the United States Coast Guard. Bertholf's exemplary career included Alaskan and Arctic missions, exploration, service on international commissions, managing the merging of the Revenue Cutter Service and Life-Saving Service into the U.S. Coast Guard, and leading the Coast Guard in World War I.[1] Commandant Bertholf served an 8-year term while most commandants served four, with the exception of World War II era Commandant Russell R. Waesche, who served for 10 years.

Ellsworth Bertholf was born in New York City in 1866, one year after the Civil War ended. Cadet Bertholf graduated from the School of Instruction in 1887, was stationed as a midshipman on the USRC *Levi Woodbury* for two years, and then commissioned as third lieutenant in 1889. Lt. Bertholf would serve on and command cutters along the Pacific Coast from California to Alaska, and then receive an appointment to study at the Naval War College in Rhode Island.

In 1897 he joined Dr. S.J. Call and 1st Lt. David H. Jarvis in a cross-country relief party in sub-zero Arctic cold and danger. The Revenue Cutter crew went to the rescue of 200 iced-in whale-hunting sailors off Point Barrow in the Alaska Overland Expedition of 1897–1898.

After earning a gold medal for that harrowing feat, Bertholf made a 1901 trip across the ice and snow of Russian Siberia to acquire reindeer for northern Alaskan Inuit natives as a domesticated food source. Bertholf's Arctic missions and exemplary achievements led to his appointment as commander of the USRC *Bear* and subsequent exploits on the Bering Sea Patrol.[2]

Given his exemplary service record, in June 1911 Captain Bertholf was assigned to command the U.S. Revenue Cutter Service. President Woodrow Wilson sought to economize and enhance efficiency so, guided by Captain Bertholf, Wilson merged the Life-Saving Service and Revenue Cutter Service into the U.S. Coast Guard in 1915, and appointed Bertholf the Coast Guard commandant.

Captain-Commandant Bertholf had previously served as a delegate to the International Conference on Safety at Sea (1912), helped create the International Ice Patrol and the North Atlantic International Ice Observation Patrol, assisted in the monitoring of vessel anchorage and movements for safety at sea,[3] and systematized the mission of port security.

As Captain-Commandant of the Revenue Cutter Service during the 1915 merger, Ellsworth Bertholf became the first Commandant of the United States Coast Guard (United States Coast Guard).

During World War I, Bertholf was promoted to the flag rank of commodore. After his 1919 retirement, Bertholf became vice president of the American Bureau of Shipping. In 1921, upon his death, Commandant Bertholf was buried with honors at Arlington National Cemetery in Virginia.[4]

Bertholf's role in preparing the Coast Guard for U.S. entry into the war in 1917, and its port security and wartime missions, will be chronicled in subsequent pages, as will his fight to separate the Coast Guard from the wartime U.S. Navy to maintain the autonomy of the service.

In his classic history of the Coast Guard from 1790 to 1915, Capt. Stephen H. Evans described the 1897–1898 Overland Expedition and lead-

6. The U.S. Coast Guard Is Born (1911–1919) 63

ership role that Lt. Ellsworth Bertholf played with his Revenue Service colleagues in the rescue of the stranded whalers off Point Barrow, Alaska. Evans cited the request by President William McKinley for volunteers to mount the Arctic expedition.

Captain Francis Tuttle sailed the USRC *Bear* as far north into Alaskan waters as the sea ice permitted, and called for volunteer cutter men to embark on the 1500 mile overland trek on dog sleds. Alaskan civilians, seasoned Inuits, and a pastor provided essential assistance along the way.

The starving whalers were found and saved by the reindeer meat and health measures initiated by Dr. Jarvis. The courage and skills of the Revenue Cutter crew resulted in the safe return of the whalers to warmer United States waters. Commendations and medals were awarded to the rescuers for the "heroic service rendered."⁵

The drive to finally combine the Life-Saving Service and the Revenue Cutter Service sprang from a word coined by President William Howard Taft: "unifunctionalism." According to its philosophy, no two governmental bodies should share a mission (Library of Congress).

Bertholf was later selected the first Revenue Cutter Service officer to attend the Naval War College in Newport, Rhode Island, at the time Captain Alfred Thayer Mahan (U.S. Navy) was on the faculty. Mahan's book *The Influence of Sea Power Upon History* (1890) argued that the U.S. Navy should have an expanded global presence to contest foreign navies. Historian David Helvarg wrote that Bertholf concluded the Revenue Cutter Service would then assume responsibility for the control and defense of U.S. coastal waters.⁶

In 1912, Commandant Bertholf faced the power of the Commission on Economy and Efficiency in the administration of President William H. Taft. The commission recommended the abolition of the Revenue Cutter Service, and the transfer of its stations, boats, cutters, and missions to the U.S. Navy and other federal agencies.

A tragic event insured the continuation of the Revenue Cutter Service. The White Star passenger liner SS *Titanic*, a vessel owned by industrial magnate J.P. Morgan, hit a North Atlantic iceberg with the loss of more than 1500 lives. Congressional hearings investigated the tragedy and interviewed survivors. National newspaper publicity focused attention on maritime safety issues. Congress then passed laws that required enough lifeboat space to accommodate all passengers and crew on board ocean vessels, constant ship radio watches, evacuation drills, and the creation of the International Ice Patrol with ship surveillance and reports on the location and direction of the giant icebergs. The U.S. Navy initiated the patrols, but concluded it did not have the ships to spare for such missions. With its Alaskan ice patrol experience, the U.S. Revenue Cutter service stepped into the North Atlantic gap and put its cutters to work.

In contemporary times, the U.S. Coast Guard has patrolled the ice belt in huge C-130 cargo aircraft. Historian David Helvarg predicted remote-sensing satellites would supplement and perhaps replace the C-130 patrols.[7]

Treasury Secretary Franklin MacVeagh had jurisdiction over the U.S. Life-Saving Service and U.S. Revenue Cutter Service. MacVeagh asked Life-Saving Service Chief Sumner Kimball and Revenue Cutter Service Captain-Commandant Bertholf to preserve the essential functions of the two agencies by combining the non-military Life-Saving Service with the military Revenue Cutter Service. Eventually, civilian Life-Saving Service personnel assimilated into the military ranks.

The coordination plan was submitted to Congress and approved by the Senate (1914) and House (1915). The Act to Create the Coast Guard placed the service under the Treasury Department and placed under U.S. Navy control in time of war, "as the President may direct." President Wilson signed the act on 25 January 1915. The president appointed Captain Bertholf to the post of captain-commandant of the U.S. Coast Guard.[8]

The career of Captain-Commandant Bertholf would be commemorated with the construction of the National Security Cutter *Bertholf*,[9] a state of the art 418-foot cutter. The *Bertholf* (WMSL-750) was launched in 2006, commissioned in 2008, and home-ported at Alameda, California.

Maritime historian C. Douglas Kroll wrote that Bertholf was appointed the first commandant of the Coast Guard over 22 senior officers,[10] which

6. The U.S. Coast Guard Is Born (1911–1919)

stimulated animosity and jealousy on the part of several of his commissioned colleagues and cost the commandant future support.

In 1918, Captain-Commandant Bertholf was promoted to commodore. Bertholf incurred additional intra-service hostility when he refused to support the preference of a majority of Coast Guard officers to have the postwar service remain under the jurisdiction of the U.S. Navy. Bertholf concluded that efficiency and mission specialization required the service to remain autonomous despite the likelihood of increased U.S. Navy prestige, pay, and benefits, and expanded mission and promotion opportunities.

But Bertholf acted on principle, not popularity, and was motivated out of concern for Coast Guard enlisted personnel who might be relegated to secondary status by transfer to the U.S. Navy. The Coast Guard was returned to the Treasury Department in 1919, the year Bertholf retired.[11]

If some of his ambitious and disappointed commissioned colleagues failed to appreciate the commandant, the U.S. Coast Guard hierarchy had not. The 1897–1898 Overland Expedition is embedded in Coast Guard lore and commemorated in the U.S. Coast Guard Cutter (USCGC) *Bertholf*. His courageous Arctic compatriots are also honored: Captain David H. Jarvis with the USCGC *Jarvis*, and Dr. Samuel J. Call (U.S. Public Health Service) with the Call Medical Clinic at U.S. Coast Guard Training Center Cape May, New Jersey.[12]

Commandant Bertholf's administrative skills were evident early in his tenure. In 1911 the U.S. Treasury Department compartmentalized the U.S. Revenue Cutter Service into the following divisions: law, operations, construction, engineering, supply, and ordnance. A captain headed each division. Bertholf established regional offices in New York, Boston, San Francisco, and Port Townsend. Administrative autonomy was granted to regional commanders. Customs collectors were excluded from jurisdiction over the revenue cutters in their respective ports,[13] finally ending the troubled history of port politics.

When Congress passed the Act to Create the Coast Guard in January 1915, the assets of the U.S. Revenue Cutter Service and fledgling U.S. Coast Guard were significant. As of 20 January 1915, combined assets included 270 stations, 10 launches and harbor tugboats, 44 vessels and boats of various types, and 25 oceangoing Revenue cutters. As of 28 January, when President Wilson signed the Coast Guard bill, Revenue cutters became Coast Guard cutters. The Coast Guard bill provided for a service complement of 4,093 enlisted, warrant officer, and commissioned officer personnel.

The service had a national headquarters in Washington, D.C., 17 regional districts and commands, and an officer-training academy. Irving H. King succinctly summarized the contributions of the Revenue Cutter

Service and Life-Saving Service: as of 30 June 1914, the "services had destroyed (or towed) 32 derelicts (abandoned, drifting, marooned vessels ashore or at sea), rescued 5,238 persons from peril, assisted 2,147 vessels with a total of 10,983 persons on board, and a combined value (vessels and cargo) of $24,386,191. The cost of operating both services was $4,781,949."[14]

The Revenue Cutter Service was assigned the responsibility of tracking and monitoring the location of icebergs in the North Atlantic, reporting iceberg information by radio, and making written reports for the safety of the international maritime community. Commandant Bertholf's *Reports of Vessels on Ice Patrol in the North Atlantic* (1913) added significantly to knowledge about icebergs: their numbers, locations, physical size and characteristics, and weather and sea patterns. The report was based on information contributed by revenue cutter ice patrol captains like Capt. Charles E. Johnston (USRC *Seneca*) and Capt. Aaron L. Gamble (USRC *Miami*).

The cutters *Seneca* and *Miami* steamed out of East Coast ports to the North Atlantic iceberg zones and relieved each other after being replenished with coal and other supplies at U.S and Canadian ports along the Atlantic Coast. Radio reports were transmitted to major Atlantic Coast radio stations, the Hydrographic Office in New York City, ships at sea, and in written reports sent to headquarters in Washington, D.C.

While on the ice patrol, cutter crews performed the missions of assisting ships and crews at sea, alternating sail and steam power to conserve coal, and coping with the heavy seas, frigid weather, and North Atlantic fog.

The icebergs ranged in frequency from 30 to 100 between Greenland and the Grand Banks in the first cutter patrol season, with sizes estimated from 200 to 400 feet long, heights up to 70 feet, and one calculated at 150 feet. Bergs drifted with the ocean currents. One was charted for a distance of 32 miles in a single day. With fog and variable seas, one cutter report advised all ships at sea that "the vigilance of the officer of the watch be unremitting."[15]

The national and international maritime organizations forwarded their appreciation of the Revenue Cutter Service Ice Patrol to Treasury Secretary William G. McAdoo and Commandant Ellsworth P. Bertholf. At an international conference in London, to which Bertholf was a delegate, 14 maritime nations agreed to contribute funds to support the costs of the Revenue Cutter Service Ice Patrol. President Wilson ordered the cutter service, and later the Coast Guard, to continue the patrols.[16]

Missions were complex and demanding, and expanded on Commandant Bertholf's watch. Responsibilities included the enforcement of neutrality, immigration, navigation, quarantine, and smuggling laws; policing

6. The U.S. Coast Guard Is Born (1911–1919)

and patrolling regattas and other maritime events; saving lives and property at sea and ashore; and providing medical service to commercial fisherman. Some cutters carried U.S. Public Health Service medical doctors. Other cutters had medical manuals and trained crews. Cutter crews interdicted Chinese immigrants and the opium trade. The Revenue Cutter Service continued military training and ordnance upgrades to be prepared for integration with the U.S. Navy in wartime and on various national defense and security missions.[17]

Missions in challenging weather and heavy seas resulted in the loss of two grounded cutters in Alaskan waters in 1910 and 1914. Commandant Bertholf understood the losses, given his own cutter command experience in the largely uncharted, foggy, icy, high seas environment of the North Pacific. Coast Guard historian Irving King succinctly concluded, "The surprising thing is that cutters navigated these waters for so many years with so few mishaps. One could rationally say the same about the loss of just fourteen cutters in the 124-year history of the Revenue Cutter Service."[18]

Ellsworth Bertholf's contributions to the Life-Saving Service, Revenue Cutter Service, and Coast Guard, are difficult to exaggerate. His long naval career is a testimonial to exemplary seamanship, command presence, and principled leadership.

Bertholf started his maritime career with an appointment to the U.S. Naval Academy as the result of high competitive examination scores, the encouragement of his New Jersey high school principal, Professor Nelson Haas, and the recommendation of Congressman John Hill. But Bertholf's subsequent expulsion from the U.S. Naval Academy for excessive demerits, insubordination, and the hazing of a peer cadet were not an auspicious start to a naval career. Similar infractions and reprimands inexplicably occurred after Bertholf applied and was admitted to the U.S. Revenue School of Instruction, and then stationed as a cadet on board the training ship *Salmon P. Chase*. Despite the demerits and reprimands he accumulated between 1882 and 1887, cadet Bertholf was well trained on the USS *Constellation* and the USRC *Salmon P. Chase*.

Bertholf finally received a third lieutenant commission in 1889, a process delayed because of disciplinary problems, and the obligatory retaking of essential examinations. High scores on the required examinations and a good interim record earned while Bertholf served as a deck watch officer on the ocean-going USRC *Levi Woodbury* provided the fortunate naval aspirant a belated commission and professional start to what would become an exemplary career as a line officer, cutter commander, U.S. Life-Saving Service inspector, and the first U.S. Coast Guard commandant.[19]

Bertholf acquired command experience as an executive officer on several Revenue cutters in the North Pacific, including the USRC *Bear* that he would later command.

In 1895, 2nd Lt. Bertholf was ordered to attend the Naval War College in Newport, Rhode Island, where he studied under prominent U.S. Navy instructors, and learned naval tactics, strategy, seamanship, history, and ordnance—knowledge that would help him coordinate Revenue Cutter and Coast Guard missions with the Navy during his time as the commandant during World War I.[20]

In 1907, Captain Bertholf and his family journeyed to San Francisco to take command of the USRC *Bear*. The famed wooden-hull auxiliary sail and steam powered cutter was under repair in preparation for duty in the challenging weather, fog, unchartered waters, and the heavy seas in Bering Sea waters.

Electric illumination and wireless communications modernized the 198-foot revenue cutter. On that tour of duty, Bertholf and his skilled and disciplined crew handled law enforcement and rescue missions; coordinated with magistrates, courts, and U.S. marshals; and enforced seal protection laws against armed Japanese crews and vessels. Violators were fined, prosecuted, and imprisoned. Contraband and vessels were confiscated.[21]

Between 1910 and 1911, Capt. Bertholf returned the USRC *Bear* to California, assumed command of the USRC *Morrill* at Detroit, Michigan, on the Great Lakes, and expressed interest in succeeding retiring Commandant, Captain Worth G. Ross. In June 1911, the U.S. Senate confirmed Captain Ellsworth Bertholf as captain-commandant of the U.S. Revenue Cutter Service.[22]

President Woodrow Wilson and Congress declared war on Germany because of that nation's unrestricted submarine (U-boat) warfare against U.S. commercial vessels that carried goods to Britain.

The U.S. Coast Guard was transferred to the control of the U.S. Navy for the duration of the Great War. Commandant Bertholf cooperated with the U.S. Navy in shared and mixed crews, training, and cutter patrols across the Atlantic. The Coast Guard increased its ranks through the national draft (conscription) and shortened enlisted and officer training programs.

Coast Guard cutters engaged in anti-submarine warfare missions using deck guns and depth charges and escorted Allied (British, American, French) merchant ships across the Atlantic and into the Mediterranean Sea. The service distinguished itself in missions at home and abroad. The USCGC *Onondaga* became the U.S. Coast Guard Academy training vessel

6. The U.S. Coast Guard Is Born (1911–1919)

to replace the *Itasca* that was assigned as a cruising cutter with the U.S. Navy Fleet.

Other cruising cutters, ranging from 165 feet to 205 feet in length, added to the wartime legacy of the Coast Guard and U.S. Navy. The cutters included the *Ossipee, Algonquin, Yamacraw, Manning, Tampa,* and *Seneca.*

On the domestic front, the assets of the U.S. Lighthouse Service (stations and vessels) and the stations of the former U.S. Life-Saving Service enhanced the patrol and communications systems.

The station crews were on the lookout for German U-boats and ships in distress from storms, accidents, and enemy torpedoes. Captain Godfrey L. Carden, captain of the Port of New York, administered a system of Coast Guard patrols, shipboard inspections, fire fighting, and explosive loading detachments that laid the foundations for the port and harbor security operations that emanated from the Espionage Act of 1917. Captain Carden contributed to the establishment of the U.S. Coast Guard as the premier port security agency at home and abroad from World War I to the present.

The shorelines of New York and New Jersey were kept free of tragedies by Capt. Carden's Coast Guard teams. "Captains of the Port" were also established at the strategic shipping centers of Sault Ste. Marie (Michigan), Norfolk (Virginia), and Philadelphia (Pennsylvania).

Captain-Commandant Bertholf placed 1st Lt. Russell R. Waesche in charge of the division of communications at U.S. Coast Guard Headquarters in Washington, D.C. The future World War II commandant developed an intricate electronic communications network that connected East Coast Navy and Coast Guard assets and other federal agencies in a system fully operational by 1919.

Coast Guard air assets were expanded during the war. Aviation pioneers like Lt. Elmer F. Stone and Lt. Norman B. Hall flew missions in borrowed aircraft. Stone and Hall were directed by Bertholf, along with other Coast Guard aviators, to attend the U.S. Navy School of Aviation at Pensacola, Florida. Congress authorized the construction of Coast Guard airbases along the Great Lakes and ocean coasts. Coast Guard officers commanded naval air stations in the U.S. and France.

On 26 September 1918, USCGC *Tampa* was torpedoed with the loss of 111 Coast Guard members. Another 81 of the 8,835 Coast Guardsmen who served in the war would also perish.

After the war ended in 1918, several U.S. Navy and Coast Guard officers favored keeping the service in the Department of the Navy as a separate entity, similar to the status of the U.S. Marine Corps. Bertholf appeared before a congressional committee and argued successfully against the plan. The U.S. Coast Guard returned to the jurisdiction of the U.S. Treasury in 1919, the year Commandant Bertholf retired.[23]

After his retirement, Captain Ellsworth Bertholf, with the support of both the U.S. Treasury and U.S. Navy secretaries, moved to New York City with his wife, Emilie Innes Sublett Bertholf, and accepted a position as vice president with the American Bureau of Shipping.

The bureau, its significance and missions enhanced by Bertholf's knowledge and reputation, advised the merchant shipping industry on standards of ship construction, crew training, licensing, safety, technology, and transportation. Expertise and ship inspections were believed by informed observers and maritime insurers to have kept shipping safer, and lessened the frequency of accidents and maritime tragedies.

While Bertholf was serving in the American Bureau of Shipping, he learned about the transfer of the U.S. Coast Guard from the wartime U.S. Navy back to the U.S. Treasury Department as per the 28 August 1919 executive order of President Woodrow Wilson.

Then, on 11 November 1921, the seemingly healthy and active former commandant died of a heart attack at the age of fifty-five. *The New York Times* commemorated the career and contributions of "Commodore E. P. Bertholf ... Arctic Hero ... known on every coast of the United States and Alaska."

U.S. Coast Guard Headquarters in Washington, D.C., commemorated Bertholf's career and ordered that official remarks be read at every Coast Guard unit muster. In mid–November, in ceremonies performed by U.S. Navy and U.S. Coast Guard personnel and civilian clergy, Bertholf was buried with honors at Arlington National Cemetery. In 1928, near Bertholf's grave, in the words of historian C. Douglas Kroll, a monument was placed at the site to be named "Coast Guard Hill" that commemorates "the U.S. Coast Guardsmen killed in action in World War I [and] lists the names of all those lost aboard [the U.S. Coast Guard cutters] *Seneca* and *Tampa*."[24]

7

Rum Runners and Depression (1919–1936)

William Edward Reynolds was born on 11 January 1860, in the year preceding the outbreak of the American Civil War (1861–1865). The Maryland native earned appointment as a U.S. Revenue Service cadet in May of 1878. On 17 June 1880, Third Lt. Reynolds began his duties as a commissioned officer.

His first major assignment occurred in 1881 as a member of a rescue sled team on the north shore of Russian Siberia, as a crewmember of the 140-foot U.S. Revenue Cutter (USRC) *Corwin* sled team that searched for the missing exploration steamer SS *Jeannette*. In 1898, during the Spanish-American War, Lt. Reynolds assumed command of USRC *Louis McLane*, named, like the *Corwin*, after a treasury secretary. The *Louis McLane* was assigned to the North Atlantic Fleet.

Reynolds earned his captain's stripes in 1903. During World War I, Capt. Reynolds was named the chief of staff of U.S. Naval District Twelve headquartered in San Francisco. In 1919, Capt. Reynolds was assigned to U.S. Coast Guard Headquarters at Washington, D.C., and later appointed captain-commandant with promotion to commodore.

Subsequently, Reynolds was promoted to rear admiral, as per act of Congress on 12 January 1923. Reynolds retired in 1924 after a distinguished 45-year career. Admiral Reynolds died in 1944, near the end of World War II.[1]

Captain Alex Larzelere, author of *The Coast Guard in World War I*, cited then Capt. William E. Reynolds as one of several Coast Guard officers assigned to the staff of U.S. Navy district commanders. In April 1917, Reynolds was placed in command of the Coast Guard's Pacific Coast southern division and reported for duty with the U.S. Navy. Reynolds commanded Twelfth Naval District harbor patrols, and then was appointed chief of staff to the commandant of the 12th Naval District for the duration of the war.[2]

In the immediate post-war period (1919–1923), the Coast Guard was restored to peacetime status, but its leaders had to battle in the political thickets to thwart efforts to keep the service under the control of the War Department and U.S. Navy.

Commandant William Reynolds and Treasury Secretaries Carter Glass and David Houston fought off politicians, Navy officials, and even some Coast Guard officers to maintain the independent status of the Coast Guard. President Woodrow Wilson issued an executive order in August 1919 directing the U.S. Coast Guard to resume its peacetime missions under the jurisdiction of the U.S. Department of the Treasury.[3]

Commandant Reynolds led the USCG in the early controversial years of Prohibition when the service enforced the unpopular laws prohibiting the sale of alcoholic beverages. In the years of the commandant's leadership, the number of the cadets at the U.S. Coast Guard Academy expanded from 23 in 1920 to 72 in 1923.[4]

In their book on U.S. Revenue Cutter patrols and rescues in the Bering Sea and Arctic regions, Truman R. Strobridge and Dennis L. Noble described the environment in which Lt. Reynolds and his cutter crew colleagues operated: "Officers and crews had to suffer long hours in an extremely hostile environment ... lookout watches in the ice pack (where) polar winds howl across the frozen sea and seem to cut into your very soul. One wonders if ... 3rd Lt. William E. Reynolds [ever pictured himself] mushing over the frozen Siberian environment with a dog sled in search of whalers" as officers and men did in search of stranded mariners.[5]

First Lieutenant William E. Reynolds was named by the Treasury Department to be a member of the court-martial board and prosecuting officer in the 1896 military trial of the controversial cutter commander Michael A. Healy. The heralded commander of the USRC *Bear* was charged with drunkenness on board the vessel and putting the ship, crew and mission at risk in hazardous circumstances.

Lt. Reynolds had served with then 1st Lt. Healy on the USRC *Corwin* in 1881, when he placed the U.S. flag and claimed Wrangell Island for America. Reynolds had significant experience in Alaskan and Arctic waters, having participated in the search for the crew of the polar exploration vessel SS *Jeannette.*

The final guilty verdict against Capt. Healy resulted in the decision of Treasury Secretary J.G. Carlisle to punish Healy by reduction to the lowest position on the Revenue Cutter Service captain's list, a four year suspen-

7. Rum Runners and Depression (1919–1936)   73

sion from rank and command, a public reprimand to be communicated to all revenue cutter officers, and a final warning to Healy of dismissal from the Revenue Cutter Service for any subsequent intoxication incidents.[6] Lt. Reynolds administered his prosecutorial responsibilities professionally and objectively in the face of alleged perjured testimony and extensive national publicity about the San Francisco proceedings.

Commandant Ellsworth Bertholf, who led the U.S. Coast Guard during its transition from the U.S. Revenue Cutter Service and through World War I, had recommended to Treasury Secretary Carter Glass that Reynolds succeed him as head of the service. William Edward Reynolds ended his career in 1924, having served with honor as commander of the Bering Sea Patrol Fleet, superintendent of construction and repair at Coast Guard Headquarters in Washington, D.C., and Twelfth Naval District chief of staff.[7] He had participated in dangerous polar rescue missions, was prosecuting officer in a controversial court-martial, and was U.S. Coast Guard commandant in a period of rapid transition, asset and personnel challenges, and multi-mission expansion.

Rear Admiral Frederick C. Billard headed the Coast Guard from 1924 to 1932. The Washington, D.C., native was accepted as a U.S. Revenue Cutter Service cadet in 1894 and then served on the USRC *Chase*.

Billard achieved the ranks of third lieutenant in 1896 and captain in 1912. During the Spanish-American War (1898), Lt. Billard was assigned to the USRC *Corwin* in the Pacific Fleet. Between 1900 and 1905, he was an instructor and navigator on the training vessel USRC *Chase*. From 1906 to 1911, Billard had served as an assistant to USRC Chief W.J. Ross.

Captain Billard was named commander of the U.S. Navy warship USS *Aphrodite* in the Atlantic in 1918 in World War I; he was assistant to the U.S. Coast Guard commandant in 1919 and appointed U.S. Coast Guard Academy superintendent in 1921. Rear Adm. Billard succeeded Commandant Reynolds in 1924.[8]

The enforcement of Prohibition (1920–1933) was administered by the U.S. Treasury Department and U.S. Coast Guard. The mission requirements of illegal alcohol interdiction caused the service to grow significantly in cutters, patrol boats, ground assets, and personnel under Commandant Billard. The purchase and construction of patrol craft and the transfer of U.S. Navy destroyers to the Coast Guard caused fiscal, logistical, tactical, and administrative challenges for the service. Admiral Billard's administrative genius matched the challenges. Billard expanded cadet and officer training programs to meet mission requirements by modifying the curriculum and infrastructure at the U.S. Coast Guard Academy.

Rear Adm. Billard served three terms as U.S. Coast Guard commandant and died at his post. Coast Guard historian R. E. Johnson observed that Billard led the service during its expanded Prohibition law enforcement mission while continuing to carry out the myriad of traditional Coast Guard responsibilities.[9]

Alex Larzelere chronicled Billard's exemplary service in World War I. While Capt. Frederick C. Billard was serving as the U.S. Coast Guard Academy superintendent, he was assigned command of the U.S. Coast Guard Cutter (USCGC) *Onondaga* at New London, Connecticut. Under Captain Billard, the training cutter *Onondaga* convoyed Coast Guard units to various stations. The *Onondaga* transported newly commissioned cadets to the cruising (oceangoing) cutters being prepared for service in European waters. The *Onondaga* then escorted U.S. Army harbor vessels from port locations to Coast Guard units for use in the war. One of Billard's missions involved the CGC *Onondaga*'s escort of the Great Lakes cutter *Mackinac* to the Atlantic coast and Long Island Sound off the port of New York City.

Captain Billard received orders to report to London in 1918 for overseas duty and command of the 302-foot USS *Aphrodite* that had a crew complement of 121 enlisted personnel and 11 officers. Billard escorted merchant vessels along the coast of France. Subsequently, the *Aphrodite* served as the flagship of a squadron that steamed out of the French port of Bordeaux. Shortly after the 11 November armistice that ended World War I, the USS *Aphrodite*

Commandant William Reynolds served in the post just after the end of World War I and during the earliest days of Prohibition (United States Coast Guard).

struck a German mine in the North Sea, but the crew managed to complete the mission. After brief hospitalization in London, Captain Billard returned to the United States in May of 1919.[10]

Rear Adm. Billard played a role in the approval of the U.S. Coast Guard marching song that got its title from the service motto *Semper Paratus* ("Always Ready"). Commandant Billard wrote the following about the pending musical piece: "*The Coast Guard* magazine is doing a commendable bit of work in publishing 'Semper Paratus.' The words, written by the late Captain [Francis Saltus] Van Boskerck [USCG] exemplify clearly and with inspiration the record and traditions of our service. May the Coast Guard anthem become as popular as the standard marches and anthems of the other branches of our military and naval services."[11]

Among the stirring historic "Semper Paratus" stanzas are: "We fight on land and sea. Through howling gale and shot and shell, to win our victory. Semper Paratus is our guide, Our Pledge, our motto too. We're 'Always Ready' to do or die! Aye! Coast Guard, we are for you!"[12]

Adm. Billard was challenged with the administration of the Coast Guard in the Prohibition era (1920–1933). Some Coast Guard personnel did "do or die" in shootouts with illegal alcohol "rum runners." The Coast Guard both suffered and inflicted fatalities on the Great Lakes and in the Atlantic and Gulf coastal regions. The shootings and arrests resulted in court cases, public demonstrations, critical newspaper editorials, retaliation against off-duty Coast Guard personnel, and public demands for Commandant Billard's resignation. C. Douglas Kroll

Rear Admiral Frederick Billard served three terms as commandant and died in office (United States Coast Guard).

summarized the impact of the Prohibition mission upon the Coast Guard concisely: "By the end of their thirteen-year-long 'Rum War,' the service had dramatically expanded in size (personnel and assets), but lost much of its hard-earned credibility with the public."[13]

The National Prohibition (or Volstead) Act of 1919 was named after its sponsor, Congressman Andrew J. Volstead. Volstead's home state of Minnesota became one of the national epicenters for alcohol transportation on land (from Canada) and on the Great Lakes. The western shore of Lake Superior encompassed the eastern Minnesota boundary and port of Duluth, northern Wisconsin (the major port of Superior), and Michigan. Rum running and enforcement activities also occurred on the Atlantic, Gulf, and Pacific coasts. Missions were carried out by harbor boats and oceangoing Coast Guard cutters. Coast Guard aircraft on land and sea and twenty reconditioned and transferred U.S. Navy destroyers were added to Coast Guard assets.

Rum running criminals and racketeers became heroes. Civilians openly flouted the law. Some state, local, and federal officials took bribes to look the other way. Congress charged the U.S. Treasury Department and its law enforcement units, the Secret Service and the U.S. Coast Guard, with the dangerous task of enforcing the unpopular law until its repeal in 1933. Federal law enforcement officials joined forces with local and state police agencies to enforce Prohibition.

U.S. and foreign smugglers ran sail and motor craft outside the national 12-mile sovereign coastal boundary and transferred contra-

Commandant Harry Hamlet was the son of a Revenue Cutter Service officer (United States Coast Guard).

band cargoes to smaller vessels for inshore landings. To carry out inland river, lake, port, and ocean enforcement in the vast maritime realm of U.S. waters, Rear Adm. Billard asked President Calvin Coolidge for $28 million to build and acquire the assets and infrastructure necessary to conduct the "Rum War." Commandant Billard calculated that the requested appropriation would facilitate the purchase or building of more than 90 small boats, 200 cabin-type cruisers, 20 brand new cutters, and the 3,500 commissioned officers and enlisted personnel needed for the assigned mission. Congress reduced Billard's appropriation to $13 million in 1924.

The *New York Times* heralded the new U.S. Coast Guard war on drug and alcohol runners. Adm. Billard recognized that the service was assigned a tremendous responsibility, and he welcomed the opportunity to expand Coast Guard responsibilities, missions, publicity, and prestige. Smaller 75-foot patrol boats and large oceangoing cutters conducted the patrols. Coast Guard personnel manned U.S. Navy destroyers. In just one incident in 1922, the USCGC *Acushnet* captured a sailing schooner off Cape Cod, Massachusetts, that was carrying 2,000 cases of liquid contraband.

The Coast Guard air fleet was expanded to do coastal and ocean reconnaissance. The Coast Guard air arm included rugged Chance Vought UO-4 float (sea) planes. U.S. Customs Service and U.S. Navy aircraft were added to the Coast Guard air fleet to accommodate the order of Treasury Secretary Henry Morgenthau to expand Coast Guard responsibilities in international border surveillance to supplement the U.S. Border Patrol.

The 1933 repeal of the 18th (Prohibition) Amendment to the U.S. Constitution found the Coast Guard in an expanded position with increased personnel, assets, and budgets. The reputation of the service in the Prohibition Era had been both positively enhanced and damaged. The bribery of civilian officials, police, judges, and even a few Coast Guard personnel reflected badly on government agencies. But the courage, determination, and professionalism exhibited by law enforcement and public safety personnel in civilian and military venues reflected positively on the enforcers, as did the danger of the missions and the casualty counts.

The U.S. Coast Guard proved it could carry out its law enforcement responsibilities and fly and sail its air and sea assets with skill and competence. The lessons learned would serve the Coast Guard and the nation well in subsequent conflicts at home and overseas in integrated missions with domestic law enforcement agencies and the other U.S. Armed Forces.[14]

While Adm. Billard administered the Coast Guard bureaucracy, missions, budgets and assets, he did not neglect the training and support of Coast Guard personnel. Having been the superintendent of the U.S. Coast

Guard Academy, Billard pushed to improve the campus and curriculum of the Fort Trumbull, Connecticut, site. Billard favored the transfer of the academy to the adjacent New London site. He supported the improvements and modernization of the engineering curriculum. Treasury Secretary Andrew Mellon laid the foundation for Hamilton Hall at the academy's New London site on the Thames River in 1931, after New London officials spearheaded the process. To meet the medical, financial, curricular, and morale needs of enlisted personnel, the League of Coast Guard Women was organized in 1924.

Commandant Billard was instrumental in facilitating access to entertainment and physical exercise for Coast Guard personnel at isolated land and oceanic patrol stations. He coordinated the development of correspondence courses and libraries so enlisted personnel could earn rate promotions. Initially the courses and examinations were based upon and contributed to by the U.S. Navy, U.S. Marine Corps Institute, and U.S. Merchant Marine. Subsequently, the U.S. Coast Guard Academy designed and administered curricular, examination, and certification procedures.

Adm. Billard was successful in planning and acquiring funds for the construction of new cutters capable of carrying out missions in the extreme and varied physical environments of the International Ice Patrol, polar regions, Bering Sea Patrol, and ice breaking on the Great Lakes. New 200 to 250 foot cutters were built in the late 1920s to mid–1930s, and continued to serve throughout World War II. Bethlehem Shipbuilding Corporation in Massachusetts built the "Lake" class cutters *Pontchartrain*, *Tahoe*, *Chelan*, *Mendota*, *Shoshone*, *Cayuga*, and *Champlain*. The cutters could do speeds of 17 knots and had 3,000 horse power. The armament would include 3 inch and 5 inch deck guns.

General Engineering and Dry Dock Co. (Oakland, California), United Dry Dock Yard (Staten Island, New York), and Bay City (Michigan) Shipyard launched these cutters in the Billard years: *Itasca*, *Saranac*, *Sebago*, *Tahoma*, *Mohawk*, *Onondaga*, *Algonquin*, *Escanaba*, and *Comanche*.

Under Billard, the Coast Guard encouraged advanced training in oceanographic studies in civilian and naval positions. That knowledge that would be effectively applied in World War II on the Greenland Patrol.

A final contribution from Adm. Billard came in 1926: the suggested use of the letter "W" in cutter hull number designations to distinguish U.S. Coast Guard ships from U.S. Navy vessels. The Coast Guard "W" would not be generally assigned to cutters, however, for another 15 years, until World War II. Commandant Billard did not live to see his "W" designation on cutter hulls. The commandant died of pneumonia in 1932 at 58 years of age.[15]

7. Rum Runners and Depression (1919–1936)

Harry G. Hamlet was the son of Capt. Oscar C. Hamlet of the United States Revenue Cutter Service. Hamlet graduated from high school in Massachusetts and took courses at the Massachusetts Institute of Technology (MIT). Hamlet was appointed a cadet in 1894, was assigned to the training practice ship USRC *Chase*, and earned an ensign commission in 1896. Ensign Hamlet was assigned to the USRC *Bear*. Several *Bear* crewmembers conducted the dangerous Arctic Relief Expedition of 1897–1898 that resulted in the rescue of starving crewmembers from four stranded whaling ships in the polar Arctic off the north Alaskan coast.

Invited to attend the U.S. Naval War College in Newport, Rhode Island, Hamlet completed his course work and was reassigned to the USRC *Bear*. When the United States entered World War I in 1917, Hamlet organized personnel training at two naval section bases, was assigned to U.S. Naval Forces in France, and held command of the U.S. Navy warship USS *Marietta* in 1918. In 1919 Hamlet and the *Marietta* crew rescued the crew of the USS *James* as the ship was sinking in heavy seas off the coast of France. For his skilled seamanship in gale force winds and high seas, Hamlet received the Congressional Gold Life-Saving Medal from the U.S. Treasury secretary and a Special Commendation and Silver Star from the U.S. Navy secretary.

In 1919 Hamlet was assigned to the ship operations and personnel divisions at U.S. Coast Guard Headquarters in Washington, D.C., and then command of the Hawaiian based USCGC *Mohave* for a Far East cruise. In 1924, during Prohibition, Captain Hamlet administered ship operations, reconditioning, and commissioning for 20 U.S. Navy destroyers that were transferred to the Coast Guard, and then commanded the U.S. Coast Guard Destroyer Force.

Captain Harry Hamlet received his four-stripe rank in 1926. In 1928 he was appointed superintendent of the U.S. Coast Guard Academy in New London, Connecticut. Four years later, President Herbert Hoover appointed Capt. Hamlet commandant of the U.S. Coast Guard.

The Great Depression of 1929–1939 forced Commandant Hamlet to cut budgets, close Coast Guard stations, reduce personnel numbers, and decommission boats and cutters. President Franklin Delano Roosevelt favored combining the Coast Guard with the Navy for ostensible economic and mission efficiencies. Commandant Hamlet and Admiral William V. Pratt, the U.S. Navy's chief of naval operations, thwarted Roosevelt's plan by demonstrating how the merger plan would be counterproductive and more expensive. Congressional objections to the proposed merger settled the question, and the Coast Guard remained under U.S. Treasury Department control.

As Coast Guard commandant, Capt. Hamlet was promoted to the rank of rear admiral, but when his term ended in 1936, Adm. Hamlet was returned to the rank of captain and assigned to the offices of the Treasury secretary and the U.S. Senate Commerce Committee as a legislative consultant for U.S. Merchant Marine policies and planning.[16]

In 1938, Capt. Hamlet submitted to mandatory retirement at the age of 64. For pension purposes, Hamlet was elevated from his previous commandant rank of rear admiral to the higher rank of vice admiral because of his exemplary 40-year service record. Adm. Hamlet died in 1954,[17] after serving his nation in World War I and living in retirement through World War II and the Korean War (1950–1953). Hamlet was buried at Arlington National Cemetery. The distinguished Coast Guard leader gained fame for his off shore sailing on the revenue cutters *Bear* and *Tahoma*, leadership at Coast Guard Headquarters in Washington, D.C., as superintendent of the U.S. Coast Guard Academy, and as U.S. Coast Guard commandant.[18]

Hamlet even contributed his literary talent to the Coast Guard heritage by writing "The Creed of a Coast Guardsman," which states in part: "I revere that long line of expert seamen [and their] devotion to duty and sacrifice [in a] service honored and respected in peace and war. I shall endeavor to be a United States Coastguardsman."[19]

The decision-making scrutiny Commandant Hamlet applied to Depression-era budget cuts is indicted by his cut list: 15 life-saving stations mostly from the New England–New Jersey–New York maritime region; 176 Prohibition-era law enforcement vessels, including 100 75-foot patrol boats; 7 former Navy destroyers; and more than 50 harbor area picket boats. More than 1,700 Coast Guardsmen, including enlisted and warrant officer personnel, were discharged, or assigned to the Civilian Conservation Corps. Numerous Coast Guard officers and enlisted personnel were reduced in ranks and rates. Those measures resulted in a significant expense reduction of around 25 percent. Nonetheless, the personnel balance totaled a Coast Guard complement of nearly 10,000, which led historian Robert Erwin Johnson to conclude, "Quite clearly, there would be no return to the situation of a decade earlier."[20]

The cost-cutting Congress again contemplated combining the Coast Guard with the U.S. Navy, but Adm. Hamlet, Roosevelt's new Treasury Secretary Henry Morgenthau, members of Congress, knowledgeable civilians, merchant marine and maritime interests, and a panel of naval officials successfully argued in favor of maintaining Coast Guard and Treasury Department autonomy.[21] The analysts, however, as per historic precedent and law, stressed the importance of continuing the historic cooperative missions and integration of the U.S. Coast Guard with the U.S. Navy and the other U.S. Armed Forces in time of international conflict and national security threats.

The heroic rescue work Hamlet did as commander of the 189-foot USS *Marietta* in coming to the aid of the sinking USS *James* off the stormy French Atlantic coast was previously mentioned. Captain Alex Larzelere explained the rest of the story in his book *The Coast Guard in World War I*. The treacherous stormy seas put several U.S. Navy vessels at risk of sinking. Some did. Others were on the verge of broaching. Radio calls from naval ship commanders for help taxed the towing and rescue skills of the *Marietta* crew. Capt. Hamlet's ship maneuvers and orders to naval escort vessels resulted in several ship salvages and sailor rescues. U.S. Navy Secretary Josephus Daniels commended the professional leadership and seamanship skills of the Coast Guard commanders of the 24 combat vessels in the European maritime theater of operations.[22]

The 45 rescued USS *James* crewmembers sent a letter of gratitude to Capt. Hamlet and his 10 officers and 130 enlisted men: "Your valor, heroic measures, and daring chances [resulted in the fact that] not a man of the *James* was lost."[23] Captain Hamlet and his crew exhibited the exemplary courage and code of the Coast Guard search and rescue heritage in peace and war from the historical past to the present.

Prior to his requesting and receiving orders for an overseas command in the European maritime theater, Hamlet had been assigned to command U.S. Navy Section Base 6 in New York. Of that assignment, the Third Naval District chief of staff, Capt. Louis R. De Steiguer, wrote the following about Hamlet to Rear Adm. John D. McDonald, commandant of the Third Naval District: "Captain Hamlet has been most successful in the training of men. I know of no finer type of officer than Captain Hamlet. The Third Naval District has been most fortunate in having his services. He has never failed us in the many difficult problems that have come up at that station, both as a section base [for vessel docking and repair] and as an operating station."[24]

8

The Coast Guard in the World War II Era (1936–1946)

Russell R. Waesche, Sr., was born in Maryland in 1886, was educated in the public schools of that state, and completed one year of study at Purdue University in Indiana. Waesche was accepted into the U.S. Revenue School of Instruction as a cadet in 1904, and earned his officer commission in 1906.

Ensign Waesche initiated his sailing career with the Revenue Cutter Service over the next five years at stations in the North Atlantic, on the Inland Seas of the Great Lakes, and then off the shores of the Pacific Northwest. Between 1911 and 1918, Waesche was commander of the USRC *Pamlico*. From 1915 through World War I, Waesche served at U.S. Coast Guard Headquarters in Washington, D.C.

In the decade following World War I, Waesche's assignments included a repeat command of the *Bothwell*, that, like other Revenue cutters, became Coast Guard cutters after 1915, the *Snohomish*, and the naval destroyers *Beale* and *Tucker*. He had assignments at Philadelphia Navy Yard as a Destroyer Force gunnery officer, and then back at U.S. Coast Guard Headquarters as chief ordnance officer.[1]

Waesche developed the Coast Guard Institute correspondence course system for enlisted personnel and warrant officers to achieve rank and rate advancement. The innovative officer changed Coast Guard field force organization structures, and was appointed to the War Plans Division of the U.S. Navy. This experience served Waesche well during World War II when, as commandant, he coordinated Coast Guard and U.S. Navy instructional, tactical, logistical, and combat operations.

In 1935, Commander Waesche was promoted to the position of aide to the commandant, Adm. Harry G. Hamlet. In 1936, Cmdr. Waesche was

8. The Coast Guard in the World War II Era (1936–1946)

promoted to rear admiral and appointed to succeed Adm. Hamlet as commandant of the United States Coast Guard.[2]

In 1939, Commandant Waesche carried out President Franklin Roosevelt's pragmatic order to integrate the civilian U.S. Lighthouse Service into the military structure of the U.S. Coast Guard. The plan proved to be fortuitous for the service and the nation during World War II and after. The commandant did not neglect the domestic responsibilities of the Coast Guard. During his tenure, Waesche expanded Coast Guard missions on the Great Lakes and other major lakes and rivers. Emphasis was placed on aids to navigation, maritime safety, ship inspection, and icebreaking to extend the shipping season for wartime domestic and overseas needs.

Waesche prepared the Coast Guard for war and integration with the U.S. Navy, but preserved the identity and autonomy of the Coast Guard during and after World War II. The commandant led the wartime expansion of the Coast Guard. Members of the service crewed 750 cutters, 290 U.S. Navy boats and ships, 255 U.S. Army vessels, and 3,500 small craft. During World War II (1939–1945) Coast Guard cutters, boats, aircraft, and shore station personnel performed peacetime, national security, combat, search and rescue, and anti-submarine and convoy escort patrol missions in every maritime theater of war. Admiral Waesche earned awards and commendations, and the gratitude of federal officials and leaders of the other U.S. Armed Forces, especially the U.S. Navy. After the war, Waesche administered the return of the Coast Guard to the U.S. Treasury Department.[3]

Coast Guard files contain a variety of photographs from the career of the distinguished commandant. Among them: Waesche as a member of the U.S. Revenue Cutter Service Academy (School of Instruction) at Arundel Cove on Curtis Bay, Maryland, ca. 1906; a player on the Revenue Cutter Service baseball team; in cadet and officer uniforms in various circumstances, one as 3rd Lt. Waesche, 1907; Lt. Cmdr. Waesche, as commanding officer with the crew of the USS *Beale* in Prohibition enforcement; with U.S. Coast Guard Women's Reserve Commanding Officer Dorothy Stratton; and in uniform coming out of a hatch of a World War II landing craft.

A final photograph illustrated the close coordination of the Navy and Coast Guard in this descriptive caption: "Vice Admiral Russell R. Waesche, Commandant of the U.S. Coast Guard, is sworn in as a full Admiral by Rear Admiral Thomas Gatch, Judge Advocate General of the U.S. Navy, as Mrs. Waesche and a group of high-ranking officers in the Coast Guard look on."[4]

After serving an unusually long term as U.S. Coast Guard commandant, Adm. Waesche retired in 1946. He died less than one year later and was buried with honors at Arlington National Cemetery.[5]

The Coast Guard's Lt. Frank Erickson was serving with the U.S. Navy and assigned to the air control tower on Ford Island, Hawaii, when Japanese naval and air forces struck Pearl Harbor on 7 December 1941. Seeing the carnage on land and sea, Lt. Erickson became a proponent of the fledgling Sikorsky rotor-wing helicopter for search and rescue and surveillance missions. Lt. Erickson corresponded with the aircraft inventor. Commandant Waesche became interested, witnessed a helicopter flight in 1943, and convinced the U.S. Navy to allow the Coast Guard to develop the rotor-wing craft for Navy and Coast Guard missions. Lt. Erickson became a helicopter pilot and training instructor.[6]

That would not be the only time the innovative commandant was ahead of the curve in planning and administration. In honor of his historic achievements, a Legend-class National Security Cutter was posthumously named after him[7]: the 418-foot *Waesche* (WMSL-751). The *Waesche*, commissioned in 2010, was one of 8 Deep Water National Security Cutters scheduled for construction at Northrop Grumman Shipbuilding in Pascagoula, Mississippi.

Russell R. Waesche, Sr., revealed examples of innovative leadership early in his career. President Woodrow Wilson, anticipating the possibility of U.S. involvement in war with the Germany, and aware of that nation's submarine threat, created the Interdepartmental Board on Coastal Communications in 1916. The board was ordered to assess coastal defense systems, stations, and communications networks for the saving of life and property and to enhance national defense.

The Coast Guard was tasked with improving its telephone communication systems and networking with shore stations, lighthouses, and light ships (floating lighthouse stations at sea). The logistical and technical challenges were enormous. Lines, circuits, copper wiring, transmission facilities, and commercial telephone networks were developed and expanded. Captain Alex Larzelere, the author of the role of the Coast Guard in World War I, wrote how, after the U.S. declared war on Germany in 1917, the U.S. Navy ordered the coastal communications system placed under the supervision of the Coast Guard commandant.

U.S. Coast Guard Headquarters in Washington, D.C., met the challenge by expanding its small communications division under First Lieutenant R. R. Waesche, who was subsequently promoted to the rank of captain. Waesche increased the personnel complement of warrant officers and enlisted and civilian personnel who were made responsible for a system that would include hundreds of "miles of overhead lines (and) sub-

8. The Coast Guard in the World War II Era (1936–1946)

marine [beneath the sea] cable owned and maintained by the U.S. Coast Guard."[8]

Vice Admiral Waesche administered fortuitous additions to the Coast Guard just before the United States entered World War II. Changes occurred rapidly and effectively because Commandant Waesche was willing to listen to civilians and military colleagues, from the Coast Guard and the other branches of the U.S. Armed Forces.

Captain Dorothy C. Stratton was the first female commissioned officer of the United States Coast Guard. Captain Stratton influenced Adm. Waesche to administer structural and bureaucratic modifications. Stratton earned a Ph.D. in administration from Columbia University, and joined the Purdue University faculty as a professor of psychology and dean of women.

As World War II drew the United States into combat, Stratton joined the U.S. Navy Women's Reserve, otherwise known as Women Appointed for Voluntary Emergency Service (WAVES). Stratton was commissioned a lieutenant after completing U.S. Navy training at Smith College in Northampton, Massachusetts.

C. Douglas Kroll traced the inspirational life of Captain Stratton from her civilian professional years to the officer's distinguished Coast Guard career and post-service achievements. Kroll described how Navy Lt. Stratton served as assistant to the commanding officer at the WAVES radio school in Madison,

Commandant Russell R. Waesche carried the Coast Guard through the trying years of World War II (United States Coast Guard).

Wisconsin, until orders sent her to Washington, D.C.

In November 1942, President Franklin D. Roosevelt signed into law the establishment of the U.S. Coast Guard Women's Reserve. Lt. Cmdr. Dorothy Stratton transferred to the Coast Guard and became the director of the women's reserves.[9]

Adm. Waesche was amenable to Lt. Cmdr. Stratton's rationale for naming the members of the Coast Guard Women's Reserve. Stratton explained, "The motto of the Coast Guard is Semper Paratus—Always Ready. Why not call the members of the Women's Reserve SPARS? A spar is a supporting beam and that is what we hope each member of the Women's Reserve will be. I like SPARS because it really has meaning." And it was done.

World War II produced new breeds of Coast Guard heroes, like Signalman First Class Douglas Munro, the service's only Medal of Honor recipient (United States Coast Guard).

Lt. Cmdr. Stratton's administrative skills earned her promotions to commander and then captain. Captain Stratton organized a program that recruited, trained, and supported 10,000 enlisted and 1,000 commissioned SPARs in most of the rates and ranks of the Coast Guard, thus freeing up males to go overseas as the women filled essential and skilled domestic billets.

Captain Stratton received accolades and commendations from Adm. Waesche and U.S. Navy Secretary James Forrestal. Dorothy Stratton left the Coast Guard in 1946, and served as a director in the International Monetary Fund and director of the Girl Scouts of America. The Women's Officer Professional Association named a leadership award after Capt. Stratton. She passed away at the still active age of 107 in 2006. In 2008,

8. The Coast Guard in the World War II Era (1936–1946)   87

the USCG named the National Security Cutter *Stratton* (WMSL-752) in her honor.[10]

Admiral Waesche heeded the suggestion of Hollywood screenwriter, civilian sailor and yachtsman Malcolm Boylan. In 1934, Boylan suggested forming a civilian Coast Guard "reserve" of skilled boat operators to teach boaters rules of the maritime road, conduct boat safety inspections, and monitor the increasingly popular sport of recreational boating on America's coasts, rivers and lakes.

Boylan's letter made its way up the Coast Guard chain of command. The letter was not immediately acted upon, but was read with interest by a young assistant to Coast Guard Commandant Adm. Harry G. Hamlet, Commander Russell R. Waesche. In 1939, recalling Boylan's "Founder's Letter," and concerned with increasing the number of Coast Guard and support personnel in the face of the coming war, Commandant Waesche assigned subordinates to draft plans for a U.S. Coast Guard reserve force.

Congress supported the plan. On June 23, 1939, President Roosevelt signed into law a bill to establish a civilian reserve to assist the Coast Guard in training and monitoring civilian boaters in navigation and boat safety, and doing search and rescue patrols. The

Under Commandant Waesche's watch, the Coast Guard mined the potential leadership contributions of women in the service. Lt. Dorothy Stratton, head of the U.S. Coast Guard Women's Reserve (SPARS), ably provided what Waesche sought (United States Coast Guard).

civilian reserve was divided into flotillas under well-trained civilian leadership in assigned districts throughout the nation. The initial civilian Coast Guard Reserve became the U.S. Coast Guard Auxiliary in February 1941, when Congress created a military U.S. Coast Guard Reserve, like the other U.S. Armed Forces.

Malcolm Boylan was appointed the civilian "commodore" of Coast Guard Auxiliary District Eleven on the California coast.[11] The uniformed Coast Guard Auxiliary has existed from World War II to the present. During the war, auxiliarists performed boating safety, surveillance and harbor security missions. Some were members of the U.S. Coast Guard Temporary Reserves with limited military status.

Admiral Waesche is credited with supporting and administering the wartime U.S. Coast Guard Reserve, SPARS, Auxiliary, and civilian employees that evolved into essential elements of what would later be called "Team Coast Guard."

Professor Robert Erwin Johnson is a noted University of Alabama historian, eminent naval historian, and author of the classic Coast Guard history *Guardians of the Sea* (1987). Johnson's extensive research from official Coast Guard sources, and his own World War II service as a petty officer on the 240-foot cutter *Haida* (WPG-45) in the north Pacific, gave the author the academic and pragmatic credibility to assess the contributions of Adm. Waesche from the commandant's Revenue Cutter Service days through 1946.[12]

Johnson ferreted out Waesche's papers at the U.S. Coast Guard Academy. These included Waesche's own written list of characteristics for effective leadership long before he was appointed the Coast Guard commandant. The traits included general confidence in the commandant nominee's "sense of justice and fairness," the ability to effectively articulate the missions and needs of the Coast Guard to Congressional committees, and "vision, balance and judgment," all qualities that Waesche would exhibit, Johnson insisted, as commandant of the U.S. Coast Guard.

Treasury Secretary Henry Morgenthau nominated Waesche, in Johnson's words, "on 14 June 1936 ... over twenty captains and four commanders." Upon his appointment, Adm. Waesche took the unprecedented step of visiting Coast Guard stations, cutters, and commanders to explain Coast Guard policies, and elicit complaints and suggestions. Admiral Waesche inquired about and responded to conflicts that occurred between the field commands and U.S. Coast Guard Headquarters in Washington, D.C.[13]

In 1938, the U.S. Coast Guard was given the responsibility for training U.S. Merchant Marine personnel who would be tasked with shipping goods, personnel, and equipment around the globe in the increasing like-

8. The Coast Guard in the World War II Era (1936–1946)   89

lihood of U.S. entry into World War II. This included aspiring civilian merchant seamen, radio operators, and officers trained under Coast Guard auspices in New York City at Hoffman Island; New London, Connecticut (Fort Trumbull); Alameda, California (Government Island); and at sea on the merchant steamer *American Seaman* and the Coast Guard cutters *Kimball, Yeaton,* and *Northland*.[14]

Older cutters were decommissioned in the 1930s to prepare the way for the new 327-foot oceangoing (deep water) cruisers in an enhanced construction program supported by Adm. Waesche. The "327s," as R.E. Johnson described them, were "good looking ships with raked bows, cruiser sterns ... flush decks ... short broad [smoke] stacks ... a [float plane] aircraft handling crane ... two 5-inch 51-caliber guns [and] increased armament."[15] Twin screws (propellers) made the 327s more maneuverable. The 327s were named after secretaries of the Treasury, so were referred to as "Secretary" or "Treasury" class cutters. These World War II combat cutters would later be heralded, and included the *Campbell, Duane, Ingham, Taney, Spencer, Hamilton,* and *Bibb*.[16]

The cutters served with distinction in combat as destroyer escorts for merchant ships, in search and rescue missions, as anti-submarine warfare vessels, as Coast Guard and Navy flagships, in radio communications centers, and as command headquarters for commanding officers of all of the U.S. Armed Forces.

Even with war clouds gathering in Eurasia and the Caribbean, Mediterranean, Atlantic and Pacific maritime theaters, the Coast Guard did not neglect its continuing domestic missions of fire fighting, ship inspections, dangerous cargo loading, search and rescue, port security, and national defense.

Natural disasters in 1936 and 1937 included hurricanes from coastal North Carolina to New England. Coast Guard crews on land and on water rescued disaster victims. Coast Guard aircraft surveyed the storm and flood fronts, radioed for search and rescue teams, and warned people on land and water about emerging threats. In the natural disasters on Waesche's watch, hundreds of lives were saved, thousands of people were transported to safer locations, disabled boats were towed, communication lines were established and repaired, looters were deterred or apprehended, and hundreds of heads of cattle were coaxed to dry land.

In 1938, Coast Guard personnel and land and sea assets responded to a hurricane that struck New York (Long Island) and New England. As in previous and future natural disasters, the service transported government and Red Cross officials and a myriad of relief workers and volunteers to strategic sites.

Stranded victims and vessels in distress were aided. The Coast Guard delivered mail in the midst of the natural disasters. Several Coast Guard facilities and vessels were damaged and destroyed. Coast Guard personnel suffered casualties in the rescue and relief missions.[17]

In the midst of its domestic and national defense missions, the 250-foot USCGC *Itasca* (WPG-321), its crew and Cmdr. Warner K. Thompson were involved in radio communications, tracking, and search efforts with Navy ships and aircraft for missing aviator Amelia Earhart and navigator Fred Noonan. The search area was off Howland Island in the Central Pacific.[18] Speculation, conspiracy theories, and criticisms of the Earhart global flight and failed search efforts persisted for decades after the 1937 event. Private attempts to locate the remains of Earhart, Noonan and the downed aircraft continued into the 21st century.

Admiral Waesche responded to Congressional criticism about the involvement and expense of the Coast Guard in the tracking and search missions connected to the Earhart flight. The commandant estimated the *Itasca* fuel cost at $2,000 and asserted, "One of the principal duties of the Service is to answer all calls for assistance at sea. The search from July 2nd to July 17th [1937] was strictly in line with the prescribed duties of the Coast Guard."[19]

In 1939, two years before the United States entered the war, Coast Guard and Navy ships and aircraft embarked upon the "Neutrality Patrol" in the North Atlantic. The patrols were not perceived to be neutral to the German government or U-boat captains who shot torpedoes at naval vessels suspected to be tracking Nazi submarines and radioing their positions to the British Royal Navy and merchant convoys. The Coast Guard placed weather station cutters in the Atlantic to update merchant and naval vessels on sea and weather conditions. These Ocean Station cutters also did search and rescue missions.

The Coast Guard was sent to Danish Greenland after the German invasion of Denmark to protect the island's resources and prevent the Germans from setting up radio stations from which to alert patrolling U-boats about weather conditions and merchant convoy positions. Commander Edward H. "Iceberg" Smith headed the Greenland Patrol. Commander Smith, an oceanographer, supervised search and rescue and combat missions on land, sea, and air in the extreme weather and ice conditions of polar Greenland on the island's dangerous Ice Cap and in its frigid, ice-packed waters.

The "327s," and smaller cutters like the 216-foot icebreaker USCGC *Northland* (WPG-49), performed heroic missions and captured German operatives in September of 1941, three months before the U.S. entered the

8. The Coast Guard in the World War II Era (1936–1946)

war. Coast Guard aviators flew U.S. Navy PBY bomber patrol floatplanes on reconnaissance, supply, and transportation missions.

Adm. Waesche initially resisted, but later complied, with President Roosevelt's Lend-Lease Act and "Destroyer Deal" with the United Kingdom. Roosevelt gave 10 of Waesche's valuable cutters to Britain to aid Prime Minister Winston Churchill in the fight against Nazi Germany in the Mediterranean Sea.

Besides managing and articulating Coast Guard assets, missions, tactics, and logistics with the other U.S. Armed Forces and the U.S. Merchant Marine, Adm. Waesche communicated directly with President Roosevelt and his advisors about overseas and domestic operations. On the home front, Adm. Waesche directed port security, beach patrols, and the inspection of domestic and foreign ships in U.S. ports. Sensitive ethnic and race relations in the then segregated U.S. Armed Forces had to be dealt with. The Coast Guard led the way in race relations. The small service had historically placed blacks and other minorities in responsible enlisted and officer positions on cutters, in the pre-war U.S. Life-Saving Service and U.S. Lighthouse Service, and during World War II in the SPARS and on combat vessels.

Waesche was particularly creative in purchasing and building sea, air, and land assets and the infrastructure necessary to meet the expanded wartime missions.[20] It was his idea to recruit the tough and skilled coastal fishermen and adapt their well-suited sea craft for the Greenland Patrol.

An instrumental contribution to the war effort was the development of LORAN, the radio-beamed Long Range Aid to Navigation system. The Coast Guard, with the encouragement and assistance of Navy and civilian technicians, corporations, universities, and Canada and Britain, developed, maintained and manned a radio signal triangulation system that tracked the location of air and sea craft. Adm. Waesche chose Lt. Cmdr. Lawrence Harding, a Coast Guard expert on radio and aerial navigation, to coordinate the project.

Coast Guard manned LORAN stations were built, supplied, and operated at isolated insular and mainland sites in the Pacific and Atlantic during World War II, and for decades after,[21] to guide civilian, commercial, and military aircraft and ships. The electronic aid to navigation system would be replaced, not without controversy, in the late 20th century by the satellite directed Global Positioning System (GPS).

Adm. Waesche oversaw Coast Guard personnel on land and sea and in their cooperative missions with the other U.S. Armed Forces. The administrative complexity of the missions is difficult to synthesize. Coast Guard personnel crewed U.S. Navy and U.S. Army vessels, their own boats and cutters, transport ships, buoy tenders, destroyer escorts, frigates, and icebreakers, and flew Navy and Coast Guard aircraft.

Coast Guard crews carried out dangerous landing craft operations under heavy fire on enemy shores in vessels that ranged from lengths of 30 to more than 300 feet long. Coast Guard reservists and active duty personnel suffered significant casualties while serving the nation in the multi-theater war.

After the war, Adm. Waesche administered the problematic demobilization process and re-established Coast Guard autonomy in the transition of the service from U.S. Navy jurisdiction back to the U.S. Treasury Department.[22]

Commandant Waesche exhibited eclectic leadership skills at a time when the Coast Guard was required to expand its asset, personnel, and mission requirements in the domestic and global maritime war. The quality of Waesche's leadership is exemplified by three official testimonials author R. E. Johnson cited. The first is from the final annual report of Adm. Ernest J. King (U.S. Navy), chief of naval operations and commander-in-chief of the U.S. fleet in World War II: "The (U.S. Navy) Fleet, Shore Establishment, Marine Corps, Coast Guard, and Seabees ["Construction Battalion, CBs] each contributed its full share to victory."

U.S. Navy Secretary James V. Forrestal offered this testimonial about Adm. Waesche: "During the arduous war years, the Coast Guard has earned the highest respect and deepest appreciation of the Navy and Marine Corps. Its performance of duty has been without exception in keeping with the highest traditions of the naval service."

And this from Adm. King's deputy, Adm. Richard S. Edwards, on Commandant Waesche's retirement: "No one knows better than I do how much the Navy owes to the Coast Guard in general and you in particular, not only for the achievements in the war but also for the painstaking preparation in the years leading up to the war.... I salute the lowering of your flag with a heartfelt 'Well Done.'"[23]

The skills and knowledge Adm. Waesche exhibited during the war included the management of personnel training, asset acquisition, tactics, strategy, and logistics; and the articulation of Coast Guard missions with the War Department, U.S. Navy, U.S. Army and U.S. Army Air Force, U.S. Marine Corps, U.S. Merchant Marine, and the wartime Allied nations.

A survey of the geographic land and maritime regions of World War II military operations illustrates the challenges. The multi-continental and maritime theaters of operation, port security, navigation, aviation, and transportation were extensive. The geographic realm included the Gulf of Mexico, Caribbean, Atlantic and Pacific Oceans, Great Lakes, and Mediter-

8. The Coast Guard in the World War II Era (1936–1946) 93

ranean Sea. Mainland and insular theaters included North Africa, Sicily, Italy, Normandy (France), Aleutians, Coral Sea, Pearl Harbor, Greenland, Guadalcanal, Iwo Jima, New Guinea, and the Philippines.[24]

Author, historian, editor, and executive director of the U.S. Life-Saving Service Heritage Association John Galluzzo described the enhanced World War II Coast Guard mission concisely: "The maritime Service expanded its port security mission, performed antisubmarine patrols at sea and in the air, experimented with military helicopters in life-saving missions, and was an essential element of America's amphibious warfare machine."[25]

Among the essential Coast Guard contributions to World War II amphibious warfare were the skilled coxswains who ran ship-to-shore and port-to-port landing craft. Galluzzo explained it: "The U.S. Navy had never focused its training efforts on small boats and landing craft. The Coast Guard, and its predecessor, the U.S. Life-Saving Service, had been handling small boats in varied surf conditions since the middle of the 19th century. Their coxswains were ideally suited for taking the helm of the thousands of [landing craft] which rolled out of the Higgins Industries boat yard in New Orleans." As Galluzzo noted, "Medal of Honor recipient Signalman First Class Douglas Albert Munro (USCG) died at the helm of a Higgins boat while [redeploying] U.S. Marines from Guadalcanal" in 1942.[26]

Commandant Waesche's achievements are so extensive they defy summation. Those contributions include administering the 1939 merger of the U.S. Lighthouse Service into the Coast Guard to manage aids to navigation (buoys, lighthouses, lightships, and sound systems) which guided military and merchant vessels to their stations. Coast Guard cutters, boats, and assorted craft had to be constructed, repaired, and fitted for radio communications, armament, ordnance, radar, sonar, and antisubmarine warfare explosive depth charges.

Waesche's wartime leadership resulted in his being the recipient of several U.S. Armed Forces and Allied Nations commendations and medals. Those awards included the Distinguished Service Medal and the Navy Commendation Ribbon. The United Kingdom presented Adm. Waesche with the Order of the British Empire. The Polish government awarded the commandant the Polanda Restituta.[27]

Adm. Waesche served Presidents Franklin Roosevelt and Harry Truman during the war. Perhaps his most significant legacies were helping to integrate U.S. Navy and Coast Guard operations with regular consultation and his contributions to the schools of instruction to take advantage of the personnel and assets of the respective sea services.[28]

Commander Gary M. Thomas has served as an active duty commander at sea and at a LORAN shore station. As the executive director of the Foundation for Coast Guard History, Cmdr. Thomas has contributed to the preservation of Coast Guard history and added to its mission legacy. It is from that background that Cmdr. Thomas neatly synthesized the historical legacy of the service. He wrote that for more than 200 years, "the USCG has been part of America's national defense organization and participated in every major war and engagement. From the early days of sailing cutters to the newest National Security Cutter, the USCG has played an important part in protecting our nation. Whether landing U.S. Army and U.S. Marine personnel in Europe and the Pacific ... or ... manning the worldwide LORAN navigation system ... the USCG [has continued] to be an integral part of our nation's defense."[29] It is that magnificent legacy that Adm. Waesche contributed to and expanded.

Lt. Malcolm F. Willoughby wrote a magnificent history of the role of the Coast Guard in World War II. The Naval Institute Press published Willoughby's *The U.S. Coast Guard in World War II* in 1957 and a revised printing in 1989. Willoughby noted that in 1956, Vice Admiral Alfred C. Richmond, commandant of the Coast Guard, credited Adm. Waesche with ordering "the establishment of the Historical Section of the Coast Guard charged with the duty of preparing and preserving the records of the events that were to follow"[30] in the World War II era. It was from the materials developed and published by the History Section, Commandant Richmond asserted, that Lt. Willoughby chronicled his classic history.[31]

Lt. Willoughby credited Capt. Ellis Reed-Hill, Capt. Samuel F. Gray, Lt. Cmdr. Frank R. Eldridge, and more than 20 other civilian and Coast Guard enlisted and commissioned men and women with the research and writing of the ship and shore station monographs that enabled the author to compile his complete ashore and afloat domestic and overseas history. Willoughby included several naval histories and civilian works to provide specialized information for his 348-page Coast Guard history.[32] Willoughby spends several pages of that history on the contributions of Adm. Waesche to the war effort with profiles and photos.

Among tributes to Commandant Waesche in Willoughby's book was this one from Adm. Chester W. Nimitz, the U.S. Navy Pacific Fleet commander: "Admiral Russell R. Waesche, the wartime Commandant of the United States Coast Guard, was a man I held in the highest esteem. It was my privilege to have many of his combatant units under my command during the War [and they acquitted themselves] in the highest traditions of their Service ... worthy of their motto, '*Semper Paratus*': Always Ready."[33]

Admiral Nimitz went on to pay tribute to the Coast Guard domestic missions of public safety, port security, and search and rescue, and iden-

8. The Coast Guard in the World War II Era (1936–1946)

tified those missions as equally important to the war effort. Nimitz reiterated the administrative skills and dedication of the wartime commandant, and his and the Coast Guard's "selfless devotion to duty as part of the Navy's fighting force."[34]

Rear Admiral Russell R. Waesche, Jr., the commandant's son, graduated from the Coast Guard Academy in 1936, then served ashore, and then afloat on several cutters, and overseas during and after World War II. Rear Adm. Waesche commanded the USCGC *Mohave* on the Greenland Patrol in 1943–1944. Prior to that seagoing command, Waesche, Jr., served as an inspector in the construction of 180-foot buoy tenders in Duluth, Minnesota. He retired in 1971.[35]

9

The Post-War and Cold War Eras (1946–1962)

James Francis Farley was born on 22 June 1889 in Oxford, Ohio. Farley graduated from Ithaca High School in New York in 1908. From 1908 through June 1912 he was a cadet at the Revenue School of Instruction. Upon earning his commission, Third Lt. Farley commenced active duty in the U.S. Revenue Cutter Service. From 1913 to 1919, Farley served during the mission expansion period of the Revenue Cutter Service and U.S. Coast Guard in the World War I era.[1]

World War I commenced in Europe in 1914. The United States remained neutral until 1917, when President Woodrow Wilson and Congress declared war on Germany because of German submarine attacks on American vessels and on the British ship RMS *Lusitania* (1915) that was carrying U.S. passengers and contraband cargo.

Lt. Farley served on the U.S. Coast Guard cutters *Mohawk*, *Seminole*, *Onondaga*, and *Yamacraw*, while the latter cutter was assigned to the U.S. Fleet Patrol Force. Lt. Farley sailed on convoy escort duty in the Mediterranean between the British colony of Gibraltar and home seaports in the United Kingdom. His service in the Great War earned Farley the Victory Medal and Escort Clasp.

From 1919 to 1925, Farley served as New York Division accounting officer, was posted to sea duty on the USCGC *Scaly*, and subsequently to the cutters *Seneca*, *Gresham*, *Morrill*, and then the *Mohave* out of Honolulu. In 1925, Lt. Farley was appointed ordnance officer at U.S. Coast Guard Headquarters in Washington, D.C. He earned the rank of lieutenant commander in 1926 and was promoted to commander in 1931 and captain in

9. The Post-War and Cold War Eras (1946–1962)

1941, just before the Japanese attack upon Pearl Harbor, Hawaii. Farley was appointed commodore, then rear admiral in 1943. In 1946, Admiral Farley was named commandant of the Coast Guard.[2]

Between 1925 and 1935, Cmdr. Farley served with the destroyer force that enforced Prohibition laws on the American Gulf and Atlantic coasts. Commander Farley skippered the U.S. Coast Guard destroyers *McCall* and *Wilkes*, and earned a reputation in gunnery practice. In 1933–1934, Cmdr. Farley commanded the cutters *Pontchartrain* and *Modoc*.

In 1937 Cmdr. Farley was transferred to Coast Guard Headquarters as a communications officer. In that capacity, Farley represented the Coast Guard and the United States at several international telecommunications, broadcasting, and radiotelegraph conferences, and became a member of the Defense Communications Board.[3]

In 1942, Capt. Farley was appointed Eighth Naval District Coast Guard commander at New Orleans, Louisiana, where he earned the Legion of Merit. In 1943 he returned to U.S. Coast Guard Headquarters to serve as assistant chief operations officer and then chief personnel officer. With full promotion on 1 January 1946, Adm. Farley succeeded World War II Commandant Russell R. Waesche.

As commandant, Admiral Farley had to compete with the exemplary reputation of Adm. Waesche. The "pipe smoking Uncle Joe" successor to Waesche was never as popular as his predecessor, but Farley became noted for tending to the problems of Coast Guard personnel and administering the post-war demobilization of the service. Farley skillfully administered the cutter ocean station and weather platforms and search and rescue responses, and enhanced the LORAN and Bureau of Marine Inspection missions.

Commandant Farley ended his term of office on 31 December 1949 and retired on 1 January 1950, after 42 years of distinguished military service. On 25 November 1974, Farley died from throat cancer and was buried at Arlington National Cemetery.[4]

When Captain Dorothy Stratton left the Coast Guard in 1946, Admiral Farley presented the SPAR leader with the Legion of Merit. In recognition of the award, U.S. Navy Secretary James Forrestal commended Capt. Stratton for her contribution to women in military service, the Coast Guard, and the nation.[5]

In the post-war period, Congress began looking for cost-cutting efficiencies. Some lawmakers suggested that the global missions of the Coast Guard be reconsidered in peacetime and that the service stick to homeland waters more in keeping with its name. Defenders of the Coast Guard's wartime missions and expanded global reach argued that the service was the best federal institution to carry out marine safety, law enforcement, and national security missions.[6]

Commandant Farley looked for economic efficiencies in life-saving, lighthouse and lightship stations, LORAN sites, and aids to navigation installations in each Coast Guard district. Several navigation aid stations were disestablished. The number of patrol boats and cutters were increased to meet the needs of port security missions[7] during the Korean conflict and evolving Cold War.

The increased port security missions necessitated the recruitment of additional Coast Guard personnel to carry out ship and marine safety inspections. To meet the needs of the service, Adm. Farley initiated the controversial but pragmatic policy of commissioning experienced U.S. Merchant Marine officers into the Coast Guard.[8]

Admiral Merlin O'Neill succeeded Adm. Farley as U.S. Coast Guard commandant, serving from 1950 to 1954. Throughout his career, O'Neill rapidly advanced in rank as ensign (1921); lieutenant (1925); lieutenant commander (1929); commander (1940); captain (1942); commodore (1945); rear admiral (1946); vice admiral (1950); and full admiral (1954). He served on the U.S. Coast Guard cutters *Gresham*, *Haida*, and *Algonquin* in the 1920s, and sailed on three Bering Sea Patrol missions.[9]

O'Neill's early career included a cruise on the USCGC *Mohave* and assignment at the Philadelphia Navy Yard to oversee the conversion of the U.S. Navy destroyer USS *Ericsson* for Coast Guard interdiction duty. Between 1925 and 1927, O'Neill served as executive officer and then commander of that cutter. In 1927, he joined the faculty of the U.S. Coast Guard Academy in New London, Connecticut, and did summer training cruises with the cadets.[10]

From 1930 to 1942, O'Neill served as commander of the destroyers *Monoghan*, *Cassin*, and *Herndon* on interdiction missions off the Atlantic coast; as operations officer at Coast Guard Headquarters in Washington, D.C.; United States delegate to the London International Whaling Conference; and director of the civilian Coast Guard Auxiliary.[11]

In World War II, O'Neill commanded the Coast Guard crewed attack transport USS *Leonard Wood* (APA-12). USS *Leonard Wood* Coast Guard crews experienced combat in the Mediterranean Sea off North Africa and Sicily (Italy), and in the Pacific Ocean off the Marshall and Gilbert Islands. For outstanding combat seamanship, logistics, and tactics, O'Neill earned the Navy Unit Commendation, and the Legion of Merit in action against enemy submarines, aircraft, mines, and shore side enemy gunfire.[12]

Malcolm F. Willoughby traced O'Neill's war career in his classic history *The U.S. Coast Guard in World War II*. According to the author, rank

9. The Post-War and Cold War Eras (1946–1962)

advancements placed Commander O'Neill and then Captain O'Neill in command of the attack transport USS *Leonard Wood* as part of the Western Naval Task Force in the Mediterranean. USS *Leonard Wood* served as a U.S. Navy flagship. Captain O'Neill earned the Legion of Merit for leadership and heroism in combat in the Mediterranean (North Africa–Sicily) Theater of Operations.[13]

In the Pacific Solomon Islands campaign, Captain O'Neill commanded the USS *Leonard Wood* in Northern Attack Force (TF52) under Rear Adm. Richmond K. Turner of the U.S. Navy. Captain O'Neill also commanded the flagship USS *Leonard Wood* as part of the Attack Force Reserve Group of Transport Division 20 in the Kwajalein Atoll insular campaign.[14]

Commandant John F. Farley succeeded Commandant Russell R. Waesche and oversaw the post–World War II demobilization of the Coast Guard (United States Coast Guard).

Coast Guard coxswains became noted in World War II for seamanship skills and courage in landing craft operations in the Pacific. It was significant and symbolic, therefore, that in 1944 O'Neill assumed the position of commanding officer of the Coast Guard Amphibious Training Unit at the U.S. Marine Corps Base Camp Lejeune in New River, North Carolina. Following that one-month assignment, O'Neill was named commander of the Fifth Coast Guard District with headquarters at Baltimore, Maryland. As 5th District commander, O'Neill was captain of the port and commander of the Marine Inspection Office, the Coast Guard base, and a recruiting station.

In 1945, O'Neill was appointed assistant chief of the Finance and Supply Division at U.S. Coast Guard Headquarters in Washington, D.C., appointed to the rank of commodore, and assigned to command the strategic Norfolk, Virginia, U.S. Coast Guard Station.¹⁵

As of 1 February 1946, Rear Adm. Merlin O'Neill became the assistant commandant of the U.S. Coast Guard, as per the nomination of President Harry Truman and U.S. Senate confirmation. On 1 January 1950, Adm. O'Neill succeeded Adm. Joseph F. Farley as commandant with the rank of vice admiral.¹⁶

By 1950, the Coast Guard completed its post–World War II demobilization orders with approximately 23,000 personnel, a variety of boats, craft, and stations, 177 cutters, and more than 420 lighthouses. The Korean War (1950–1953) expanded Coast Guard domestic port security and overseas missions as the Cold War between the Union of Soviet Socialist Republics, its satellites, and the People's Republic of China heated up. President Truman issued an executive order that increased Coast Guard port and national security responsibilities. Port security procedures were initiated to better protect harbors, support overseas military missions, and investigate merchant mariners suspected of Communist sympathies. That national security mission got the U.S. Coast Guard positive and negative attention,¹⁷ and involvement in judicial litigation.

The role of the U.S. Coast Guard in the Korean War was significant. Scott T. Price, an associate historian at U.S. Coast Guard Headquarters in Washington, D.C., traced its contribution in *The Forgotten Service in the Forgotten War: The U.S. Coast Guard's Role in the Korean Conflict*. Price described Coast Guard missions in South Korea

Commandant Merlin O'Neill served in that post during the Korean War (United States Coast Guard).

9. The Post-War and Cold War Eras (1946–1962)

from 1946, when the service began to train the South Korean maritime defense force, through 1953 and the end of the war.

As United Nations forces led by the United States fought to expel Communist North Korea from South Korea, and the People's Republic of China from the Korean peninsula, the Coast Guard manned LORAN stations near the Pusan Perimeter, in the Japanese archipelago, and elsewhere.

Coast Guard cutters performed transportation, search and rescue, and weather station duties. The Coast Guard supported the Korean War mission with its expertise in aids to navigation, port security, and merchant marine inspection. More than 20 Coast Guard cutters and their crews served in the Korean theater and earned the Korean Service Medal. Cutters docked at Japanese ports and established or expanded U.S. Coast Guard stations and air detachments on the islands of Midway, Guam, Wake and the Philippines. Cutter crews persevered in gale force winds, heavy seas, and other challenges to ships, technology, and seamanship.[18]

Serving two terms as commandant, Admiral Alfred Carroll Richmond fought successfully to block the merger of the U.S. Coast Guard Academy with the U.S. Merchant Marine Academy (United States Coast Guard).

The Korean War stimulated Congressional appropriations to support an expanded U.S. Coast Guard Reserve force that had been diminished by post-war demobilization. Cold War propaganda between the Communist Bloc and the West led to the transmission of pro–Western Voice of America broadcasts. Coast Guard and specialized civilian personnel manned the radio station ship USCGC *Courier* off the coast of Greece.[19]

At the time of Commandant O'Neill's retirement in June 1954, the

Coast Guard personnel complement totaled more than 29,000. The civilian support staff numbered about 5,000. The Cold War made Coast Guard asset and mission expansion necessary to cover traditional domestic missions and meet the evolving requirements of national security at home and abroad.[20] Commandant Merlin O'Neill contributed the leadership necessary to meet the demands and needs of the service during that critical historical period.

In his survey of Commandant O'Neill's tenure, historian Robert Erwin Johnson credited the admiral with meeting the initial needs of post-war demobilization, and then turning about to increase air, sea, shore, and personnel assets in response to added domestic and international missions assigned to the service in the Cold War and Korean War.

Professor Johnson credited Adm. O'Neill with preparing the civilian Coast Guard Auxiliary to carry out the boat safety instruction, inspections, and search and rescue missions required by increased civilian motor and sail boat traffic, accidents, and casualties on America's coastal and inland waterways.[21]

Admiral Alfred Carroll Richmond succeeded Commandant O'Neill. Commandant Richmond served as the military head of the U.S. Coast Guard from 1954 to 1962. Born in Waterloo, Iowa, in 1902, Richmond pursued his education in Virginia and entered the college of engineering at George Washington University in Washington, D.C.

As a teenager Richmond worked at the U.S. Naval Observatory, was accepted as a U.S. Coast Guard Academy cadet in 1922, and graduated as an ensign in 1924.

Richmond steadily earned his officer ranks: ensign (1924); lieutenant (jg) (1926); lieutenant (1928); lieutenant commander (1932); commander (1942); captain (1943); rear admiral and assistant commandant (1950); vice admiral and commandant (1954); full admiral (1960); and retirement from the Coast Guard (1962).[22]

The 1920s was a busy and productive decade for Richmond. During that period, he served as an aide to the commandant at headquarters in Washington, D.C.; aide to the commanding officer of the Special Patrol Force against "Rum Runners" off the New York coast; and in the Special Service Squadron off the Massachusetts coast. In the late 1920s, Richmond served on the staff of the U.S. Coast Guard Academy; on the USCGC *Mojave*; with cadets on the USCGC *Shaw*; navigation officer on the USCGC *Pontchartrain*; and executive officer on the USCGC *Wainwright*.

In the 1930s, Richmond served at the Philadelphia Navy Yard; as executive officer on the USCGC *Herndon*; directed small arms training out of U.S Coast Guard Headquarters; and was executive officer aboard the USCGC *Haida* on Alaska, Bering Sea, and Arctic patrols. In the late 1930s, Richmond returned to duty at Coast Guard Headquarters, graduated in law from George Washington University, and was a delegate at the International Whaling Conference in London, England.[23]

The decade of the 1940s encompassed Richmond's diverse assignments and achievements during the pre-war, wartime, and immediate post World War II era. Richmond was assigned to Bethlehem Steel Company at Baltimore, Maryland, where he supervised the modification of what was to become the USCGC *American Sailor* for its role as the merchant marine training vessel he would later command.

Richmond commanded the Maritime Service Training Station in Port Hueneme, California. When the *American Sailor* was transferred to the federal War Shipping Administration, Richmond assumed command of the USCGC *Haida* for convoy escort duty out of Juneau, Alaska, and was the examining officer in the Merchant Marine Inspection Office out of New York City at the Third District Coast Guard Office.

Assigned overseas in 1943, Richmond was put in charge of the Merchant Marine Hearing Unit in London, where he administered and enforced laws and regulations on Coast Guard ships, boats, and crews, and investigated incidents, accidents, injuries and deaths involving U.S. Naval Forces in the European Theater. Richmond earned the Bronze Star Medal for his service with U.S. Naval Forces and U.S. Merchant Marine ships during and after the Allied invasion of the French province of Normandy in 1944.

In 1945, Richmond returned to administrative planning and budgetary responsibilities at U.S. Coast Guard Headquarters in Washington, D.C. In 1950, Rear Adm. Alfred C. Richmond was appointed assistant commandant and subsequently chief of staff of the United States Coast Guard.[24]

In 1954, Vice Admiral Richmond was named commandant of the U.S. Coast Guard to succeed Vice Admiral Merlin O'Neill. Admiral Richmond was appointed to a rare second term in 1958, and promoted to full admiral in 1960 by new legislation that required that rank to be given to all future commandants. Commandant Richmond represented the United States at several international maritime conferences and assisted in the crafting of policies and regulations on maritime commerce and safety.[25]

The decade of the 1960s expanded Adm. Richmond's eclectic career. The commandant was nominated for executive positions at international lighthouse conferences and chaired a national committee for the prevention of oil pollution at sea.

In May 1962, in a change-of-command ceremony on the Potomac River aboard the legendary World War II combat ship, the USCGC *Campbell*, Adm. Richmond turned his responsibilities over to Admiral Edwin

J. Roland to complete a long career of distinguished service and numerous awards. Admiral Richmond died in March of 1984 and was buried in Virginia at Arlington National Cemetery.[26] But before his demise, Richmond had more to accomplish.

Admiral Richmond had served the interests and missions of the Coast Guard well. The commandant was credited with successfully opposing President Dwight David Eisenhower's plan to merge the U.S. Coast Guard Academy with the U.S. Merchant Marine Academy at King's Point, New York. Eisenhower, a highly respected World War II commander and U.S. Army chief of staff, was motivated by reasons of efficiency and economy. Richmond assembled a committee to do a feasibility study of Eisenhower's proposal. The study concluded that to mix the different missions of the sea service academies would be inefficient and actually increase costs. The firm opposition of U.S. representatives from Connecticut and New York helped sink the unification proposal.[27]

Maritime historian Robert Erwin Johnson served on the USCGC *Haida* in World War II on convoy escort, anti-submarine warfare, and search and rescue patrols off Alaskan and in the Bering Sea. Quartermaster Johnson carried out his navigation and deck watch duties diligently, as chronicled in his book, *Bering Sea Escort: Life Aboard a Coast Guard Cutter in World War II.*

Johnson traced commander Richmond's time as skipper of the *Haida*, Richmond's seafaring skills in icy, stormy seas, and the commander's concern for the safety and welfare of the crew. Johnson portrayed Cmdr. Richmond as personifying military presence and bearing and destined for higher command.[28]

While Coast Guard commandant, Admiral Richmond wrote the foreword to the 1957 edition of Malcolm F. Willoughby's classic history, *The U.S. Coast Guard in World War II.* In the month prior to the Japanese attack upon Pearl Harbor, President Franklin Roosevelt signed the executive order that placed the U.S. Coast Guard under the jurisdiction of the U.S. Navy. In the foreword, Richmond described that tumultuous period, and the "preparation ... integration ... multiplicity of assignments, [and] demands on personnel and equipment that led to a brilliant record of accomplishment that now finds its way into national and Coast Guard history."[29]

Commandant Richmond credited the wartime leadership of World War II Commandant Russell R. Waesche, and "the debt of gratitude the thousands of us who knew or served under him" owed but could "never hope to repay."[30] Richmond paid tribute to the staff at the Historical Section of the Coast Guard, and the skill and dedication of author Malcolm

F. Willoughby for writing the book and preserving this significant period of Coast Guard history.[31]

Admiral Richmond had served at Coast Guard Headquarters in several administrative capacities before becoming commandant. With his law degree, Richmond was the first commissioned U.S. Coast Guard legal specialist. Richmond mastered budgetary matters and presented annual budget proposals to cost conscious congressional committees.[32]

The U.S. Navy and U.S. Coast Guard had mutual interests in maintaining huge icebreaker ships to support costly Arctic and Antarctic supply, transportation, and defense missions. Admiral Richmond, his Navy counterparts, and Eisenhower's Treasury Secretary Douglas Dillon encouraged inter-service cooperation and planning for the use and maintenance of the icebreaker missions. Proposals to construct nuclear powered icebreakers were considered too costly and unnecessary by federal officials and the U.S. Navy and Coast Guard.

By 1965, the Navy and Coast Guard began negotiations that eventually placed icebreaking services exclusively within the Coast Guard. The Treasury and Defense Departments agreed with the transfer of all U.S. Navy icebreakers to the U.S. Coast Guard. This policy objective vindicated President Franklin Roosevelt's previous decision to assign exclusive icebreaking duties on inland and coastal waterways to the Coast Guard. The expanded icebreaking missions required increased Coast Guard budgets, icebreaker acquisition and construction, and the recruitment of hundreds of additional personnel and U.S. Public Health Service medical and dental officers.[33]

On Commandant Richmond's watch, the Coast Guard icebreakers *Northwind* and *Eastwind* assisted the U.S. Navy and Royal Canadian Navy in monitoring and maintaining the Distant Early Warning (DEW) line of radar and other military stations in Canadian waters. In 1957, the U.S. Coast Guard cutters *Storis*, *Bramble*, and *Spar* traversed the Arctic Ocean north of Canada to assess the practicality of the historic Northwest Passage objective. The cutters were joined by the Canadian icebreaker HMCS *Labrador*. The cutters *Spar*, *Storis*, and *Bramble* entered the maritime history books as the first U.S. ships to traverse Arctic waters north of the North American continent from the Atlantic to the Pacific.

Under Richmond, the Coast Guard initiated the use of LORAN-C that expanded the range of its predecessor, Long Range Aid to Navigation-A; and the Automated Merchant Vessel Reporting System (AMVER), by which U.S. and foreign merchant vessels shared position reports to Coast Guard vessels, provided radio stations that allowed civilian and military vessels to plot ship positions and aid vessels in distress, and assist crew members who required medical attention.[34]

Admiral Richmond's historic two-term (eight year) tenure was matched only by his World War II predecessor, Adm. Russell R. Waesche. Richmond was credited with upgrading and building shore stations, sea and air assets, and expanding domestic and overseas missions. The Coast Guard would reflect the influence of Richmond's leadership for more than a generation after his retirement.[35]

10

Vietnam, DOT, "Bender's Blues," and Fisheries Patrols (1962–1982)

The next generation of U.S. Coast Guard commandants spanned the decades from the 1960s into the early 1980s. Commandants Roland, Smith, Bender, Siler and Hayes, like their predecessors, responded creatively to limited budgets, expanded domestic and international missions, and combat in Southeast Asia.

Edwin John Roland was born in Buffalo, New York, in 1905. Appointed as a U.S. Coast Guard Academy cadet in 1926, Roland earned a bachelor of science degree in engineering and an ensign commission in just three years in a challenging schedule that included academics, military training, and an athletic regimen of baseball, basketball and football. He led victorious Coast Guard Academy football teams against Army, Marine and Navy gridiron athletes.

From 1929 to 1934, Lt. (jg) Roland served as gunnery officer on the Coast Guard destroyers *Shaw* and *Wilkes* in Prohibition enforcement. In addition to those assignments, Roland was the gunnery officer and navigator aboard the USCGC *Escanaba*. In 1934 Roland returned for a four-year stint at the Coast Guard Academy as assistant coach and mathematics and physics instructor. While at the academy, Roland led a cadet summer cruise on the USCGC *Cayuga* and assisted in refugee evacuation in the European Spanish Civil War. From 1938 to 1940, Roland was executive officer and then commander of the cutter *Nemesis* out of the Florida port of St. Petersburg, and then assigned to the Eighth District Office at New Orleans, Louisiana.[1]

In his World War II service from 1942 to 1944, Roland headed the enlisted personnel division at U.S. Coast Guard Headquarters in Washington, D.C.; commanded an Escort Division that led convoys to the Mediterranean Sea; and was stationed on the flagship USS *Vance* with Coast Guard crewmembers. In 1944 Commander Roland skippered the Great Lakes heavy-duty icebreaker *Mackinaw* (WAGB-8) out of Cheboygan, Michigan, in missions to facilitate the transportation of supplies and the passage of U.S. Navy, Army, and merchant ships to their wartime locations. Roland's service earned him Coast Guard and Navy commendations.[2]

Roland finished out the post-war 1940s as operations chief and chief of staff at Great Lakes Ninth District Headquarters in Cleveland, Ohio, and commanded the legendary World War II USCGC *Taney* out of San Francisco. In the 1950s, Roland was the commandant of cadets at the Coast Guard Academy; studied at the National War College at Fort McNair in Washington, D.C., and served in the office of the chief of staff at Coast Guard Headquarters in Washington, D.C. Following that assignment, Rear Admiral Roland commanded the First Coast Guard District at Boston. In the 1960s, Roland commanded the Eastern Area of the United States and Atlantic Ocean and the Third Coast Guard District at New York City. In 1962, Vice Adm. Roland assumed the duties of assistant commandant of the Coast Guard from Washington headquarters, and became commandant that same year. Commandant Roland retired from the U.S. Coast Guard in 1966.[3]

In the early 1960s, Adm. Roland received commendations, awards, and medals from the secretary of the Treasury, U.S. Coast Guard, and U.S. Navy for his leadership and response to requests to train crews and provide patrol vessels for coastal surveillance missions in the Vietnam War. Commandant Roland went to Saigon to meet with Naval Coastal Surveillance Forces upon the arrival of several 82-foot patrol boats (cutters) to the port of Da Nang for Coast Guard Squadron One.

On the home front, Roland administered the extensive Cuban migrations into Florida waters, and in 1963 initiated the construction of the 210-foot medium endurance USCGC *Reliance* (WMEC-615) that was built at Todd Shipyards in Houston, Texas. In the late 1960s, Roland served as U.S. representative at the London merchant ship safety and standards conventions in Britain.[4]

New York City Mayor Robert F. Wagner honored Adm. Roland with the City Medallion in recognition of the commandant's service as Eastern Area and Third Coast Guard District commander. Roland's contributions are symbolized by the awards, honors, commendations, ribbons and medals bestowed upon him by civilian, military, and international organizations; he earned expert rifle and pistol shot medals during his career.[5]

10. Vietnam, DOT and Fisheries Patrols (1962–1982)

A review of several aspects of Roland's career substantiates the accolades and honors he earned. Commandant Roland sent the Coast Guard into combat in Vietnam in operations that involved eight years of coastal and riverine operations, port security, ATON, smuggling interdiction, transportation, and the insertion of U.S. Navy, Army, Marine, and Special Forces units.

Admiral Roland advocated sending the Coast Guard to Vietnam to preserve "the military credibility" of the service.[6] Roland initiated combat skills training for Coast Guard personnel and was encouraged to do so by his friend and military colleague U.S. Marine Corps Commandant General Wallace M. Greene,[7] who appreciated the history of the joint Coast Guard, Marine and Navy combat missions in the Pacific in World War II.

Commandant Roland went to Subic Bay in the Philippines on 17 July 1965 to inspect Coast Guard patrol boats and crews before they headed out into monsoon rains and heavy seas with a Navy support ship for the Vietnamese port of Da Nang. Admiral Roland subsequently deployed more WPBs (82-foot Coast Guard Patrol Boats/cutters), 44-foot motor lifeboats, and 40-foot utility boats for search and rescue, aids to navigation and combat missions, and additional large oceangoing cutters to supplement Squadron One on Market Time patrols.

In a July visit to Saigon, Vietnam, Adm. Roland visited Squadron One cutter crews and responded to the request of Rear Adm. Norvell G. Ward of the U.S. Navy for experienced Coast Guard port security teams to deal with defense and explosive loading operations in vulnerable ports. Treasury Secretary Henry W. Fowler and Adm. Roland quickly responded to Department of Defense requests for the Coast Guard to set up a LORAN-C radio communication chain in Vietnam. Despite logistical and tactical challenges, the Coast Guard built and manned the strategic LORAN network.[8]

On his watch, Commandant Roland increased the North Atlantic and Bering Sea fisheries patrols and added three medium endurance cutters to respond to the increasing encroachment of Soviet and Japanese fishing vessels.

Admiral Roland and Treasury Secretary Fowler objected to no avail when President Lyndon B. Johnson ordered the transfer of the Coast Guard from the Treasury Department to the newly established Department of Transportation (DOT). Commandant Roland acquiesced when he was assured that under DOT, the service would continue its military role.[9]

Historian Robert E. Johnson described the initial resistance by Adm. Roland to the transfer and Roland's description of an exchange with President Johnson at the White House: "We opposed [the transfer] rather violently." Lyndon Johnson responded: "The transfer did not need legislation," and, he, as president, "could transfer transportation functions from the Coast Guard to DOT" if the USCG remained in the Treasury Department. Commandant Roland therefore decided to accept the transfer to DOT to avoid the "dismemberment" of the service.

The 1967 transfer from Treasury to Transportation occurred after Roland's retirement, historian Johnson explained, but "Admiral Edwin J. Roland deserves much of the credit for the ease with which the transfer was made, and for the fact that the service lost nothing in the process." Moreover, Johnson concluded, Roland "was personally responsible for bringing about the state of military readiness that made possible the rapid response to the Navy's request for assistance in Vietnam, which helped maintain the Coast Guard's [military] integrity when it left the Treasury Department."[10]

Admiral Roland's successor was Commandant Willard J. Smith, who served from 1966 to 1970. The Michigan native followed the career tradition of his father, Warrant Officer Oscar Smith. Willard Smith entered the U.S. Coast Guard Academy as a cadet in 1930 and graduated as Ensign Smith in 1933. His career advancement proceeded at a respectable pace as lieutenant junior grade in 1936; lieutenant (1939); lieutenant commander (1942); commander (1944); captain (1955); rear admiral (1962); full four-star admiral (1966), and then commandant from 1966 to 1970.

Under Commandant Edwin Roland's watch from 1962 to 1966, the Coast Guard began its first cutter construction program since World War II (United States Coast Guard).

Willard Smith's career missions in chronological order were first as a line officer on the USCGC *Saranac* out of Galveston, Texas; aide to the commandant at U.S. Coast Guard Headquarters in Washington from 1936 to 1939; and flight training at Pensacola Naval Air Station

10. Vietnam, DOT and Fisheries Patrols (1962–1982)

in Florida, where he earned aviator status in June 1940.¹¹

During World War II Smith was attached to Coast Guard Air Station San Francisco and supervised new construction of that facility. Smith also served on anti-submarine patrols in the Pacific as part of Navy Patrol Squadron VP-44. In addition to those assignments, Smith conducted aerial surveys of Alaska, and received a Coast Guard commendation for landing a PBY floatplane at sea to get a U.S. Navy officer off of a ship and to a shore side Navy hospital. Smith finished out the war as an aide to the U.S. Coast Guard commandant.¹²

During Commandant Willard J. Smith's tenure the Coast Guard made the leap from the Department of the Treasury to the new Department of Transportation (United States Coast Guard).

From the end of World War II to 1962, Smith handled a plethora of specialized assignments in exemplary fashion. Smith commanded Coast Guard Air Station Traverse City, Michigan; studied at the Armed Forces Staff College in Norfolk, Virginia; attended LORAN classes at the aids to navigation school in Gorton, Connecticut; was the commanding officer at U.S. Coast Guard Station Guam; and commander of the Western Pacific Section.

Then Smith commanded the Great Lakes icebreaker *Mackinaw* out of Cheboygan, Michigan; headed the administrative management division at U.S. Coast Guard Headquarters in Washington, D.C.; returned to the U.S. Coast Guard Academy staff for three years; and was operations chief at Thirteenth Coast Guard District headquarters in Seattle, Washington.

In 1962, now Rear Adm. Willard J. Smith was appointed superintendent of the U.S. Coast Guard Academy. Admiral Smith would earn the Legion of Merit for his leadership in modernizing the technology and management curriculum; improving campus and building infrastructure; commanding the training sailing cutter *Eagle* at the international tall-mast marine parade in New York City (1964); and hosting Commandant Edwin J. Roland and members of Congress and the Executive branch on the *Eagle*. After his tenure at the academy ended in 1965, Rear Adm. Smith assumed command of the Ninth Coast Guard District at Cleveland, Ohio, and administered personnel and operations in the vast Great Lakes "Inland Seas" maritime region.[13]

Admiral Smith had been appointed commandant of the Coast Guard in June 1966, replacing Adm. Roland. The change of command ceremony occurred on the legendary 327-foot World War II USCGC *Campbell* at the Washington, D.C., Navy Yard.

Commandant Smith received numerous commendations and awards for his service achievements, including recognition for facilitating the transfer of the Coast Guard from the Department of the Treasury to the Department of Transportation, and several World War II campaign, national defense, and distinguished service awards. Admiral W.J. Smith died in April 2000.[14]

As commandant, Admiral Smith coordinated Coast Guard activities with the Department of Defense and the U.S. Armed Forces in Vietnam before and after the Coast Guard was transferred to the DOT. In March 1967, U.S. Navy Secretary Paul H. Nitze wrote to the Treasury Department requesting additional Coast Guard support. Assistant Treasury Secretary Joseph W. Barr replied that the Coast

Commandant Chester Bender helped usher in a new era for the Coast Guard, one in which marine environmental protection became a regular mission of the service (United States Coast Guard).

10. Vietnam, DOT and Fisheries Patrols (1962–1982)   113

Guard was conferring with the Navy about assigning five more large cutters to Vietnam after appropriate consultations with area and district Coast Guard commanders.

In response, Commandant Willard J. Smith deployed five 311-foot-long endurance cutters to South Vietnam to strengthen Market Time patrols. Smith also reached an agreement with the U.S. Air Force to train volunteer Coast Guard aviators to fly U.S. Air Force helicopters in the Air Force Aerospace Rescue and Recovery Service to rescue downed aviators in Vietnam. The agreement was signed by General John P. McConnell, Air Force chief of staff, and Admiral Smith in March 1967.

In 1969, the chief of naval operations requested that the Coast Guard transfer two high endurance cutters to the Navy for subsequent transfer to and the training of South Vietnamese Navy personnel. Naval Vice Admiral Elmo Zumwalt wanted the cutters for the 5-inch deck guns that were capable of firing shells up to 7 miles in support of U.S. and Vietnamese ground forces. The Navy Secretary, Joint Chiefs of Staff, Dept of Transportation Secretary John Volpe, and Commandant Smith were all involved in the transfer of the cutters to the Navy first because the Coast Guard did not have the legal authority per se to transfer ships to another nation.[15]

Admiral Chester R. Bender succeeded Adm. Willard J. Smith and served as Coast Guard Commandant from 1970 to 1974. The West Virginia native had transplanted to Florida and was appointed a cadet at the U.S. Coast Guard Academy. Bender was a member of the academy boxing team. He graduated in 1936.

Ensign Bender served as a line officer on Atlantic patrols on the cutters *Mendota* and *Bibb*. Then Bender transferred to the *Ossipee* on the Great Lakes. During World War II, Bender took flight training at U.S. Naval Air Station Pensacola, Florida, and did anti-submarine warfare patrols out of Coast Guard Air Station Elizabeth City, North Carolina.

In 1943–1944, Lt. Commander Bender commanded an air-sea rescue squadron out of Coast Guard Air Station San Diego (California), and became liaison officer and rescue advisor at the Far East U.S. Air Force Headquarters in the Philippines. Among the many commendations and ribbons Bender would acquire throughout his career, the air-sea rescue missions earned him the Bronze Star Medal.[16]

Between 1945 and 1960, Bender was posted at U.S. Coast Guard Headquarters in Washington, D.C., in the Air-Sea Rescue Agency and was pilot and aide to the commandant. Then, Commander Bender was appointed executive officer at U.S. Coast Guard Air Station St. Petersburg, Florida, until he was assigned to command Coast Guard Air Station Traverse City, Michigan. In 1955, Bender headed the division of war plans at

Coast Guard Headquarters. Later he was the commander of Coast Guard Air Detachment Barber's Point, Hawaii, after which he commanded the 311-foot USCGC *Bering Strait* out of Hawaii on Pacific patrols.

The decade of the 1960s found Bender performing a continued variety of assignments. Bender was the readiness and mobilization officer for the Western Area commander at San Francisco, and then chief of administrative management and program analysis in Washington, D.C. President Lyndon Johnson promoted Bender to Rear admiral in 1964 and gave him the Great Lakes command in Cleveland, Ohio. In 1965, Rear Adm. Bender was named superintendent of the U.S. Coast Guard Academy. There, Bender expanded academy construction projects and established the U.S. Coast Guard Museum. In 1967, he commanded the Twelfth Coast Guard District and Western Area (Pacific) Command out of San Francisco.[17]

From 1970 to 1974, President Richard M. Nixon nominated now full four star Adm. Bender to the post of commandant to succeed Adm. Willard Smith. Adm. Owen W. Siler would succeed Commandant Bender in 1974, but before his retirement, Bender had more to achieve.

Commandant Bender developed policies and techniques to better control marine pollution, and became an international leader in that arena. Bender pioneered innovative law enforcement, marine safety, and environmental protection operations. Admiral Bender became especially noted for his modification of the traditional enlisted Coast Guard uniform. The distinctive new uniform would become known as "Bender's Blues."[18]

In 1968, Rear Adm. Bender had suggested to Commandant Smith that Coast Guard personnel should wear uniforms distinctly different from U.S. Navy uniforms. Admiral Smith was described as not interested. When Bender became commandant in 1970, the Coast Guard uniform proposals were studied by a panel and distributed throughout the service.

Bender thought the traditional enlisted uniform and "Dixie Cup" head cover demeaned older enlisted personnel and detracted from the authoritative image of Coast Guard law enforcement and boarding crews. The Bender hat (cover) would have the visor look of officers and chief petty officers. Commandant Bender believed that his suggested "Coast Guard Blue" uniform would be professionally unique and inspiring. Enlisted personnel widely supported the proposed uniform modifications. Transportation Secretary John Volpe approved of the changes in the uniforms, and "Bender Blues" became policy.[19]

Commandant Bender's successor was Owen Wesley Siler, who served in that capacity from 1974 to 1978. Born in Seattle, Washington, in 1922, Siler graduated from Santa Maria Junior College (1940) in California, was appointed to the U.S. Coast Guard Academy that same year, and graduated

10. Vietnam, DOT and Fisheries Patrols (1962–1982)   115

in 1943 from a concentrated wartime curriculum with a bachelor's degree in engineering. Ensign Siler was immediately ordered to duty in the Pacific on the assault transport USS *Hunter Liggett*, from which he experienced combat shore landings. Siler served two years on the *Hunter Liggett* with responsibilities in gunnery, deck watch, and navigation. In 1945, Siler was assigned to the assault troop transport USS *Bayfield* and took part in the occupation of Japan.[20]

In 1946, Siler was assigned to Alameda Coast Guard Training Station in California, and then was navigation officer on the wartime combat ship *Taney*. In 1947, Siler was stationed at the Eleventh District Coast Guard Station in Long Beach, California.

The Coast Guard's expanding missions taxed the service during the mid– to late 1970s, but Commandant Owen Siler provided sturdy leadership during that time, navigating the way for the service to become "maritime, military and multi-missioned" (United States Coast Guard).

From 1947 to 1962 Siler took aviator training at the U.S. Naval Air Bases in Pensacola, Florida, and Corpus Christi, Texas. Then, in 1948, Siler did search and rescue and air patrols from the Coast Guard Air Station at Port Angeles, Washington. In 1952, Siler studied at the Naval Flying School in Corpus Christi, followed by an assignment at Coast Guard Air Detachment Barber's Point, Hawaii. Siler finished out the 1950s as an assistant to the Coast Guard Commandant in Washington, D.C., and from 1959 to 1962 he commanded U.S. Coast Guard Air Station Corpus Christi.[21]

Through the 1960s, Siler continued his career advancement in a variety of specialized assignments: search and rescue chief at Seventeenth District Headquarters in Juneau, Alaska, and executive and then commanding officer at Coast Guard Air Station Miami, Florida. Then Siler studied at the National War College in Washington, D.C.; had leadership posts in the management division at Coast Guard Headquarters in Washington, D.C.; and graduated with a master's degree from George Washington University in international affairs.

In the 1970s, Captain Siler was appointed rear admiral and commander, Second Coast Guard District in St. Louis, Missouri, where he received honors for leading a mission to control a deadly barge chlorine spill. In 1974, President Nixon nominated Siler for higher command. Rear Admiral Siler became commandant upon the retirement of Adm. Bender.

Admiral Siler ended the Ocean Stations program, as cutters on weather patrol were replaced by advanced technology; minority recruiting was emphasized; the new "Bender's Blues" uniforms were distributed to all service members; women cadets were accepted for flight training and admission to the U.S. Coast Guard Academy; and Coast Guard fisheries management and law enforcement missions were extended by Congress out to sea in a two million mile maritime domain area for 200 miles off the ocean coasts of the United States.

Deep-water port construction in the Gulf of Mexico allowed increased oil tanker access and expanded Coast Guard port security and inspection responsibilities. Coast Guard helicopters and cutters performed icebreaking and escort missions for equipment barges in the oil-rich North Slope off the north Alaskan site of Point

Commandant John B. Hayes fought the ages-old battle to keep the Coast Guard separate from the Navy, while concurrently working to keep the service properly funded to achieve its many mission goals (United States Coast Guard).

Barrow. The USCGC *Polar Star* was commissioned in 1976; Coast Guard petroleum Strike Teams managed tanker oil spills in Asian, Latin American, and North American (Chesapeake Bay, Florida) waters; and the Coast Guard developed technologies and strategies to identify oil polluting companies and tankers. It also blockaded coastal Florida waters to interdict contraband drug smuggling.[22]

The Coast Guard, from the time of the Revenue Marine and Revenue Cutter Service, had been engaged in smuggling and contraband interdiction missions that were greatly expanded in the Prohibition period of the 1920s and early 1930s. In 1976–1977, the U.S. Coast Guard, the Drug Enforcement Administration (DEA), and the U.S. Customs Service coordinated their drug interdiction efforts. By the end of 1977, Coast Guard forces had seized dozens of contraband vessels with cargoes worth hundreds of millions of dollars.

Admiral Siler and Coast Guard units, with partner agencies, responded to increasing incidents of yacht highjackings and robberies. Commandant Siler issued warnings and disseminated security and prevention instructions.

Changes were occurring because of the technological and administrative changes made by Adm. Siler in the aids to navigation (ATON) program. The operation of ATON stations ashore (lighthouses) and afloat (lightships) had been done manually by Coast Guard personnel. Gradually, the light stations were automated, and large navigation buoys replaced lightships and light structures off shore. Radio transmissions led to the transfer of Coast Guard personnel from ATON to other duties. LORAN-C became the federally supported navigation technology in the Coastal Confluence Zone along the U.S. seaboard, Great Lakes, and Canada in coordination with the navigation format of the Department of Transportation.

LORAN-C was intended for civilian use, as opposed to the World War II and Korean War LORAN stations which supported military operations. The Canadian Coast Guard constructed and administered LORAN-C stations in coordination with U.S. stations. Some LORAN stations were operated overseas and in foreign nations under the aegis of the Department of Defense.

Admiral Siler was dedicated to modernizing Coast Guard air, land and sea assets and infrastructure. Nearly a dozen seagoing cutters had been built in the World War II era of the 1930s and 1940s, as were several Coast Guard aircraft. Siler made his case to federal agencies and officials when federal spending was being significantly reduced. Nonetheless, under Commandant Siler, two new 399-foot polar icebreakers, several

140-foot icebreaking tugs, and 160-foot construction and dredging Coast Guard tenders were constructed. Under Siler's supervision, several 270-foot cutters, 41-foot motor lifeboats, and 32-foot waterway, port and harbor boats were built. The World War II era 180-foot buoy tenders and 95-foot patrol boats were rebuilt and upgraded. The innovations led to more efficient use of crews and assets.[23]

Commandant Siler expanded the Coast Guard billets that women could train for and made the U.S. Coast Guard Academy the earliest service academy to enroll female cadets. The first two female Coast Guard aviators completed flight training in 1977. Under Siler, female commissioned officers and enlisted personnel were assigned to the U.S. Coast Guard cutters *Morgenthau* and *Gallatin*. Shore stations were composed of mixed-gender crews. Coast Guard Reservists and civilian Coast Guard Auxiliary personnel were given expanded opportunities in boat safety and search and rescue missions. Reservists had more opportunity for active duty. Coast Guard representatives were involved in international maritime conferences and United Nations issues.

Search and rescue stations were upgraded or newly constructed in New England, Florida, and on Lake Superior, including at U.S. Coast Guard Station Bayfield on the Chequamegon Bay of Lake Superior in northern Wisconsin. Admiral Siler advocated these projects because, as he stated, "Deteriorated shore plants were inefficient ... expensive ... unwholesome ... and unsafe."[24]

Commandant Siler's leadership led to the popular perception that the Coast Guard was a premier agency for search and rescue, port security, law enforcement, environmental protection, and national defense. Adm. Owen W. Siler ended a distinguished three-decade career when he retired in May 1978.[25]

Admiral John B. Hayes was born in 1924 in New York State and entered the Coast Guard Academy in 1943. Ensign Hayes was commissioned in 1946; assigned to the LORAN Station in Matsumae, Japan; commanded the USCGC *Ariadne* in 1952; served on the cutters *Vigilant* and *Sagebrush*; and performed duties at Coast Guard Base Key West, Florida. Hayes began studies at the U.S. Naval War College in Newport, Rhode Island, in 1959. Hayes earned a master's degree in international affairs in 1964 at George Washington University in Washington, D.C. By 1966 he was commander of a Naval Task Group and Division II, Coast Guard Squadron One, in Vietnam.

After Vietnam, Cmdr. John B. Hayes was assigned to Coast Guard Headquarters in the nation's capital, and in 1968 he became Captain Hayes and subsequently commandant of cadets at the Coast Guard Academy. In

10. Vietnam, DOT and Fisheries Patrols (1962–1982) 119

1973, Rear Adm. Hayes returned to Coast Guard Headquarters, and then was assigned as commander of the Seventeenth U.S. Coast Guard District out of Juneau, Alaska. In 1978, Admiral Hayes was appointed Coast Guard commandant and served at that post from 1978 to 1982.[26]

Commandant Adm. Hayes had to adjust to congressional budget cuts and fight off proposals to permanently place the U.S. Coast Guard under U.S. Navy control. Hayes counteracted the service merger ideas by citing the diverse duties of the multi-mission Coast Guard. A joint board was established to facilitate communications, training, and mission articulation. The Coast Guard, with the support of Congress, increased its drug interdiction missions with U.S. Customs and the Drug Enforcement Administration, and increased contraband interdiction seizures.

Admiral Hayes hosted a conference with Caribbean political leaders to forge cooperative policies and teamwork in drug and illegal immigration enforcement, search and rescue, and safety at sea. The migration issue became more prominent with increased Haitian migration and illegal attempts to enter the United States. Coast Guard cutters and crews responded to the mass migration of Cubans heading for the United States in the 1980 Mariel Boatlift incident, and saved hundreds of lives at sea in the process.[27]

The career of Admiral John Briggs Hayes was chronicled after his retirement in an extensive interview for the U.S. Coast Guard Oral History Project, conducted by Lt. (jg) Michael Mansker on 8 October 1985, three years after Adm. Hayes retired from active service. Lt. Mansker's perceptive questions and summation provided an exemplary chronicle of the career of Adm. Hayes, and illustrated the eclectic skill set, training, and mission diversity required of Coast Guard officers in the myriad of mission responsibilities.

The career of Adm. Hayes included rigorous studies and training at the U.S. Coast Guard Academy, command of Coast Guard shore stations and cutters afloat, overseas duties, advanced academic studies, and leadership positions in port security (as a captain of the port), law enforcement, aid to navigation responsibilities ashore and on a buoy tender, and a variety of Coast Guard missions from the beginning of his Coast Guard career as an academy cadet, to becoming the top commanding officer in the U.S. Coast Guard.

Admiral Hayes earned a variety of medals, awards, and campaign ribbons from assignments in U.S. waters and overseas. The awards and commendations included the World War II Victory Medal, Legion of Merit with Combat "V" device, Coast Guard Expert Rifleman Medal, Republic of Korea and Republic of Vietnam Citations, National Defense Medal,

Navy Distinguished Service Medal, Coast Guard Distinguished Service Medal, and the Secretary of Treasury Commendation Medal.

Among his many interesting postings, Adm. Hayes was liaison officer to the U.S. House of Representatives in an appropriations investigation group (1961) and commanding officer of the LORAN Transmitting Station in Matsumae, Japan, in 1951. Administering the logistics for the Matsumae LORAN station required extraordinary creativity, as Hayes explained: "We had to use an LST [Landing Ship Tank] to transport the Loran trailers because the tunnels leading from the docks at Matsumae were not high enough to handle the trailers. We had to borrow a tractor from the [United States] Army and get it to Matsumae over the Japanese rail line. We had to dig trenches for cables and electric lines between trailers in the frozen ground in adverse [winter] weather. I had ten enlisted personnel and myself [then a young officer], and that was the whole command."[28]

The U.S. Coast Guard has long been noted for the responsibility given to its rated non-commissioned officers (NCOs) and commissioned officers. Lt. Mansker inquired about those responsibilities. The former commandant responded: "Coast Guard commissioned officers, petty officers, and warrant officers are head and shoulders above their counterparts in the other services in exercising leadership and in decision making skills. A young lieutenant in command of a patrol boat is given a very substantial amount of authority to go with his or her responsibility." Admiral Hayes said petty officers and commissioned and warrant officers were invariably "operating in a real world environment ... responding to real life situations that can be immediately evaluated."[29]

11

Militarization, Middle East, Interdiction and Ecology (1982–1994)

From 1982 to 1994, three commandants led the U.S. Coast Guard: Admirals James S. Gracey, Paul A. Yost, Jr., and J. William Kime.

James S. Gracey, a Newton, Massachusetts, native, graduated from the U.S. Coast Guard Academy with an ensign commission, bachelor's degree in engineering, and awards for superior proficiency in tactics, drill, and seamanship. From 1949 to 1951, Gracey was a U.S. Coast Guard Academy instructor, and then officer of the deck on the 311-foot *Barataria*, an ocean station cutter out of Portland, Maine. Rounding out his professional education, in the early 1950s, Gracey attended provost marshal, fire protection, and explosives loading schools.

In the early 1950s, he also served at the captain of the port office in Boston, Massachusetts, studied at the LORAN School in Groton, Connecticut, and commanded LORAN Station Ocean Cape in Yakutat, Alaska. Then Gracey taught tactics at the Coast Guard Academy, coached basketball, studied business administration at Harvard, did a stint at Coast Guard Headquarters in Washington, D.C., and commanded the *Mariposa*, a buoy tender home-ported at New London, Connecticut. The *Mariposa* did aid to navigation missions off Connecticut and Long Island, and icebreaking on New York's Hudson River.[1]

The following decades were similarly productive for Gracey. Between 1965 and 1977, he was comptroller out of the St. Louis, Missouri, Coast Guard headquarters; project officer at Governor's Island, New York City, during the transition at the site of the U.S. Army Base at Fort Jay to Alameda, California; and then served as executive officer at the base. In 1969, Captain Gracey headed the programs division at headquarters, earned flag rank in 1974, and was chief of staff at Fifth Coast Guard District Headquarters in Portsmouth, Virginia. Then Rear Adm. Gracey took command of the Ninth (Great Lakes) Coast Guard District in Cleveland. In that capacity, Adm. Gracey served on a navigation board and assisted in the resolution of Great Lakes pilotage conflicts between the U.S. Department of Transportation and the government of Canada.[2]

From 1977 to 1982, Adm. Gracey returned to national headquarters as chief of staff. He completed tours of duty as Pacific Area and then Atlantic Area commander; and advanced to full admiral and commandant of the Coast Guard. As commandant, Gracey faced the mission expansion and budget issues of his predecessors, and recurring attempts by Congress to privatize certain Coast Guard missions, such as search and rescue. Gracey led the movement to build technologically advanced 270-foot oceangoing cutters, 110-foot patrol boats, and the advanced HU-25A Falcon aircraft.

National defense assumed increasing significance in Coast Guard missions, and included support of U.S. military operations in Grenada (1983) and the 1984 Maritime Defense Zone concept of Coast Guard military support.

Admiral Gracey directed joint Coast Guard–Caribbean drug enforcement missions and space shuttle support missions. In general, Commandant Gracey sought, as he asserted, "to keep the USCG afloat ... on an even keel ... and moving forward."[3]

The offshore missions of the Coast Guard evolved within the context of international treaties and increased Congressional authority to meet contemporary needs. Fishing enforcement, narcotics and immigration interdiction, and a plethora of law enforcement and national defense paradigms necessitated increased domestic and global involvement. The related ship monitoring and boarding responsibilities required tactical innovation and diplomatic outreach.

In the 1970s and 1980s, in the era of Commandants Siler, Hayes, and Gracey, the use of global positioning and computer communication technology evolved. The Coast Guard continued to adhere to complex procedures to obtain permission to board international ships on the high seas and in the domestic maritime realm.[4]

In the Prohibition era of the 1920s and early 1930s, Coast Guard interdiction of foreign vessels beyond the generally recognized 12-mile limit of national maritime sovereignty had involved litigation and the occasional release of confiscated ships and apprehended crew members. In the half-century following Prohibition, the Coast Guard acquired authority to board ships at sea after getting the permission of the master of the ves-

11. Militarization, Middle East, Interdiction (1982–1994) 123

sel, or the approval of representatives of the nation under which the ship was registered or flagged.

The Coast Guard would initiate communications, usually via radio, with the U.S. State Department and the nation of interest. Response time could range from a few hours to several days, or a week or more. In the interim, if the legality of the ship's registration or activities was suspected, Coast Guard officials might conclude the suspect vessel was "legally assimilated into statelessness" and therefore "subject to United States jurisdiction on the high seas."[5] If permission to board did not ensue, the Coast Guard cutter commander could follow the vessel of interest until permission was granted, or the vessel entered U.S. waters and could then be boarded[6] with appropriate legal authority, procedures, and force.

Admiral Paul Alexander Yost, Jr., was placed in command of the United States Coast Guard on 30 May 1986. Yost's previous post had encompassed the overlapping positions of commander of the Atlantic Area, commander Third Coast Guard District New York City, and commander of the Maritime Defense Zone Atlantic. Prior to his appointment as Coast Guard commandant in 1986, Yost had administered operations in a maritime realm that included the Atlantic, Gulf of Mexico, and Caribbean maritime zones, and coastal defense under the U.S. Navy Atlantic Fleet commander. Prior to 1986, Adm. Yost served as chief of staff at U.S. Coast Guard Headquarters in Washington, D.C., directing planning, budgeting, and programs; and Eighth District Commander in New Orleans, Louisiana.[7]

Commandant Yost revealed his grasp of U.S. Coast Guard history and the contributions of the service in his foreword to the reprinted (1989) edition of Lt. Malcolm F. Willoughby's history, *The United States Coast Guard in World War II* (Naval Institute Press, 1957). Yost traced Coast Guard air and sea missions in every theater of war and chronicled the national security and maritime training contributions the service made on the domestic front. Admiral Yost concluded, "World War II was the test of fire that forged the modern Coast Guard," called Willoughby's work "a classic," and commended "the Naval Institute Press for helping [the U.S. Coast Guard] launch our bicentennial celebration" on 4 August 1989.[8] As a young officer, Yost made his own significant contributions to national security in naval combat operations in Vietnam as commander of Task Group 115.3 (1969).

In 1975, Yost was operations chief in the Seventeenth Coast Guard District, Alaska, then special assistant in the Department of Transportation, and an alternative representative in the United States Law of the Sea delegation. From 1966 through 1974, Yost served as captain of the port in Seattle, Washington, special assistant to the chief counsel at Coast Guard

Headquarters in Washington, D.C., administrator in the Aids to Navigation Division; and before that, commander of the USCGC *Resolute* out of San Francisco, California.

After graduation from the U.S. Coast Guard Academy in 1951, Yost compiled a catalog of academic achievements from that date to 1964, earning master's degrees in international affairs (George Washington University in Washington, D.C.) and mechanical engineering (University of Connecticut); doing graduate work in business administration; and graduating from the Naval War College (Newport, Rhode Island).[9]

Given his Vietnam combat experience, it was understandable that Commandant Yost emphasized and expanded naval defense operations in the Coast Guard, but not without criticism. Admiral Yost added missile launchers to high endurance oceangoing cutters and expanded drug interdiction and national security missions with the Defense Department, Drug Enforcement Administration, U.S. Customs, and foreign military and law enforcement agencies. The commandant increased Coast Guard operations in the Persian Gulf, and joint search and rescue and border cooperation with the Union of Soviet Socialist Republics (USSR)[10] during a limited thawing period of the Cold War.

Admiral Yost did not neglect natural and human caused disasters on the home front. At the commandant's direction, the Coast Guard responded to hurricanes in the Gulf of Mexico, a California earthquake, and oil spills off the California and Alaskan coasts. The oil spills from the U.S. tankers *Exxon Valdez* (Alaska) and the *American Trader* (California) led Congress to pass the Oil Protection Act (1990) and expand Coast Guard responsibilities in environmental protection and oil tanker inspection and regulation.

The several medals and commendations he earned illustrate Paul Yost's personal and professional achievements during a long Coast Guard career. Among them are the Silver Star, two Distinguished Service Medals, Legion of Merit with combat "V," United Nations Service Medal, Navy Meritorious Unit Commendation, and the Presidential Unit Citation.[11] In that regard, Yost's Vietnam service requires further explanation, and illustrates the significant role the U.S. Coast Guard has played in national defense missions with its U.S. Armed Forces counterparts.

Yost exhibited courageous and inspirational combat leadership in the Vietnam War. Yost was among three future Coast Guard commandants who served in Southeast Asia. He earned the Silver Star for his response to an April 1969 enemy ambush on the Bo De River. Fatalities occurred in the nine-vessel U.S. Navy Swift Boat mission, during which Yost rescued the crew of a grounded patrol boat under shore-side enemy fire.[12]

U.S. Navy, U.S. Navy SEALS, U.S. Army and Army Special Forces,

11. Militarization, Middle East, Interdiction (1982–1994) 125

U.S. Coast Guard personnel, and the navy and marines of the government of South Vietnam conducted operations against Viet Cong units in peninsular, forest, and riverine regions of the Mekong Delta. The logistical units and missions were called Silver Mace and Sea Float, the latter consisting of pontoon barges anchored in strategic river areas. Enemy supply missions were intercepted in those naval operations. Commander Paul A. Yost operated from Sea Float infrastructure in patrol boat, surveillance, and junk (native boat) interdiction missions.[13]

Commandant James Gracey kept the Coast Guard "afloat ... on an even keel ... and moving forward" (United States Coast Guard).

Commander Yost deliberately put himself in harm's way on Coast Guard patrol boat and Swift Boat missions, because he had concluded, "If you led missions, you planned them well. People who didn't lead missions could get into a habit of sloppy planning. To keep myself involved, and keep the risk factors very well known to me, I tried to lead between a third and a half" of the missions.[14]

Admiral Yost took lessons, strategies, and significance from his time in Vietnam: "From Vietnam, we learned that we [in the Coast Guard] should be very aware of our military mission, [and realize] the Coast Guard is a capable war-making service with the expertise and experience to run patrol boats. In wartime the Coast Guard ought to be there as a source of boats, experience, and people."[15]

As Coast Guard commandant, Admiral Yost was criticized for his increased militarization of the Coast Guard in ordnance and weapons emphasis, elements of which would be reduced by his successors. But Yost was vindicated after the 11 September 2001 terrorist attacks upon the United States. In 2003, the Coast Guard was transferred from the Department of Transportation to the newly formed Department of Homeland Security and given an expanded national defense role at home and overseas.[16]

While serving as Eleventh Coast Guard District commander out of Long Beach, California, in 1990, Admiral John William Kime became the 19th commandant of the U.S. Coast Guard. Kime served in that capacity from 1990–1994. At the time of his elevation to commandant, Adm. Kime was contemporaneously commander of the U.S. Maritime Defense Zone Pacific (Central California Sector), and coordinator in the Office of National Drug Control Policy in the Pacific Region.

The 1957 Coast Guard Academy graduate earned advanced degrees in naval architecture and naval engineering from Massachusetts Institute of Technology. Admiral Kime's career included deck and engineering posts on the USCGC *Casco*, Commander of the LORAN Station at Wake Island in the Pacific, appointment to the Merchant Marine Technical and Naval Engineering divisions at U.S. Coast Guard Headquarters in Washington, D.C., U.S. negotiator at the International Maritime Organization conference in London, where he assisted in drafting codes for liquefied gas tanker transports, head of the structural design program for the Polar class icebreakers; and engineering officer on the USCGC *Boutwell*.[17]

Commandant Paul Yost expanded the military culture of the Coast Guard, a move vindicated by the changes made to the service after the terrorist attacks of September 11, 2001 (United States Coast Guard).

In 1977, J. William Kime graduated with distinction from the Industrial College of the United States Armed Forces, and then transferred back to Coast Guard Headquar-

11. Militarization, Middle East, Interdiction (1982–1994)

ters as assistant director of the Merchant Marine Technical Division. He also served as a member of the United States delegation in London to the International Conference on Tanker Safety and Pollution Prevention. The following year, Kime assumed command of the Marine Safety Office in Baltimore, Maryland, and in 1981 was appointed deputy chief of the Office of Marine Environment and Systems at Coast Guard Headquarters.

Like most Coast Guard officers, Kime received periodic orders to move to other assignments. From 1982 to 1984, Captain Kime served as chief of operations in the Seventh Coast Guard District out of Miami, Florida. In that capacity, he supervised Caribbean area drug interdiction missions.

Though he sought to significantly demilitarize the Coast Guard, Commandant J. William Kime's tenure will mostly be remembered for the service's role in the first Gulf War (United States Coast Guard).

In 1984, Kime was promoted to flag rank, and in 1986 was chief of marine safety, security, and environmental protection at Coast Guard Headquarters in Washington, D.C., in addition to attending marine safety and environmental conferences. Given his many positions, accomplishments, and promotions, it is little wonder that Adm. Kime earned a variety of service medals, ribbons, and commendations[18] for, as naval commanders say, "a job well done."

Admiral Kime earned the Defense Service Medal and Legion of Merit in recognition of his professional achievements, and leadership as commandant in responding to the breakup of the Soviet Union and several Communist governments in Eastern Europe.

The commandant administered support missions for U.S. military operations in the Middle East and specifically in the Persian Gulf during Desert Shield and Desert Storm.[19] Despite his involvement in military operations, Commandant Kime terminated Admiral Yost's Coast Guard drug interdiction operations deep in the Latin American forests, and removed Yost's harpoon missiles from Coast Guard high endurance cutters.[20]

Coast Guard historian David Helvarg contrasted commandant philosophies and leadership styles succinctly: "Strong personalities compete to leave their imprint on the institution, and sometimes lead erratic course corrections." Examples of such sea changes, Helvarg explained, would include "the shift from the militarizing mission of Adm. Paul Yost (1986–1990) to the environmental and corporate management ethos of his successor, Adm. William Kime (1990–1994)."[21]

12

Maritime Outreach, Asset Innovation and War on Terror (1994–2002)

Between 1994 and 2002 the Coast Guard departed from its primarily domestic and humanitarian missions to replicate its historic World War II national security responsibilities of port security at home, and national defense missions overseas with the other U.S. Armed Forces and international institutions and defense and security forces.

The overseas missions were primarily in response to the War on Terror that commenced after the terrorist attacks upon the United States on September 11, 2001 ("9/11"). The leading Coast Guard commandants in that initial time frame were Admirals Robert F. Kramek and James M. Loy.

Admiral Kramek graduated from the U.S. Coast Guard Academy as an ensign in 1961 with a bachelor of science degree in engineering. Kramek's career assignments before serving as Coast Guard commandant (1994–1998) included command of the *Midgett*, U.S. Coast Guard Base Governor's Island (New York City), U.S. Coast Guard Districts Seven and Thirteen, and chief of staff at headquarters in Washington, D.C. As Seventh District commander, Kramek was the regional drug interdiction coordinator and head of the Haitian immigration task force.

Kramek did graduate work at the University of Alaska, University of Michigan, and Johns Hopkins University. He earned master of science degrees in marine and mechanical engineering and management. Kramek graduated with distinction from the U.S. Naval War College in Newport, Rhode Island, and from National Defense University at Fort McNair in Washington, D.C. Admiral Kramek earned his flag rank in 1986, and was appointed commandant of the Coast Guard in June 1994.[1]

Kramek expanded drug enforcement and immigration interdiction efforts in the Caribbean region (Puerto Rico, Virgin Islands, Lesser Antilles) in Operation Frontier Shield and Operation Gulf Shield in the Gulf of Mexico. The expansion included law enforcement, search and rescue training, and mission articulation with the nations in that maritime realm in Operation Trade Winds and Operation Unitas. The regional maritime outreach included Coast Guard training and operations with Latin American coast guard and naval units.[2]

Under Kramek, international outreach and training missions occurred with previous Cold War adversaries, including former republics of the Soviet Union, Latvia, Lithuania, Estonia, and Ukraine. The coordinated plan with Slavic Europe was code named Operation BALTOPS (Baltic Sea Operations). The U.S. Coast Guard helped these newly sovereign nations train their own fledgling coast guards.

In addition, it worked with the border guards of the Russian Federation on search and rescue and fisheries enforcement patrols. The U.S. Coast Guard also engaged in oil spill response training and exercises with Canada.[3]

On Kramek's watch, the service responded to oil spills off the New England coast and the Houston (Texas) Ship Canal. During his tenure search and rescue responses were sent to downed Alaskan Airlines Flight 301, TWA Flight 800, and a private American aircraft shot down by Cuba. In Operation ABLE MANNER, the Coast Guard rescued more than one thousand Haitian refugees at sea.[4]

Commandant Kramek met budget challenges with

Assuming command of the Coast Guard after the fall of the Berlin Wall, Commandant Robert Kramek expanded outreach and training opportunities with former Cold War adversaries (United States Coast Guard).

12. Maritime Outreach and War on Terror (1994–2002)

Congress, administered the building of new buoy tenders to enhance expanded aids to navigation missions, and increased training operations at the U.S. Coast Guard Academy Leadership Training Center.[5]

Coast Guard commandants have historically done an outstanding job matching personnel and missions with changing technological, international, socioeconomic, ecological, and national security circumstances. In 1988, Commandant Robert Kramek placed future commandant James M. Loy on staff to design responses to anticipated events. Several five-year strategies were developed to anticipate demographic, energy, and international changes. One significant element of Coast Guard planning was the development of the concept of "Maritime Domain Awareness."[6]

Admiral Kramek directed technological innovations on the domestic scene in search and rescue, port security, law enforcement, infrastructure, and boat and cutter innovation. He witnessed the launching of the new Juniper class cutters designed to replace the World War II 180-foot buoy tender cutters, four of which were still serving on the Great Lakes. Several of the 16 new 225-foot Jupiter class cutters were assigned to ports on the East Coast.

In addition to the Jupiter Class buoy tenders, Marinette Marine Corporation in Wisconsin received a federal contract to build what were called Keeper class shore and inland cutters. Keeper class cutters were named for the famed U.S. Life-Saving Service and U.S. Lighthouse Service keepers whose courage and competence enriched the Coast Guard legacy.

Commandant James Loy was at the helm when the 2001 terrorist attacks struck New York City and Washington, D.C. (United States Coast Guard).

The first Keeper class cutter was the *Ida Lewis* that had a 1997 delivery date.[7]

In his post-retirement career, Admiral Kramek applied his maritime knowledge and leadership skills as a member of the American Bureau of Shipping (1998–2006) in Houston, Texas.[8] Admiral Kramek's administrative expertise and vision continued the Coast Guard leadership tradition, as did the career and tenure of his successor, Admiral James M. Loy (1998–2002).

Ensign James M. Loy graduated from the U.S. Coast Guard Academy in engineering in 1964. Loy went on to command the USCGC *Point Lomas* in Vietnam, and cutters *Valiant* (Galveston, Texas) and *Midgett* (San Francisco). Admiral Loy had flag assignments as commander of the Eighth Coast Guard District in Louisiana and chief of personnel and training at Washington, D.C., headquarters.

As chief of staff (1996–1998), Adm. Loy modified management structure and planning and budget procedures. Prior to becoming commandant, Loy had been the Atlantic Area commander, and directed Coast Guard operations in the 1994 Haitian and Cuban migrations.[9]

Commandant Loy (1998–2002) increased the Coast Guard personnel complement and improved retention. Loy led the way with the modernization of Coast Guard air and sea assets in the Integrated Deepwater System acquisition project.

Loy enhanced his own leadership skills in postgraduate studies at the University of Rhode Island, where he earned master's degrees in public administration and history and government, and at Wesleyan University in Connecticut. Loy also attended the Armed Forces Industrial College at Fort Leslie J. McNair in Washington, D.C., and interned at Harvard University in Cambridge, Massachusetts, at the John F. Kennedy School of Government.

In his illustrious career Loy earned numerous medals, awards, and commendations, including the coveted Combat Action Ribbon.[10] The American Society of Public Administration presented its 2001 Leadership Award to Admiral Loy in 2001. He earned a maritime leadership award from the United Kingdom in 2000, and in that same year an award from the National Association for the Advancement of Colored People. In 2001, Loy received the Military Leadership Award from the Sailors, Marines, and Airmen Club.[11]

Admiral Loy retired in 2002, and served subsequently in national security capacities in the Transportation Security Administration (TSA) under Transportation Secretary Norman Mineta,[12] before the U.S. Coast Guard was transferred to the newly established Department of Homeland Security in 2003.

12. Maritime Outreach and War on Terror (1994–2002) 133

When terrorists struck targets in the United States on 11 September 2001, in New York City, Shanksville, Pennsylvania, and at the Pentagon in Washington, D.C., Commandant Loy directed a national Coast Guard response on ocean, coastal, inland, and Great Lakes waters, and met with civilian and commercial port authority officials. Regular, reserve, and auxiliary personnel stepped to the fore with their diverse experience and skills in partnership with local, state, and federal public safety and law enforcement units.

Great Lakes Coast Guard units increased security and ship boarding missions within hours of the attacks. The Coast Guard conducted joint patrols with Canadian and U.S. military and law enforcement agencies. The Ninth District (Great Lakes) commander, Rear Adm. James Hull, directed his maritime security forces and called the U.S. Coast Guard Reserve to active duty.

The civilian Coast Guard Auxiliary provided support at Maritime Safety Offices and shore and air stations, and patrolled inland waterways. Great Lakes defense, economic, and power plant infrastructure was monitored and protected. With the creation of the Department of Homeland Security in 2003 and the transfer of the Coast Guard to that agency, Great Lakes personnel were sent to the Middle East in the War on Terror and integrated missions with the U.S. Navy. National security became a Coast Guard priority. Adm. Loy led that mission evolution as commandant, and subsequently as a civilian leader in national security agencies.[13]

Jim Loy knew what Coast Guard leadership and command was all about on the home front overseas. During the Vietnam War, Loy did 15 months in that combat theater on 82-foot patrol boats, and earned a Bronze Star. As United States military forces withdrew from Indochina, Loy trained South Vietnam naval forces on Coast Guard cutters that were to be transferred to the naval personnel of South Vietnam.[14]

The U.S. Coast Guard has coordinated its missions with the U.S. Navy since the earliest days of the Service. Commandant Loy continued that alliance. On "9/11," the chief of naval operations asked Loy how the U.S. Navy could assist the Coast Guard. It was mutually decided that Coast Guard cutters should be present in New York Harbor, and the U.S. Navy should operate farther out to sea in other capacities.[15]

Admiral Loy was diligent about maintaining and expanding Coast Guard budgets and assets to meet new mission requirements. During his tenure as commandant, Loy met senior officer leadership who had blue-water (ocean) command experience to replace the aging cutter fleet. "When it was clear that [cutters which served more than] fifty miles off shore were aging ... we went through strategic planning, and did a mission study with all of our federal customers ... talking about twenty-five years down the road."[16]

Loy and his Coast Guard colleagues then launched what would become a multi-billion dollar "integrated approach" management plan with ship builders and high technology companies for "Deepwater" assets that included logistics, aircraft, communications, and proposed new National Security Cutters. After his retirement from the Coast Guard, Loy continued his contributions to the Deepwater mission as a lobbyist for a Washington, D.C., firm headed by former defense secretary William Cohen.[17]

The complexity of the subsequent projects, competition between associated industries and interest groups, and cost overruns led to conflict, public controversy, and Congressional hearings that forced more stringent oversight and fiscal and management reforms. The Coast Guard assumed greater management control over the projects, and contributed more of its nautical engineering and naval architecture expertise. The U.S. Navy was brought in to contribute its big project and sea faring experience and technological expertise.[18] The Deepwater program generally progressed on target to produce and improve the next generation of assets to meet the evolving domestic and overseas requirements of the multi-mission Coast Guard.

James M. Loy responded decisively to the terrorist threat to the maritime infrastructure of the United States, and was acutely aware of the possibility of the potential of terrorists using ships and small watercraft to attack harbor and urban infrastructure, and ships in U.S. ports. In a speech at a secret intelligence meeting in 2002, Adm. Loy asserted that U.S. ports and strategic waterways constituted 25 percent of the gross domestic product (GDP) of the United States. Loy explained the need for better intelligence about foreign threats, and the need for timely intelligence about ships, terrorists, strategic cargo, possible targets, and technology. To acquire that knowledge database, Loy advocated intelligence exchanges between the Coast Guard and domestic and overseas intelligence agencies, and the cooperation of shipping company operatives.[19]

National defense reporter and author Bill Gertz lauded President George W. Bush and his administration for the 2002 announcement about the proposed cabinet-level Department of Homeland Security (DHS). Dozens of federal agencies were to be moved into this national security agency to coordinate U.S. defense, national security, and intelligence assets in the War on Terror.

The transfer of the Immigration and Naturalization Service, U.S. Customs Service, Federal Emergency Management Agency (FEMA), Border

Patrol, Secret Service, and the U.S. Coast Guard was planned. The Border Patrol would be transferred from the Department of Justice, U.S. Customs from the Department of Treasury, and the U.S. Coast Guard would be moved to the Department of Homeland Security from the Department of Transportation. The Transportation Security Administration, formed in 2001, was transferred to the DHS in 2003.[20]

General Michael Hagee was the commandant of the United States Marine Corps from 2003 to 2006. General Hagee subsequently served as president and CEO of the Admiral Nimitz Foundation and National Museum of the Pacific War in Fredericksburg, Texas. Following their respective retirements from the Marine Corps and Coast Guard, Gen. Hagee and Adm. Loy appeared together at a public forum on national security. The two retired service commanders discussed the essential role of the civilian and military communities in national security.

The former commandants agreed that economic development and diplomacy were necessary elements of the defensive and offensive phases of national security. They agreed that the War on Terror required military and diplomatic strategies, international assistance to developing nations, fighting disease and poverty, and controlling the proliferation of weapons of war.[21]

Following his tenure as Coast Guard commandant, Adm. Loy and historian Donald T. Phillips co-authored *Character in Action: The U.S. Coast Guard on Leadership* (Naval Institute Press, 2003). Admiral Loy described the immediate leadership responses the Coast Guard contributed to its port security mission after the 11 September 2001 attacks.

Loy credited Coast Guard regular, reserve, and auxiliary units for rapid, professional responses to the attacks from the Great Lakes to the interior rivers and coastal waters. He explained the coordinated missions with local and federal authorities.[22] Admiral Loy's perspectives, insights and recollections on Coast Guard leadership and mission response are historically and administratively significant.

Admiral Loy described the 1500 miles of international maritime border between Canada and the United States, and the strategic infrastructure the Coast Guard protects. That maritime domain stretches from the St. Lawrence River to the Great Lakes of Superior, Michigan, Huron, Ontario and Erie.

In coordination with Canadian military and law enforcement agencies, large ships were monitored and inspected. Nuclear and other power plants and water intake systems in Chicago and other Great Lakes metropolitan areas were inspected and secured. Coast Guard enlisted and commissioned personnel were transported from Ninth District Headquarters in Cleveland, Ohio, to New York City and Washington, D.C., to assist in planning logistical and tactical responses.

Great Lakes captains of the port joined their regional counterparts to increase harbor security at strategic locations. Coast Guard Reserve units were called to active duty in a "Team Coast Guard" alliance, Loy explained, that allowed "the United States Coast Guard to double its forces overnight."[23]

Among the building blocks of effective leadership skills, traits, and mission success Loy and Phillips reviewed are adherence to enunciated values, teamwork, cultivating relationships, good communications, and honoring and teaching institutional history to instill pride and understanding within the organization and its personnel.[24]

To get strong leaders, Phillips and Loy advised finding people who exhibit intelligence, energy, self-confidence and character; are team players that promote the group over themselves; focus on detail, and accept personal accountability. Team members must commit to standards of excellence and have the courage to initiate an objective removal process to expel members who cannot or will not do their jobs.

Caring relationships among team members, the authors asserted, inspire higher performance levels and elevate morale. Outside alliances should be developed to enhance productivity and expand the knowledge and experience base. Keep rules to a minimum. Be decisive. Provide technical training. Give energetic younger members the freedom to participate and act. Mentor personnel and be tolerant of mistakes.

Consult people in the field for their insight and experience before implementing policies that affect and direct them. Let field personnel know they are respected and appreciated and are part of the team. Work for consensus, cooperation, and input instead of just telling subordinates what they must do. Spotlight achievement and success by giving people credit for their contributions, and offer successful personnel awards and promotions.

A handshake, smile, and thank-you are positive reinforcers. The teachings of historical examples to broaden perspectives and learn from experience are elements of what Loy meant by teaching the history and traditions of the institutional mission.[25]

Admiral Loy offered numerous historic and contemporary examples of enlisted, officer, auxiliary, and civilian leadership decisions and actions in a variety of Coast Guard missions. Donald T. Phillips supported his observations with numerous management examples. The cross-professional experience of the two authors provided an outstanding intellectual and pragmatic leadership guide.

13

U.S. Navy and Coast Guard Articulation and Homeland Security (2002–2006)

Cadet Thomas H. Collins graduated from the U.S. Coast Guard Academy in 1968. Collins subsequently earned master's degrees in liberal studies and business administration, and became a faculty member in humanities at the U.S. Coast Guard Academy in New London, Connecticut, the hometown of his spouse, Nancy Monahan.

Lt. Collins initiated his career as deck officer on the U.S. Coast Guard Cutter (USCGC) *Vigilant*, and then served as the commanding officer of the USCGC *Cape Morgan* out of Charleston, South Carolina. Collins was then assigned deputy commander of Group St. Petersburg, Florida, and subsequently captain of the port of Long Island Sound in New Haven, Connecticut.

Other assignments included commander, Pacific Area and Eleventh Coast Guard District (Alameda, California), and the Fourteenth Coast Guard District in Honolulu, Hawaii. Prior to becoming the vice commandant at U.S. Coast Guard Headquarters in Washington, D.C. (2002–2006), Collins headed the Office of Acquisition, where he directed systems worth $3 billion and contributed significantly to formulating the concept of the Integrated Deepwater System project to modernize Coast Guard ship and aircraft assets for ocean missions.

Commandant Collins utilized new technologies and developed strategies to enhance Coast Guard mission performance. Admiral Collins earned a variety of medals and commendations in his career, including the Coast Guard Distinguished Service Medal and Legion of Merit.[1] He managed the transition of the Coast Guard from the Department of Transportation to the new Department of Homeland Security in 2003. The transition and function of the Coast Guard within the DHS had positive mission results, and complex mission and budget problems.

On 24 April 2002, then Vice Commandant and Vice Adm. Thomas H. Collins was interviewed at his Washington office by Chief Petty Officer Peter Capelotti (USCGR) for the U.S. Coast Guard Oral History Program. The oral history program was part of the Operation Noble Eagle Documentation Project.

CPO Capelotti asked Vice Adm. Collins perceptive questions about his career, coming appointment as Coast Guard commandant (which would commence in June 2002), and lessons learned from the Coast Guard response to the 11 September 2001 terrorist attacks on New York City, the Pentagon in Washington, D.C., and the downed United Airlines Flight 93 near Shanksville, Pennsylvania.[2] The 33 courageous passengers and crew tried to regain control of the Boeing passenger aircraft from the 4 terrorists. The airliner crashed, leaving no survivors.

Vice Admiral Collins described his support role in assisting and representing Adm. Jim Loy, Coast Guard commandant (1998–2002). Collins commended Loy for his immediate post–9/11 communications and articulation with captains of the port; mission planning with District Coast Guard commanders and civilian public safety and security personnel; the maritime rescue and transportation of New York City area civilians; ship inspections; monitoring and boarding passenger liners coming into U.S. ports; mobilization of air and sea assets; cooperation with the U.S. Navy and the chief of naval operations; and active duty call-up of Coast Guard Reserve personnel.[3]

On 9/11, the Coast Guard was still under the jurisdiction of the Department of Transportation, so missions and budget concerns had to be approved and coordinated with the DOT.

In response to the interviewer's questions, Adm. Collins enunciated an appreciation of the eclectic training of Coast Guard personnel that allowed them to transition from the duties and missions they were on to adapt to the port security and national defense roles that had to be immediately assumed: "We directed over 50 cutters that were deployed on fisheries and counter-drug missions into most of the major ports around our country for a number of weeks."[4]

The domestic maritime domain that the Coast Guard patrols is extraordinarily expansive in geographic and logistical terms. Admiral Collins informed his interviewer that the Coast Guard had to contend with more than 350 U.S. ports and 95,000 miles of domestic coastline, and monitor and inspect foreign ships and crews in contiguous waters

13. Service Articulation and Homeland Security (2002–2006) 139

and at port facilities. Incoming foreign and domestic merchant ships carry tens of thousands of containers. That huge task, Collins explained, required the Coast Guard to partner with a variety of security agencies.[5]

When asked about articulation with the U.S. Navy, Vice Adm. Collins explained that there is at least "one meeting every six months with the NAV-GUARD [Navy–Coast Guard Board] co-chaired by myself and the Vice Chief of Naval Operations, and selected flag officers [who discuss] Homeland Security issues and [domestic and overseas] partnerships." In addition, the Coast Guard commandant frequently meets at the Pentagon. "When the [U.S. Armed Forces] Chiefs meet with the President, the Commandant attends with them, and has monthly luncheon meetings with the CNO ... so there is continual dialogue."[6]

Commandant Thomas Collins saw the service through yet another departmental transition, this time from the Department of Transportation to the newly-formed Department of Homeland Security (United States Coast Guard).

Vice Admiral Collins went on to explain that maritime security and domestic defense involved national sovereignty issues, and included fisheries enforcement and drug and immigration interdiction. Collins asserted, "Drugs are the cash cow for terrorist operations."[7]

In the April 2002 interview, Adm. Collins alluded to the eventually implemented legislation introduced by Senator Joseph Lieberman to consolidate security agencies into a Cabinet-level homeland security office.

Collins correctly predicted that the Immigration and Customs Services would be part of the mix, as would, of course, the U.S. Coast Guard.[8] The Department of Homeland Security was activated in 2003 under Secretary Tom Ridge. On 6 August 2003, in celebration of the 213th birthday of the Coast Guard, Commandant and full Admiral Thomas H. Collins introduced Ridge, the civilian head of the Department of Homeland Security and the Coast Guard.

Collins described the traditional missions of the Coast Guard as "search and rescue, marine safety, environmental protection, drug interdiction, fisheries enforcement, domestic and polar icebreaking, aids to navigation, and migrant interdiction." Collins explained the national security missions of "supporting Operation Liberty Shield at home; defending America's ports and infrastructure; and the deployment of 11 cutters, 4 port security units, and over 1250 people overseas in Operation Enduring Freedom and Iraqi Freedom," alongside "America's superb military, and our coalition partners."[9]

Commandant Collins expressed the pride the service had when the Coast Guard joined the Department of Homeland Security, and he highlighted Secretary Ridge's background as ideally suiting him for the position. Ridge had served as a U.S. Army infantryman in Vietnam, and then on the home front as a district attorney, congressman, and Pennsylvania governor.

Former Pennsylvania Governor Tom Ridge accepted the job as the first civilian secretary of the Department of Homeland Security, the home of the Coast Guard since 2003 (Department of Homeland Security).

Admiral Collins then traced the chronology of the Homeland Security Department: "In October of 2001, following the tragic events of September 11, [Ridge] was sworn in as the first Director of the Office of Homeland Security, and on January 24 he became the first Secretary of Homeland Security,"[10] having been appointed to those positions by President George W. Bush.

Commandant Collins did not neglect the "Inland Seas," as the Great Lakes District Nine maritime region is called. Admiral James M. Loy (commandant, 1998–2002) had initiated the building of the next generation of Great Lakes icebreaking buoy tenders. Admiral Collins continued the expansion and upgrading of Coast Guard air and sea platforms. Manitowoc Marine Group's Marinette Corporation awarded a subcontract to ABB Marine to produce electric propulsion systems scheduled for 2005 delivery. A new Great Lakes Coast Guard cutter was scheduled to replace the World War II era USCGC *Mackinaw*. The new high technology cutter would have a 360-degree steering capability and no intrusive, problematic mechanical gears.[11]

Admiral Collins played a critical role as public spokesperson for the Coast Guard in sessions with government officials. In late July 2002, Commandant Collins and five retired Coast Guard commandants (Admirals Loy, Kramek, Kime, Yost, and Gracey) met with President George W. Bush at the White House to discuss homeland security, national defense, and the projected Deepwater Program for asset modernization; and the acquisition of funding and personnel for the new missions. The commandants endorsed a recommendation to Congress for the Coast Guard to be transferred from the Department of Transportation to the Department of Homeland Security.[12]

Commandant Collins has been credited with leading "a command that has seen the Coast Guard through its largest transition since becoming a unified service in 1915," and for having been "personally committed to making effective use of emerging technologies, and developing innovative methods to improve Coast Guard mission performance."[13]

The innovative programs would include coordination with the U.S. Navy in the National Fleet Agreement that "tailored integration of multimission platforms, infrastructure, and personnel" in processes designed to "synchronize research and development, fiscal stewardship, procurement, doctrine development, training, and the execution of operations."[14]

Under Adm. Collins and his successors, the Coast Guard would continue its historic partnership with the U.S. Navy. Commandant Collins signed the expanded National Fleet agreement with Admiral Vern Clark, chief of naval operations, to coordinate policies for national defense and the global War on Terror.[15]

The modernization and mission plans involved the expansion of shore infrastructure, and maritime and air assets. The Integrated Deepwater System project, for example, upgraded Coast Guard aviation, and included the construction of twin-engine CASA CN235–300M maritime patrol aircraft for medium-range missions. The HC-130H Hercules aircraft would be equipped with advanced command and control communications systems.[16]

Thomas Collins had a reputation of being "more cerebral" than his predecessor, the more outgoing, political, and pragmatic Admiral James Loy. Commandant Collins had the responsibility of administering port security missions in a nation with more than 95,000 miles of coastline and 361 ports where 7,000 ships make 50,000 port calls per year. His supporters credited Collins with understanding what small boat and cutter personnel know, do, and endure from his own experience as a captain of the port, and as patrol boat and area commander.[17]

On 22 November 2002, early in his tenure as commandant, Adm. Thomas Collins gave a presentation before the U.S. Commission on Ocean Policy. In that address, Collins reiterated the potential post–9/11 threats to port security, shipping, and other marine missions the Coast Guard superintends, including pollution control, illegal fishing, migrant and drug interdiction, and search and rescue.

Admiral Collins explained the capacities and requirements the service needed to manage its expanded missions; the acquisition of the personnel, assets, and budgets necessary to carry out expanded responsibilities; and the significance of the proposed Department of Homeland Security, and transfer of the Coast Guard into it. Collins went on to explain how the military structure of the Coast Guard facilitated its contributions as demonstrated throughout its history and in contemporary times.

The commandant responded to concerns that mission expansion in national security and defense could diminish the Coast Guard's ability to carry out its traditional domestic missions. Collins referred to the 1999 Inter-Agency Task Force on the Coast Guard's Roles and Missions. The panel concluded the Coast Guard must continue those missions, because the transfer of some service duties to other agencies would be inefficient, costly, and counterproductive.[18] Increased demands would require increased budgets, the commandant asserted, and Collins commended President George W. Bush for his proposed fiscal year 2003 budget increase that would enhance, Collins claimed, Coast Guard operational capabilities.[19]

Commandant Collins explained to the U.S. Ocean Policy Commission the importance of the proposed Deepwater program, and the need for supplementing the antiquated National Distress System with the state of

13. Service Articulation and Homeland Security (2002–2006)   143

the art Rescue 21 System of communications with updated coastal command and control. Rescue 21 would allow interconnection with Homeland Security units, and local, state and federal public safety, law enforcement, and paramedical agencies.

Admiral Collins provided an update on the plans to rebuild the port security, maritime safety, and small boat life-saving capacities of shore stations. He described the establishment of Marine Safety and Security Teams and Strike Teams trained to cope with chemical and biological accidents and incidents, natural disasters, terrorism, and law enforcement situations. The well-trained personnel would respond to situations with weapons, air-transportable boats, and sophisticated communications systems. As a functional precedent for such team operations, Admiral Collins alluded to the successful Strike Team response on the ground during the "9/11" devastation in New York City.[20]

14

Deepwater Project and Natural Disasters (2006–2010)

Admiral Thad Allen became the 23rd commandant of the United States Coast Guard on May 23, 2006, and would serve through 2010.

The straight-talking, take-charge leader spearheaded innovation and modernization. Allen continued that leadership style in the Deepwater Project, natural disasters in Haiti, and, before becoming commandant, in Hurricane Katrina (2005). Admiral Allen brought his talents to bear in the Gulf of Mexico British Petroleum Deepwater Horizon oil spill while commandant and in the immediate year following his retirement.

Admiral Allen was a pragmatist about the politics and reality of climate change and the physical geography of the Arctic Region. Allen pushed to have the Coast Guard develop a greater presence in the polar region in response to the international race for territorial presence, petroleum, tourism, and search and rescue probabilities in the frigid maritime region.

Allen enhanced Coast Guard relationships and mission articulation with the other U.S. Armed Forces, federal law enforcement and public safety agencies, and private sector business and security entities.[1] In his first year as commandant, Adm. Allen succinctly summarized his policy format and objectives: "The modernization and strategic transformation the Coast Guard is about looking into the future and repositioning the Service to best serve the Nation in the 21st Century."[2]

Thad W. Allen came from Tucson, Arizona. Ensign Allen graduated from the U.S. Coast Guard Academy in 1971. In his diverse career, Allen transcended the commissioned ranks and held a variety of assignments as commanding officer ashore and afloat in several Coast Guard districts and at Coast Guard Headquarters. Allen was a leader and public spokesperson in the Gulf Coast Katrina storm of 2005 and in the Gulf of Mexico

14. Deepwater Project and Natural Disasters (2006–2010)

British Petroleum oil spills. His work and notoriety in Hurricane Katrina paved the way for his 2006 appointment as commandant of the U.S. Coast Guard by President George W. Bush. Admiral Allen coordinated natural disaster responses and was appointed the national incident commander after his 2010 retirement from the Coast Guard.

In his illustrious career, Allen served as a captain of the port, patrol boat commander, Atlantic Area commander, and as commander of a LORAN Station in Thailand during the Vietnam War. Admiral Allen served as chief of staff at Coast Guard Headquarters before becoming commandant, and gained valuable experience crafting budgets and doing long range planning. He had also commanded the Seventh Coast Guard District where he led operations in South Carolina, Florida, Georgia, and the Caribbean. Admiral Allen provided immediate and effective leadership as the Atlantic Area commander after the September 11, 2001, terrorist attacks.

Commandant Thad Allen showed his leadership potential prior to receiving the top post while taking command of the Hurricane Katrina disaster response efforts in 2005 (United States Coast Guard).

Allen had command experience as the captain of the port in New York and New England, and served aboard Coast Guard cutters *Citrus*, *Androscoggin*, and *Gallatin*. Allen led search and rescue missions in the Caribbean and intelligence operations out of El Paso, Texas.

The Coast Guard returned to the Gulf Coast en masse to respond to the British Petroleum oil spill disaster during Commandant Thad Allen's years in command (United States Navy).

Allen earned a master's degree in public administration at George Washington University, and a master of science degree in management at the Massachusetts Institute of Technology. Admiral Allen proudly followed in the career footsteps of his father, Chief Petty Officer Clyde Allen. The elder Allen served in World War II as a damage control specialist on board oceangoing cutters.

On 1 May 2010, Commandant Allen was appointed National Incident Commander by President Barack Obama to direct the response to the Deepwater Horizon oil spill. Then, after 25 May 2010, when Adm. Robert J. Papp was appointed commandant of the Coast Guard, Department of Homeland Security Secretary Janet Napolitano asked Adm. Allen to continue as national incident commander for the duration of the oil spill cleanup operations.

In that capacity, Allen supervised the deployment and coordination of personnel and assets ashore and afloat. Admiral Allen had to manage Coast Guard, civilian, and federal personnel, and assets and infrastructure between the Departments of Homeland Security, Interior, and Commerce; the Environmental Protection Agency; various other local, state, and federal agencies and departments; and British Petroleum, the corporation held responsible for the oil spill.

Admiral Thad W. Allen retired from the Coast Guard on 30 June 2010, and from his incident command appointment on 1 October 2010, when the environmental cleanup afloat and ashore was terminated.[3]

Throughout his career in command positions, and as Coast Guard commandant, Adm. Allen's direct, clear, honest speaking style reflected his philosophies, objectives, and respect for Coast Guard history, traditions and missions. Those characteristics were illustrated in his many public speeches, as exhibited, for example, in his remarks to the Department of Homeland Security Fellows in New York City on 28 Monday 2008.[4] In that speech Allen concisely traced the frustrations and achievements he experienced on the ground floor at the planning and commencement stages of the new Department of Homeland Security.

The genesis of the department, Allen explained, came after "9/11/2001" when the Bush administration commenced to centralize national and border security agencies in December 2001 and January 2002. At that time, Adm. Allen was the Atlantic Area commander.

Allen recalled that the several agencies that are now part of Department of Homeland Security fought the initial unification concept, preferring to maintain mission autonomy. Then the U.S. Senate, Allen asserted, debated union membership and work rules as politics intervened in the power contest between Congressional Democrats and the Republican administration. A few people crafted legislation in back rooms. The Homeland Security Act was finally passed in 2003, and the new Department of Homeland Security Secretary Tom Ridge walked into his office on the 24th of January[5] as Adm. Allen completed his assigned responsibilities as "part of the transition team that moved [the Coast Guard] out of the DOT into the DHS"[6] when he was chief of staff of the Coast Guard.

Allen explained the complex and contentious unification process in a humorous way, describing the method of operation as "a combination of an acquisition merger, startup, and hostile takeover going on consecutively with 22 entities. Other than that, it was not a problem or hard to do!"[7] Admiral Allen described the challenges that confronted the Department of Homeland Security in its early attempts to secure air, sea, and land assets, and trying to assess intelligence information in the War of Terror that Allen perceptively concluded "is a generational war that's not going away anytime soon."[8]

In response to questions from his knowledgeable audience, Allen described the need for secure computer systems in an age of hacking into networks and cyber threats that, he said, could be mitigated by the consolidation of interactive systems and the co-location of civilian and military agencies at secure bases.[9]

The commandant was blunt and unafraid to say that the federal bureaucracy and Congressional committee overlap was an impediment to budgetary and mission efficiency: "The one area where I am always going to have a problem is the structure of Congress [that is] the biggest impediment to executing the recommendations of the "9/11" Commission.... An example: The Coast Guard operations bill this year was referred to four House committees, and they all did something different to it. The bill has been there for almost a year and has not gotten to the floor of the House."[10]

In his State of the Coast Guard Address at the National Press Club on 12 February 2010, Commandant Allen reported that the Coast Guard "was ready and resilient, as we demonstrated in the first hours and days of the Haitian earthquake, because our operational forces and command and control structure are agile and flexible ... and the authority to move forces is delegated outside our headquarters so our field commanders can act immediately. We had five cutters in the immediate area, 900 Coast Guard people in theater, evacuated 1200 American citizens, did 250 medical evacuations,"[11] and gave life-saving first responder aid to hundreds of Haitians.

Allen illustrated his experience and education in business and fiscal management by explaining that personnel reduction "and recapitalizing funding reflect hard choices that best position the Coast Guard to optimize our performance ... protect the nation ... and replace aging cutters and aircraft."[12] Allen emphasized the necessity of modernizing the cutter fleet. Some ships were 40 years old, compared to the 14 year old average of U.S. Navy ships, a situation that puts missions and crews at significant risk.[13]

On January 13, 2010, Admiral Allen demonstrated his public speaking skills, popularity, knowledge, and credibility with the other U.S. Armed Forces in a speech to the Surface Naval Association. He emphasized the importance of carrying out a 21st century cooperative strategy with the U.S. Navy and U.S. Marine Corps in security operations against human and small vessel maritime terrorism.[14]

Admiral Allen's leadership during Hurricane Katrina (2005) in the Gulf Coast states of Louisiana and Mississippi involved more than 30,000 people saved in dangerous Coast Guard boat and helicopter rescues in stormy and treacherous circumstances. Units of the other U.S. Armed Forces and civilian public safety agencies, including the Coast Guard Auxiliary and National Guard units, assisted in search and rescue and law enforcement missions.[15]

Lt. Jim Dolbow is the author of *The Coast Guardsman's Manual* (U.S.

14. Deepwater Project and Natural Disasters (2006–2010) 149

Naval Institute, 2013), a contributing writer for *Proceedings*, the distinguished periodical of the U.S. Naval Institute, an institute board member, was a legislative aid and analyst on Admiral Allen's staff, served with the Coast Guard on active duty, and is a graduate of the Naval War College and the Institute of World Politics.[16]

It was therefore interesting and significant that Lt. Dolbow, given his Coast Guard experience, recommended that it was time to appoint the Coast Guard commandant to the Joint Chiefs of Staff, and concluded that Admiral Thad Allen would be the ideal candidate for the position.[17] Lt. Dolbow had been influenced by Adm. Allen's career, command presence, and logistical and operational coordination of national Coast Guard units in response to Hurricane Katrina.

Coast Guard air, sea, and shore station crews were assembled to respond to the Katrina disaster. Great Lakes units contributed search and rescue iceboats to the subtropical Gulf Coast environment. The iceboat fan blades were located above the water surface, and therefore more functional than subsurface propellers that could get hung up on obstructions and debris. Great Lakes Sector Detroit contributed coxswains, aids to navigation teams, and other specialized crews; as did other Great Lakes stations, including units from Ohio, New York, and Wisconsin. There was also a Massachusetts Coast Guard unit from the Atlantic Coast.[18]

In his varied career, Thad Allen handled challenging and potentially dangerous situations on the home front and overseas. As a lieutenant he served in Thailand during the Vietnam War, when he and his crew raced to avoid enemy capture during the rapid evacuations in the spring of 1975. Lieutenant Allen commanded the LORAN (Long Range Aid to Navigation) Station in Lampang, Thailand.

On 30 April 1975, South Vietnam President Duong Van Minh publically announced the surrender of the capital city of Saigon to the Communist Viet Cong and North Vietnam Army. Lieutenant Allen was ordered by his commanders to destroy sensitive LORAN equipment and prepare for immediate air evacuation from the station site. The jungles around Lampang were dangerous enough because of enemy presence, the harsh vegetation, and a plethora of poisonous predator snakes.[19]

Lieutenant Allen and his crew monitored and exchanged radio communications with the military command in Bangkok, destroyed the LORAN power infrastructure, and awaited evacuation in the rapidly changing and hazardous situation.

Coast Guard historian Alex Larzelere, who served on patrol boat missions in Vietnam, described the significance of those events in his book, *The Coast Guard at War: Vietnam 1965–1975*: "Con Son LORAN

Station ceased transmission and signal SH-3 Yankee went off the air at 1246 on 29 April 1975, concluding the Coast Guard's role in Vietnam."[20] The critical contribution that Coast Guard LORAN stations made in search and rescue and navigation support throughout Indochina from the Demilitarized Zone between North and South Vietnam to Thailand came to an end as well.

Admiral Allen's career achievements led to his nomination and appointment as Coast Guard commandant. Allen's exemplary career was commemorated by his collection of numerous service medals, Gold Stars, commendations, and a plethora of leadership awards.[21]

Maritime historian David Helvarg travelled with and wrote about Commandant Allen in his book, *Rescue Warriors: The U.S. Coast Guard, America's Forgotten Heroes*.[22] Helvarg was impressed with Adm. Allen's understanding of global, environmental, and geostrategic issues, and the possibility of repercussions from alleged global warming and "Arctic meltdown." Helvarg quoted the commandant: "I am an agnostic on climate change and science and everything else. All I know is, there is water where there didn't used to be, and I have the statutory responsibilities to operate there."[23]

Helvarg was impressed by then Atlantic Commander Allen's diversion of ocean going cutters into American ports within a couple of days of the 11 September 2001 terrorist attacks, effectively, the author described, "clinching a security belt around the homeland."[24] Admiral Allen broke the "glass ceiling" for women when he appointed Vice Adm. Vivien Crea, an accomplished Coast Guard aviator, as vice commandant of the Coast Guard. Allen described Adm. Crea as "whip smart."[25]

As commandant, Admiral Allen led the largest agency in the Department of Homeland Security, with a personnel complement of 42,000 active duty men and women; 8,000 reservists; 7,000 civilian employees; and 34,000 well trained volunteer civilian members of the U.S. Coast Guard Auxiliary.

While administering the Coast Guard, Adm. Allen was a member of the Council on Foreign Relations. In 2007, the National Graduate School of Quality Systems Management at Falmouth, Massachusetts, granted an honorary doctor of science degree to the commandant.

Admiral Allen emphasized the maintenance and deployment of the Coast Guard icebreaker fleet on Great Lakes, Arctic and Antarctic waters for geostrategic, transportation, national defense, economic, and oceanographic studies.[26]

U.S. Coast Guard personnel and Adm. Allen were national heroes after Hurricane Katrina (2005). But in 2007, the Coast Guard's $24 billion

14. Deepwater Project and Natural Disasters (2006–2010) 151

Deepwater Program hit fiscal depths. David Helvarg traced the issues, problems, Congressional oversight hearings, and attempts at resolution, and chronicled Adm. Allen's direct congressional testimony about the situation.

Michael DeKort, a nautical engineer, had worked on the 123-foot Island Class cutters, and reluctantly made public the dangerous structural flaws and equipment failures of vessels he believed would put Coast Guard crews at risk. In congressional testimony, DeKort claimed contractors and at least one high-ranking Coast Guard officer initially dismissed his concerns.

Major media outlets at first ignored the story. Deepwater project contractors, Lockheed Martin and Northrop Grumman became deeply concerned about budgets, cutter and crew safety, and professional accountability. The *Navy Times*, *New York Times*, and television's *60 Minutes* published and broadcast stories of hulls buckling and technical problems at sea. Congressional (Senate and House) oversight committees scheduled hearings and interrogated the commandant.

Under critical interrogation, Admiral Allen testified about budget issues and the need for the increased involvement of ship inspectors and Coast Guard nautical engineers in construction, planning, and supervision. Allen testified how he had discussed operational changes with the chief executives of Lockheed and Northrop, and the decommissioning of eight of the 123-foot patrol boats that had received expanded hulls beyond the originally constructed 110-foot lengths. The commandant said legal action and contract modifications would be considered, and cost overruns and delays would be investigated and remedied.

Allen subsequently held accountability meetings with Lockheed and Northrop administrators. Strict Coast Guard oversight ensued over Deepwater upgrades of Coast Guard fixed-wing and helicopter aircraft, surveillance and sensor technology, and communications and computer systems. Coast Guard acquisition officers and engineers expressed concerns about the safety and stability of the composite structure designs of proposed air and sea assets. Although the contractors initially dismissed their concerns, the recommendations of the Coast Guard experts were later implemented.

Competitive bidding expanded the construction pool and expertise. In 2008, Bollinger Shipyards in Louisiana got the contract to build thirty-four 153-foot Sentinel Class Fast Response Cutters. The building of eight large 418-foot National Security Class cutters was initiated. Northrop got the contract for the latter at its Pascagoula, Mississippi, shipyard. These Legend Class cutters, named after historically famous Coast Guard personnel, would include the *Bertholf*, *Waesche*, and USCGC *Stratton*. But even these gigantic, state of the art vessels had initial hull weakness problems that were discovered, resolved, and repaired.[27]

The Coast Guard responded to the Deepwater cutter construction problems by hiring contract management specialists, and, wisely but belatedly, U.S. Navy experts from both the Naval Air Systems Command and Naval Sea Systems Command to do design and cost analysis.[28]

Among the many Coast Guard officials and members of Congress that Helvarg interviewed about Deepwater program problems was Senator Maria Cantwell. The Washington state solon was then chair of the Commerce Subcommittee on Oceans, Atmosphere, Fisheries, and the Coast Guard. Senator Cantwell appreciated the expanded missions the Coast Guard assumed after 11 September 2001, the necessity of continued maintenance funding of Coast Guard assets and personnel, the significance and seriousness of Deepwater project problems, and the necessity of their amelioration.[29]

On Deepwater, Cantwell said, "We are not out of the woods yet. This problem got way out of hand, so changes need to take place and outside agencies have a role to play. Admiral Allen did a great job with Hurricane Katrina," the senator continued, "but this acquisitions disaster is bigger than he is. He is well intended ... but wants to be free of it as soon as possible."[30]

Admiral Allen had immediately realized the seriousness of the Deepwater budget and construction issues, as indicated in his interview with Helvarg, when the commandant said, "I saw a meltdown in the organization when all of this happened, and I thought we are not taking [our eyes] off the ball [again]."[31]

In his pragmatic assessment of the aging of Coast Guard high endurance cutters and Deepwater assets, construction, budget, and timeline issues, Admiral Allen paraphrased a statement made by former Defense Secretary Donald Rumsfeld: "We have to manage with the Fleet we've got, and not the Fleet we want."[32]

15

International Outreach, Security Cutters and Arctic Expansion (2010–)

Admiral Robert J. Papp, Jr., was appointed commandant of the U.S. Coast Guard in May 2010. Admiral Papp's first vice commandant was Vice Adm. Sally Brice-O'Hara, upon whose retirement distinguished aviator Vice Adm. John P. Currier became second in command.

In late April 2012, just one month before her scheduled retirement, Adm. Brice-O'Hara assumed the role of temporary commandant while Adm. Papp recovered from surgery. Vice Commandant Brice-O'Hara, whose father had served as a U.S. Navy gunner's mate, previously served in the 14th Coast Guard District in Hawaii and then as commander of Coast Guard Training Center, Cape May, New Jersey.[1]

Prior to his appointment as commandant, Adm. Papp served as commander, Atlantic Area, and chief of staff at Coast Guard Headquarters in Washington, D.C. Admiral Papp had previously served as Ninth District (Great Lakes) commander; director of reserves and training; served afloat on the Coast Guard cutters *Papaw*, *Forward*, and *Red Beech*; and commanded the 295-foot Coast Guard Academy training barque USCGC *Eagle* (WIX-327).

Papp graduated as an ensign from the U.S. Coast Guard Academy in 1975. He earned master's degrees in strategic studies and national security at the U.S. Naval War College and in management from Salve Regina College in Newport, Rhode Island. Papp earned the Gold Ancient Mariner of the Coast Guard Medal and the honorary title of "Cutterman" that is awarded to officers with ten years or more of sea duty.[2]

In 2005, Rear Adm. Robert J. Papp, Jr., was appointed Ninth District

(Great Lakes) commander, where he superintended Coast Guard mission articulation with Canadian military, naval, and law enforcement authorities in intelligence, surveillance, and criminal apprehension. Concern about urban centers of terrorist sympathies and connections in Toronto and Windsor (Canada), Detroit and Dearborn (Michigan), and Buffalo (New York) were responded to. Investigations and contraband seizures were carried out in coordinated missions.

Two thousand undocumented immigrants were arrested between 2002 and 2004 in cooperation with Canadian and U.S. Customs and U.S. Immigration authorities. Joint patrols were conducted with the Canadian Navy, Canadian Coast Guard, and Royal Canadian Mounted Police. United States Coast Guard aircraft were utilized from Great Lakes air stations. Local, state, and federal public safety authorities participated in missions and information exchanges. Security zones were established after "9/11" around major Great Lakes ports and power infrastructure sites.

Historically, since the British-Canadian-U.S. bilateral Rush-Bagot Agreement of 1817, Canadian and U.S. naval and military presence on the Great Lakes had been limited. But, subsequent national security threats resulted in the modification of the treaty in "memorandums of understanding" concerning national security and sovereignty issues.

Canadian and U.S. officials on Admiral Papp's watch carried out international ship inspections and intelligence operations. Papp commanded several thousand Ninth District regular, reserve, civilian and auxiliary personnel. In 2006, Rear Adm. Papp was named chief of staff at Washington, D.C., Headquarters.[3]

The enormity and significance of the Great Lakes District is illustrated by the fact that when Adm. Papp assumed command of the region in 2004, the personnel complement included approximately 8,000 auxiliary, reserve, regular and civilian personnel; numerous aids to navigation stations and teams; ten cutters; 46 small boat stations; four air stations; four Sectors; four marine safety units; a plethora of radio communications systems and light stations; one LORAN station; several Great Lakes shipping ports and associated civilian port authorities; and Coast Guard captains of the port.

The Ninth District, headquartered in Cleveland, Ohio, on Lake Erie, includes 1500 miles of international border and 6700 miles of shoreline. The Great Lakes region stretches from the St. Lawrence River in the east to the nationally significant southwestern Lake Superior ports of Duluth (Minnesota) and Superior (Wisconsin). Lake Michigan is the site of numerous maritime interests, including the strategic infrastructure of the busy ports of Milwaukee and Chicago.[4]

15. International Outreach and Arctic Expansion (2010–)

In December 2010, Rear Adm. Scott Burhoe, the outgoing superintendent of the U.S. Coast Guard Academy, announced the 2011 transfer of his command to Rear Adm. Sandra L. Stosz, the first female chief of a U.S. military academy. Admiral Papp selected Stosz for the position. Rear Admiral Stosz had served as commander of U.S. Coast Guard Training Center Cape May, New Jersey, and director of the recruitment, training, and support of the 8,000-member complement of U.S. Coast Guard reservists. Admiral Stosz commended Rear Admiral Burhoe, under whose leadership the academy increased minority admissions, and was ranked first among Northeastern United States colleges by *U.S. News and World Report*.[5]

Commandant Papp proved to be a prolific and dynamic speaker, representing the Coast Guard in a plethora of events, locations, facilities, and missions. In November 2010, Homeland Security Secretary Janet Napolitano and Admiral Papp commemorated the Coast Guard heritage in World War I. The occasion was a wreath-laying ceremony at the U.S. Coast Guard World War I Memorial in Arlington Cemetery in Virginia. The Memorial was built to honor the crews of Coast Guard cutters *Seneca* and *Tampa* that were sunk in 1918. The World War I Memorial contains the names of all of the members of the U.S. Coast Guard who perished in the Great War.[6]

In Commandant Papp's February 2011 "State of the Coast Guard Address," the admiral expressed concern about mission overreach and priorities and balance. Papp described several mission related Coast Guard fatalities, and said resource and budget shortages, technology and training paradigms, and mission creep may have caused the deaths. Papp said mission assignments in the future must be weighed against resources, training, evaluations, and assurances that missions are more fully prepared and analyzed because, he concluded, "I have spoken at too many memorial services. We have had several (aviation and boat) accidents. This is unprecedented and unacceptable. We've got to do something about it."[7]

The training, success, and morale of civilian, regular, reserve, and auxiliary Coast Guard personnel were important to Adm. Papp. He emphasized those concerns in professional meetings and public speeches. The commandant honored the men and women of the U.S. Coast Guard Auxiliary at their August 2010 convention. Papp explained auxiliary support missions in pollution control, search and rescue and life saving, port security, boating safety classes, inspection, communications, and logistical support.

Just in 2010 auxiliary members saved hundreds of lives on waterways and in natural disasters, and secured several million dollars' worth of property. Commandant Papp added historical perspective by tracing contributions back to World War II, when its members patrolled American coasts and inland waterways; protected ports from espionage, sabotage, and fires; and freed up regular and reserve Coast Guard personnel for active duty wartime service at home and overseas.[8]

The commandant of the U.S. Coast Guard maintains an intensive speaking and travel schedule. Admiral Papp traveled across the United States and around the world visiting Coast Guard personnel stationed at home and overseas. He also had extensive contacts with foreign coast guards and navies.

In November 2011, Adm. Papp visited Europe and the Middle East to meet with "partner organizations" and Coast Guard members. In that month, the commandant visited Coast Guard Patrol Forces Southwest Asia in the Persian Gulf nation of Bahrain to assess the U.S. Coast Guard's support missions with the U.S. Navy. Patrol Forces Southwest Asia was established in November 2002, in response to a U.S. Navy request for 110-foot Coast Guard patrol boats in Operation Iraqi Freedom to protect on-shore and maritime Iraqi oil terminals.

Admiral Papp reiterated how the Coast Guard has historically been a military support force in national defense and port security missions and how the service advises and trains foreign naval units in defense, maritime safety, and law enforcement. Patrol Forces Southwest Asia assisted naval units in counter-piracy missions in the Indian Ocean off the Northeast coast of Africa and in combat operations in Iraq. Papp expressed pride in the Coast Guard volunteer forces that assisted the Naval Forces Central Command in defense and security operations.[9]

The commandant began his travel, ceremonial, and speaking responsibilities just months after his appointment. In the fall of 2012, Admiral Papp met with Commandant Admiral Hisayasu Suzuki of the Japan Coast Guard. The two commandants signed a bilateral agreement at the North Pacific Coast Guard Forum. The international maritime forum was formed in 2000. In 2010, the forum met in Vancouver, Canada, where the members discussed continued cooperative missions in search and rescue, illegal fishing enforcement, safeguarding maritime commerce, drug trafficking, human smuggling, and illegal immigration. The forum member nations included the United States, Canada, China, Japan, Russia, and South Korea.

"A true international cooperative spirit is represented at all Forum activities," Papp explained, and added, "What happens far out at sea impacts the United States. We have to reach further off our shores, and the Forum provides an effective way for the U.S. and other partner nations to meet this common need."[10]

In September 2010, Commandant Papp met with five female U.S.

15. International Outreach and Arctic Expansion (2010–) 157

Coast Guard Academy cadets in Washington, D.C. at the Academy Women Leadership Symposium. One observer referred to the opportunity to meet the commandant as "the intimidation factor." The cadets agreed that the congenial commandant immediately put them at ease. Questions were raised and discussions occurred about U.S. Coast Guard Academy challenges; Papp shared his recollection and understanding of the rigors of cadet training, upcoming cutter tours, accommodations, berthing space, and duty assignments. Papp promised that he would be attentive to those concerns, and invited the cadets to send him email correspondence about issues and ideas.[11]

The role of the United States Coast Guard as a military service is vividly brought to bear at annual Veterans Day commemorations. On 11 November 2010, Commandant Papp, Homeland Security Secretary Janet Napolitano, and the Master Chief Petty Officer of the Coast Guard Michael P. Leavitt honored personnel at the Coast Guard Memorial in Arlington National Cemetery.

The Coast Guard Memorial lists the names of Coast Guardsmen who gave their lives in World War I (1914–1918). "On this Veteran's Day," Adm. Papp declared, "we honor all of those who wore the uniform of our country by recognizing those who have served past and present." Secretary Napolitano added this comment at the wreath laying ceremony: "We are stronger as a country because of what they have given and what they continue to give" in the Coast Guard, the other military services, and "at the Department of Homeland Security."[12]

At his first State of the Coast Guard Address on 10 February 2011, Commandant Robert Papp addressed an eclectic audience at Bolling Air Force Base in Washington, D.C. Papp described the present state of the Coast Guard and his "charting the course" for the future of the service. Papp provided an illuminating summation of the Coast Guard mission: "No one else can do everything that we do. We protect citizens at sea, America from threats delivered by sea, and we protect the sea itself."

The commandant described the responsibilities and role of the service: "We are a military service, federal law enforcement agency, and maritime first responder." The Coast Guard, Papp said, is "locally based, nationally deployed, and globally connected."[13]

The commandant's many duties include visitations to Coast Guard stations ashore and cutters at sea. This responsibility allows the commandant to stay informed about the latest technologies, communicate with enlisted and commissioned personnel, and participate in the utilization of Coast Guard assets. Admiral Papp, as an experienced cutter commander, was admirably suited to those tasks.

In February 2011, Papp visited the patrolling USCGC *Waesche* (WMSL-751), the state of the art National Security Cutter. The *Waesche* was assigned to patrol the Pacific Ocean out of Alameda, California, and north into to the Bering Sea to carry out fisheries inspection and other maritime missions.

Papp described the superior berthing areas, workspaces, and operational capabilities of the *Waesche*; the large flight deck for helicopter landings; high visibility glass enclosed booths on the flight deck and the bridge; and the communications, ordnance, and fire suppression systems. The communications systems connected directly with the Departments of Defense, Homeland Security, and U.S. Navy units. The commandant vividly described the challenge and thrill he experienced from taking the wheel of the short-range prosecutor boat in a stern launched trial run off the *Waesche*.

Papp said the capacities and capabilities of the *Waesche* and its well-trained crew were instrumental in several narcotics interdiction missions, one of which netted 12,400 kilos of cocaine worth $400 million.

At the time of his visit to the *Waesche,* Papp mentioned Coast Guard plans for the proposed new National Security Cutters to replace the historic 378-foot high endurance cutters. Eight NSCs were planned. The operational and nearly ready NSCs as of 2011 were the *Waesche, Bertholf,* and *Stratton.* A contract was signed for the construction of the 4th NSC, the USCGC *Hamilton.*[14]

In his testimony before the House Subcommittee on Coast Guard and Marine Transportation on 1 March 2011, Adm. Papp thanked the members for their past support of budget requests for asset acquisition and modernization projects. The commandant then outlined the Coast Guard fiscal year requests.

After synthesizing the history of Coast Guard missions, Papp reviewed the achievements of Coast Guard active duty regulars and reservists, and the civilian employees and auxiliarists. Papp traced achievements in life-saving, port security, oil pollution, natural disasters, aids to navigation, and the Deepwater Horizon oil spill. The commandant informed the committee that the Coast Guard saved more than 4000 lives in the previous year, and had significant achievements in immigration and narcotics interdiction, maritime law enforcement, transportation, commerce, and national defense.

Admiral Papp outlined the air, sea, shore, and personnel assets utilized in the previous fiscal year, along with the future asset repair, acquisition, and recapitalization requests for aircraft, boats, cutters, communications, reconnaissance, and intelligence. Among the stated needs were the maintenance of the polar icebreaker fleet to meet expected expansion in scientific, oceanographic, commercial, and national defense missions and international sovereignty claims. An expanded base and infrastructure presence will be required in the Arctic region, Papp explained, and the financial considerations would require a budget exceeding $1.4 billion. Included in the cost projections were funds to support the health, welfare, and housing needs of Coast Guard personnel and their families, and extensive management expenses.[15]

In a July 2011 presentation to the U.S. Senate Committee on Transportation and Oceans, Adm. Papp reminded the lawmakers that the United States is not only a maritime but an Arctic nation. The Coast Guard, with its historic presence in the polar regions, would have increasing responsibilities given the shifting of ice and the opening of waterways. Papp said, "These new waters are spurring an increase in human activities, such as natural resource exploration (and exploitation), shipping, and ecotourism" which will "require specialized equipment, infrastructure and training" and the building of far north "coastal and shore side infrastructure, and a seasonal base to hanger our aircraft and sustain our crews" for search and rescue and other Coast Guard missions.[16]

Besides needing aircraft for expanded Arctic missions, Papp declared that the Coast Guard needed more "ice-capable ships to perform search and rescue and conduct any Arctic pollution response." Papp further explained that "vessels are sailing into the Northern Route exit into the Bering Sea through waters containing our richest fisheries, and Arctic waters rich in natural gas and oil"[17] where oil companies are bidding leases.

The United States, as of 2012, had not signed the controversial Law of the Sea Convention, the only Arctic nation not to do so. Members of Congress have argued that the document's international provisions and enforcement mechanisms would intrude excessively on U.S. sovereignty. Admiral Papp disagreed, and endorsed U.S. ratification of the treaty to better protect and get international support for U.S. maritime and commercial interests.

Commandant Papp informed the Senate committees that the Department of Homeland Security Science and Technology Directorate and the U.S. Arctic Research Commission were studying Arctic issues, and had assessed alleged future needs for the application and expansion of "infrastructure, communications, and sensors."[18] Papp appealed for support and action: "I am a sailor [and submit that] the dangers, risks and challenges of the Arctic exist. It is time to address them; and we must put to sea."[19]

In November 2011, Adm. Papp attended the International Maritime Organization (IMO) Assembly in London with the Coast Guard Deputy

Commandant for Operations, Vice Adm. Brian Salerno. Custom dictated that the delegates attend the meetings in business attire and not their service uniforms. The featured topics were counter-piracy and Arctic operations.

The IMO was established in 1958. In 2011 the organization consisted of 173 member nations. In his presentation, Adm. Papp mentioned the IMO ship and port security facility codes and the necessity of international cooperation in deterring international piracy. Papp addressed the importance of setting standards for a polar code to protect crews and ships that operate in Arctic and Antarctic waters. The code was formulated in 2010 to establish standards for cold and remote environment maritime operations, and crew training for watch standers and ice navigators. The primary objective of the polar code, Papp concluded, was to promote "safe, secure, and efficient shipping."[20]

To the U.S. Coast Guard Academy Class of 2014, Adm. Papp delivered inspirational words about the officers and traditions that preceded these cadets. In his January 2012 presentation, Papp said: "History is the story of our values that you will reflect individually and collectively as a Service."[21] Papp then traced several historical highlights of the Coast Guard, including the gallant fight of the crew of the USCGC *Taney* against Japanese aircraft at Pearl Harbor on 7 December 1941, and the story of Seaman Apprentice William Ray Flores, who stayed aboard the

Commandant Robert Papp kept the nation's politicians abreast of the Coast Guard's expanding role in Arctic waters as the international race for new sources of crude petroleum spread (United States Coast Guard).

15. International Outreach and Arctic Expansion (2010–) 161

Commandant Robert Papp gave his second state of the Coast Guard address from the deck of the USCGC *Bertholf*, a National Security Cutter in the Legendary Class, named for the first commandant of the Coast Guard (United States Coast Guard).

sinking USCGC *Blackthorn* and sacrificed his lifesaving personal flotation device and other life preservers he reached to give other crewmembers. Papp reminded the cadets that they were now "the custodians of a rich legacy of service to the Nation; a legacy that spans more than 221 years."[22]

In his second State of the Coast Guard Address in February 2012 at Alameda, California, Adm. Papp stood on the dock by the NSC *Bertholf* on Coast Guard Island. Papp informed his listeners that 95 percent of U.S. foreign trade comes by sea, and accounts for billions of dollars of gross domestic product and millions of American jobs; and that the Coast Guard secures the safety of those shipments at sea and in domestic ports. The commandant warned about the negative impact of threatened Coast Guard budget cuts, and said the service must "weather the storm" with its adaptive crew, as it has done many times before.[23]

San Francisco Chronicle reporter Carl Nolte had an upbeat impression of Adm. Papp's State of the Coast Guard presentation in front of the *Bertholf* at the cutter's homeport of Alameda, California: "It was a sight," Nolte wrote, "right out of a military recruiting poster at Coast Guard Island this week. Admiral Robert Papp stood on a platform next to three gleaming white cutters, each of them capable of long deployments in the far Pacific or Arctic."[24]

Nolte described "the new cutter's smell of paint, steel, and electronics [and] a whiff of [budget] trouble ahead"[25] that the reporter attributed to commandant's fiscal assessment of "uncertain and stormy seas" and a reduction of about $350 million from the prior year's budget that Adm. Papp said "is not an acceptable option."[26]

Upgrading the Coast Guard fleet of assorted watercraft, boats, and cutters was an essential process, Papp insisted, to meet the needs of mission expansion. The commandant's busy schedule included presiding over dedication ceremonies at shipyards to commemorate the new vessels.

In March of 2012, Adm. Papp spoke at the dedication ceremony for a new generation patrol boat: the 154-foot Fast Response Sentinel Class cutters (FRCs) that were contracted with Bollinger Shipyards in Lockport, Louisiana. The FRCs would replace the 110-foot Island Class patrol boats. The larger, more stable FRC platforms was designed to launch small boats from stern ramps, and house remotely operated weaponry. The FRC *William R. Flores,* one of the 58 patrol cutters planned for, is named after the Coast Guard seaman who gave his life saving shipmates on the sinking USCGC *Blackthorn* in 1980. The USCGC *Flores* would be home ported in Key West and Miami, Florida.

In his public presentation, Adm. Papp said, "I am honored to be part of this unique ceremony [to honor] the service of dedicated professionals who perform heroic deeds on a daily basis." The commandant described the event as a "privilege to officially dedicate cutters for the most exceptional Coast Guard men and women."[27]

The USCGC *Bernard C. Webber* commissioning ceremony took place in Miami, Florida, on April 14, 2012. Commandant Papp led the ceremonies and complimented the well-trained crew for getting the cutter on schedule to Miami. The new Sentinel Class patrol boat was one of the planned 58 ships. Papp described the cutter as having "beautiful lines, speed, seaworthiness, survivability, and over-the-horizon range with interoperational command, control and communication systems to allow it to operate seamlessly with other DHS components, and our sister services in the Department of Defense."[28]

The state of the art technology and naval engineering would only be significant, Papp explained, "if you have a proficient and well trained crew" with expertise and seamanship skills.[29] Adm. Papp highlighted Boatswain Mate First Class Bernie Webber as having displayed exceptional leadership skills when the coxswain led his brave Coast Guard crew in a 36-foot wooden motor lifeboat in hazardous seas to rescue the surviving crewmembers of

15. International Outreach and Arctic Expansion (2010–) 163

the foundering 500-foot fuel tanker SS *Pendleton* off Chatham, Massachusetts.

The SS *Pendleton* broke in two in 60-foot waves on a freezing night in the February 1952 snowstorm off Cape Cod, Massachusetts. Bernard Webber, and his crew, Adm. Papp asserted, rescued more than 30 merchant sailors at great risk to themselves while handling lifeboat CG 36500. Admiral Papp told how BM1 Webber subsequently declined the Coast Guard Gold Life Saving Medal until he was assured the two seamen and engineman second class crewmembers received the same award.[30]

The 1982 Law of the Sea Convention was signed by most of the world's maritime nations, but the U.S. Senate refused to ratify the controversial document because of concerns about encroachments on U.S. sovereignty. Opponents of the convention believed the treaty could require the United States to share resources and revenues, and subject the nation to international lawsuits and judicial arbitration. Commandant Papp had publically supported the Law of the Sea treaty in the past, and did so again before the Senate Committee on Foreign Relations on 14 June 2012.[31]

"Like the commandants before me, I am firmly convinced," Adm. Papp stated, "that the legal certainty and stability accorded by the Law of the Sea Convention will strengthen Coast Guard efforts in (1) sustaining mission excellence as America's maritime first responder; (2) protecting American prosperity; and (3) ensuring America's Arctic future."[32] Papp further explained that the convention would facilitate the security of U.S. "maritime rights, presence, and interests, including ocean resources" and the protection of America's "Exclusive Economic Zone (EEZ) that is responsible for over $122 billion in revenue annually."[33]

U.S. maritime rights and precedents allow free movement of U.S. commerce, naval support, and the protection of national security interests, Papp asserted. He added his conviction that the Law of the Sea Convention would secure American territorial sea claims out to the 12-mile limit. Papp claimed that the Law of the Sea Treaty would support the Coast Guard missions of fishing enforcement, search and rescue, narcotics and illegal immigration interdiction, national defense, and protection from international terrorism. The Law of the Sea Convention, Papp contended, would also support continued U.S. Coast Guard cooperation with the coast guards of other nations.

Vessel inspections on the high seas and cooperation with the International Maritime Organization would protect America's maritime interests, the commandant insisted, and enhance U.S. port safety and improve port security. The convention would actually increase U.S. sovereignty and national interests, said Papp.

Ocean pollution control and the expansion of America's Arctic presence would be better assured and supported by the international community if the Law of the Sea Convention were signed by the United States, according to the commandant, because the U.S. already adhered to and abided by many of the provisions of the 1982 Law of the Sea Convention, so U.S. Senate ratification of the convention would be a diplomatic triumph.[34]

Commandant Papp briefed the U.S. Senate Appropriations Committee and Senate Subcommittee on Homeland Security about Coast Guard operations in Alaska and the Arctic in August 2012.[35] The document was sourced from U.S. Coast Guard Air Station Kodiak in Alaska. Admiral Papp continued to be an articulate advocate for the expansion of Coast Guard operations in the polar region to better serve and protect U.S. economic and national defense.

The commandant informed the subcommittee members that the U.S. Coast Guard, in partnership with federal, state, local, and tribal governments, and petroleum industry officials, monitored oil industry activities in the Beaufort and Chukchi Seas. That partnership, said Papp, supports and ensures "the stewardship of the emerging maritime frontier of the Arctic."[36] The U.S. Coast Guard has managed the "stewardship" of the Alaskan-Arctic-Bering Sea frontier since the days of U.S. Revenue Cutter Service patrols that commenced with the U.S. purchase of Alaska from Russia in 1867, two years after the Civil War.

Operation Arctic Shield in 2012 involved outreach to and health care for native Arctic communities; the deployment of cutter and aviation assets, personnel, and infrastructure; and providing communications equipment necessary to facilitate Coast Guard missions. The testing of U.S. Navy and U.S. Coast Guard oil skimming equipment from a 225-foot Coast Guard buoy tender off Barrow, Alaska, provided training and practice for potential oil spill responses. Adm. Papp credited the Seventeenth Coast Guard District with formulating and administering the Arctic Shield plan.

Two MH-60 helicopters were stationed for the first time in a Barrow, Alaska, hanger ready to carry out search and rescue, law enforcement, and environmental protection missions. Two 225-foot ice capable buoy tenders and the National Security Cutter *Bertholf* were assigned for duty in the region to test "offshore operational capability," carry out oceanographic exploration, and support commercial transportation and fisheries resource management.

The Coast Guard, Papp revealed, maintained communications and operations with the Arctic nations of Canada and Russia. The commandant reiterated the challenges and opportunities of the Arctic mission,

15. International Outreach and Arctic Expansion (2010–) 165

and said the Coast Guard looked forward to working with the U.S. Congress to support Arctic operations and "protect its fragile environment."³⁷

In an August 2012 visit to Anchorage, Alaska, with Department of Homeland Security Secretary Janet Napolitano, Adm. Papp claimed that lessons learned from the 2010 Gulf of Mexico Deepwater Horizon disaster had prepared to Coast Guard for potential Arctic oil spills as Shell Oil Company prepared to drill wells using two drill ships accompanied by water craft and crews trained to cope with accidents.

During the Alaska visit, Commandant Papp conducted a tour of the 418-foot National Security Cutter *Bertholf* with Napolitano and three U.S. senators at Cold Bay in the Alaskan Aleutian Islands. Papp told the visiting dignitaries that the chances of a repetition of the magnitude of the Gulf spill were minimized by subsequent oversight planning and inspection programs, and the fact that the water depths in that region of the Arctic average about 150 feet, compared to the 5,000 foot depths in the Gulf of Mexico.³⁸

Military organizations thrive on discipline. Admiral Papp has written that proficiency is the foundation of discipline, and "mastery of craft and individual initiative" in the enlisted and commissioned ranks and ongoing training and communications are essential elements for the completion of safe and successful missions. Papp defined "mastery of craft" as exhibiting "proficiency" in the specialties for which Coast Guard active duty, reserve, auxiliary, and civilian personnel have been trained.³⁹

Personnel specialties include the ranks, rates and occupational tasks of all the members of Team Coast Guard, and involved commanding officers; boat station and cutter crews; aviation crews and mechanics; search and rescue specialists; law enforcement, engineering, office and administrative personnel; shore stations; communications, information, scientific, weather and oceanographic specialists; classroom instructors and trainers; and a variety of national defense and port security personnel.⁴⁰

Commandant Papp alluded to numerous accidents, deaths and personnel misconduct that occurred on his watch. Papp responded to those unfortunate incidents by ordering "a refocus on improving discipline through a renewed commitment to leadership and efficiency in the operational arts."⁴¹ The commandant reviewed the dangers and duties Coast Guard personnel faced in their daily missions.

To better manage the training and experiential aspects of personnel assignments, Papp initiated the policy of requiring commissioned officer and enlisted personnel to complete full duty tours at stations to maintain "tactical efficiency," instead of allowing for more frequent and interrupted assignments.⁴²

The concern of Admiral Papp for vigilance and personnel safety in the dangerous maritime environments was confirmed by the on-duty death of a Coast Guard chief petty officer and the wounding of a colleague in the attempted investigation of a suspected contraband boat off the California coast in December 2012. A Coast Guard C-130 aircraft crew spotted the suspect vessel running at night without lights, and that information was transmitted to the 87-foot USCGC *Halibut* (WPB-87340).

The small Coast Guard boat and crew were operating out of the port of Del Rey, California. Chief Petty Officer Terrell Horne died when the suspect vessel rammed the 20-foot rigid hull Coast Guard inflatable craft as it was approaching the 25-ft open hull, single engine wooden vessel. The contraband vessel and crew were eventually overtaken, and two Mexican nationals were taken into custody, brought to Los Angeles, and charged with the killing of a federal officer.

The commanding officer of the *Halibut,* Lt. Stewart Sibert, and his crew were saddened by the loss of CPO Horne. Lieutenant Sibert said Horne was an outstanding leader and confidante. Just a few months before the fatal incident, Horne helped saved the lives of three people on a disabled sailboat. "Our fallen shipmate stood the watch on the front lines protecting our nation," Adm. Papp said, "and we are all indebted to him for his service and sacrifice."[43]

In 2012, "The Year of the Chief" was celebrated at the United States Navy Memorial in Washington, D.C. Commandant Papp spoke there on 29 August 2012. Papp described the essential leadership chief petty officers contribute in the U.S. Coast Guard and U.S. Navy.[44] The chief petty officer (CPO, senior chief, master chief) sets the mood of the ship and station, Papp explained, and the rank reflects experience and leadership qualities.

The chief petty officer is the highest category of the enlisted ranks. CPOs have earned the respect of enlisted personnel and the commissioned officers as reflected, Papp said, in the oft-quoted personnel response to crew member queries about facts, procedures, and leadership: "Ask the chief!"[45]

The grade of chief petty officer was established in the U.S. Navy in the late 19th century and in the U.S. Coast Guard in the early 20th century. The Coast Guard Chief Petty Officer School is located at Coast Guard Training Center Petaluma, California.

Huntington Ingalls Industries builds ships and boats for the U.S. Navy, U.S. Marine Corps, and U.S. Coast Guard. It has employed thousands of highly skilled workers in Pascagoula, Mississippi; Louisiana, California, and Virginia.[46] Ingalls Shipbuilding was building warships in 1939, the year World War II erupted in Europe. As of 2012, Ingalls had built the

15. International Outreach and Arctic Expansion (2010–)   167

National Security Cutters *Bertholf*, *Waesche*, and *Stratton*, and was in the process of building NSC *Hamilton*.[47]

The "Keel Authentication" ceremony for the NSC *Hamilton* took place at the Huntington Ingalls shipyard in Pascagoula, Mississippi, on 5 September 2012. Admiral Papp spoke at the ceremony and thanked the shipbuilding company, civilian shipyard workers, and Coast Guard personnel for their contributions to the planning and building of the *Hamilton*, named for Alexander Hamilton, the founder and first leader of the U.S. Revenue Marine and President George Washington's secretary of the treasury.

Commandant Papp traced the evolution of the first wooden hulled, sail (wind powered) revenue cutters down to the present day cutters constructed from separately assembled units and joined into steel module hulls. Admiral Papp described the keel as the supporting spine of the hull. The completed "cold steel hull will carry," Papp said, "our nation's sons and daughters through uncertain and stormy seas and back again" on vessels constructed with the "privilege and solemn responsibility" of ship planners and builders.[48]

Admiral Papp spoke often about the courageous Coast Guard personnel who went out on the sea and in the air to perform dangerous search and rescue missions, sometimes at the cost of their lives, when other sea and aircraft are forced to stay in port or on station. One of those many Coast Guard heroes was Seaman Apprentice William R. Flores. The Hispanic hero was posthumously awarded the Coast Guard Medal in a ceremony by Fort Worth, Texas, on 16 September 2000. The ceremony took place near the family gravesite in Benbrook, Texas. Family members, friends, and Coast Guard personnel were there to honor SA Flores. Among the Coast Guard members were Eighth District Commander Rear Adm. Paul Pluta and Master Chief Petty Officer of the Coast Guard, Vince Patton.

SA Flores and 22 other Coast Guard personnel died when the 180-foot World War II era buoy tender USCGC *Blackthorn* sank in a collision with the tanker SS *Capricorn* off the entrance to Tampa Bay, Florida, on 28 January 1980. Flores drowned while refusing to abandon the sinking cutter as he threw life jackets to shipmates struggling in the water and assisted wounded and disoriented shipmates off the sinking cutter. Flores and his shipmates gave their lives to save 27 sailors.[49]

The commissioning of the 154-foot Fast Response (FRC) Sentinel Class cutter *William Flores* occurred at St. Petersburg, Florida on 3 November 2012, with Adm. Papp presiding. Papp described the stunning new multi-mission cutter.[50]

The Sentinel Class FRCs had a 9 foot 6 inch draft, 28 knot maximum speed, crew complement of 24, five day sea endurance, rough seas capability, a 25mm machine gun mount, and four .50-caliber machine guns.[51] "The Sentinel Class cutters," Adm. Robert Papp stated, are "a tribute not only to the enlisted men and women serving in the Coast Guard, but to the many heroes that preceded them. He said it would "be a critical asset in securing and protecting our nation's maritime environment."[52]

The FRCs were scheduled for a construction total of 58, to be built at Bollinger Shipyards in Lockport, Louisiana. Admiral Papp credited the owner, managers, and skilled workers at Bollinger Shipyard with caring more about their ships than just the contract and profits. "There is more to it than just a business to them," Papp asserted. "We have had a long relationship with them. They care about these ships and the people who sail in them."[53]

In his tribute to SA William Flores before the assembled audience and family members, Adm. Papp said of the heroic sailor, "Because of his sacrifice that night, others continued to live and serve their nations and their communities." Flores's heroic actions reminded Papp that members of the Coast Guard "serve in a dangerous profession, one in which we give all so that others might live."[54]

The 24th Annual Surface Navy Association Symposium occurred in Arlington, Virginia, in 2012. Commandant Papp spoke to that organization on 12 January about Coast Guard surface asset capitalization.

The audience was informed about Coast Guard Pacific missions from the Arctic through the Eastern Pacific, and how cutters serve as stewards of national security that protect and preserve the maritime domain.

Papp spoke of the 2011 diversion of the USCGC *Healy* from its polar scientific expedition to clear a 100-mile path through Arctic ice so the Russian oil tanker *Renda* could deliver one million gallons of fuel to the isolated city of Nome, Alaska. And Papp told about the USCGC *Walnut* and its 2011 delivery of emergency fresh water and a support team to the central Pacific Tokelau Islands during a drought.

Admiral Papp further illustrated the diverse missions of the Coast Guard with the story of the interdiction of seven tons of cocaine in the Caribbean Sea by the crew of the USCGC *Mohawk* and the seizure of a ton of cocaine on the first patrol of the National Security Cutter *Waesche*. Papp attributed the seizure to the skilled crew and the advanced technology on the new state of the art cutter. The commandant appropriately titled his speech, "Surface Navy: A Credible Force in Uncertain Times."[55]

Changing Arctic climate patterns are expanding the navigable waterways in the polar region, necessitating additional Coast Guard presence, operations, and infrastructure in the high latitudes, and the use of large icebreakers. Admiral Papp announced that the U.S. Coast Guard's only heavy icebreaker, the USCGC *Polar Star*, home ported in Seattle, Washington, would assume a presence in Arctic waters in 2013. The Coast Guard was seeking the services of construction companies that could do dockside repairs on the *Polar Star* and inspect, clean and repair lockers, tanks, diesel generators, boilers, gauges, thermometers, chains, gears, and associated technical and mechanical work.

The USCGC *Healy* (WAGB-20), a Medium class polar icebreaker, was thought to be insufficient by itself for the projected Arctic missions. The USCGC *Polar Star*, commissioned in 1976, was scheduled to undergo refurbishing and planned sea trials in 2012–2013, after having been laid up since 2010.[56]

The 399-foot *Polar Star* (WAGB-10) supported a crew complement of 140. The Heavy Icebreaker could accommodate two helicopters. The cutter was built in 1976 by Lockheed Shipbuilding and Construction Company in Seattle, Washington, as was its sister ship, *Polar Sea* (WAGB-11) that is no longer in commission.

The Heavy Icebreaker *Polar Star* is ideally suited to Arctic and Antarctic conditions and has served in both the Arctic and Antarctic polar regions. The *Polar Star* has three engine shafts turned by a gas turbine power plant or a diesel electric plant. It is one of the most powerful non-nuclear icebreakers in the world. Each shaft propels a four-bladed controlled pitch screw (propeller). The cutter climbs up on to the edge of an ice pack and rocks from side to side to break the ice and avoid entrapment.

Polar Star missions have included the support of scientific exploration, search and rescue, and cargo and passenger transportation. The USCGC *Polar Star* brought fuel, food, and other supplies to scientific and naval stations and served as a home base for scientists to study sea ice, oceanography, and geology. The stern and port sides of the cutter housed giant cranes that give scientists the technical and mechanical capabilities of at sea extractions and investigation.[57] The Heavy Icebreaker supported the naval mission of protecting and defending the Exclusive Economic Zone and U.S. sovereignty interests. In that respect, the Coast Guard has planned to build a new Heavy Icebreaker in the near future to supplement the *Polar Star*.

The U.S. Coast Guard assists in the formation and training of coast guards in smaller nations. Coast Guard crews visit colleagues and learn from them. On November 20, 2012, Commandant Papp visited maritime partners on the island nation of Malta in the Mediterranean Sea. He visited with U.S. Ambassador to Malta Gina Abercrombie-Winstanley, and the U.S. Coast Guard attaché at the United States Embassy. The Armed Forces of Malta, the nation's chief of defense, Brig. Gen. Martin G. Xuereb, and Malta's Maritime Squadron honored Adm. Papp. The military leaders discussed terrorism, illegal immigration, narcotics smuggling, search and rescue, maritime law enforcement and safety, national security, and training.

Master Chief Petty Officer Michael Leavitt visited with his Malta counterpart, Armed Forces Sgt. Major Warrant Officer Class 1 Geoffrey Muscat. The chaplain of the U.S. Coast Guard, Captain Gary Weeden communicated with Fr. Joseph Melli. Admiral Papp addressed the students at Malta's prestigious International Maritime Law Institute.

In his public remarks, Papp predicted, "When the students graduate and return to influential positions in their home countries, I'm certain that U.S. Coast Guard officers will be among their close colleagues as they work together to implement International Maritime Organization standards worldwide."[58]

In November 2012, Commandant Papp visited the Southeast Asian maritime nation of Singapore as a guest of the Maritime and Port Authority and Singapore's Distinguished Visitors Program. Admiral Papp conversed with authority Chief Executive Lam Yi Young, Transport Minister Lui Tuck Yew, Police Commissioner Ng Joo Hee, and the commander of the Police Coast Guard, Hsu Sin Yun. Papp then observed operations in the Port Operations Control Center, Vessel Traffic Information System, and the Integrated Tactical Training Center.[59]

In late November 2012, Admiral Robert Papp and Master Chief Petty Officer of the U.S. Coast Guard Michael P. Leavitt met with crewmembers of the 110-foot patrol boat *Aquidneck* (WPB-1309) off the Middle East nation of Bahrain.

The U.S. Coast Guard was in Bahrain as a naval support unit of the U.S. Fifth Fleet, and U.S. Coast Guard Patrol Forces Southwest Asia (PATFORSWA). Six patrol boats and 280 Coast Guard personnel were part of the operation during Papp's visit. The U.S. Central Command directed the Arabian Gulf Theater of operations.

Admiral Papp enjoyed Thanksgiving dinner in Bahrain, and commended the members of Coast Guard forces and the members of the U.S. Armed Forces in the theater of operations. Papp met with the U.S. ambassador to the Kingdom of Bahrain, Thomas Krajeski, and the police, military, naval, and coast guard officials of the host government. The Coast Guard commandant thanked them all for their support, and talked about missions and strategies. Admiral Papp then reenlisted Petty Officer Third Class Tiffany Moore, and extended PO3 Moore's Coast Guard service.[60]

The respect and concern Adm. Papp so often expressed for Coast

Guard personnel who go into harm's way were stated in his writings, speeches, Congressional appearances, and at the funerals of those who sacrificed their lives in the line of duty.

The *Navy Times* covered the story of the death of Senior Chief Boatswain's Mate Terrell Horne while pursuing a suspected Mexican contraband boat along the California coast on 2 December 2012. Two Mexican nationals were later apprehended and charged with killing the federal law enforcement officer. Horne died after the 30-foot "Panga" vessel struck his 21-foot Rigid Hull Inflatable (RHI) Coast Guard boat.

A Coast Guard C-130 plane had observed the alleged contraband running without night-lights. The 87-foot *Halibut* was ordered to check it out. CPO Horne's 21-foot RHI was dispatched from the *Halibut* and chased the Panga boat that then turned and rammed the Coast Guard craft. Petty Officer 2nd Class Brandon Langdon and Horne were thrown into the water. Two other Coast Guard crewmembers aboard the RHI were unharmed in the 1:20 a.m. collision near Santa Cruz Island.

After a chase by Coast Guard air and sea craft, the Panga was secured and the suspects were pepper sprayed and taken into custody. The accused perpetrators claimed they were taking containers of gasoline to another boat.

Drug and human contraband smugglers had been plying California coastal waters routes north of Mexico as U.S. law enforcement units monitored other routes.

BMCS Horne was an experienced and well-respected leader of whom Lt. Steward Sibert, commanding officer of the USCGC *Halibut*, said, "He was my friend, he was my confidante. He was the glue that held my crew together."[61]

On 8 December 2012, Admiral Papp spoke at the memorial service for BMCS Terrell Horne III. The service took place at U.S. Coast Guard Base Los Angeles/Long Beach in California. Commandant Papp commended the extended family represented by the Department of Homeland Security, family members, active duty, reserve, auxiliary and civilian personnel, and "our friends from local, state and federal law enforcement, and all others gathered here to honor our fallen shipmate."[62]

Admiral Papp paid respects to the grieving family members of Senior Chief Horne, and thanked the regional Coast Guard commanders and political notables present. Papp alluded to the members of the U.S. Coast Guard Band who provide comfort to mourners and inspiration to attendees at concerts and commemorations.

The commandant reminded the audience that the U.S. Coast Guard is "a military service. A profession of arms. We commit ourselves to our nation, and put ourselves in harm's way" as Senior Chief Horne did: "Without concern for himself," Papp continued, "he pushed his coxswain to safety." Senior Chief Horne, Papp concluded, "was a hero, a leader, and he made a difference."63

Commandant Papp referred to the historic "Thin Blue Line" in reference to Coast Guard personnel who have served with distinction and courage, sometimes at the cost of their lives.

Vice Commandant John P. Currier represented Commandant Papp at the Veterans Day wreath laying ceremony at Arlington National Cemetery on 11 November 2012. Vice Admiral Currier, a distinguished Coast Guard aviator, commemorated Coast Guard service in his compelling address.

Currier spoke at the Coast Guard Memorial that was built to honor contributions and the sacrifices personnel made in World War I (1914–1918). In that Great War, the Coast Guard escorted merchant convoys between North America and Europe. President Woodrow Wilson, Currier explained, commemorated the end of the War and Armistice Day on 11 November 1919. That date has since been referred to as Veterans Day.

The Coast Guard Memorial was built soon after World War I to honor fallen Coast Guard members generally and casualties from two 1918 combat events—the loss of men of the USCGC *Seneca* in the Bay of Biscay off the coast of France during a rescue attempt on a British steamer in stormy seas, and the loss of 111 Coast Guardsmen on the USCGC *Tampa* off the British Isles when that cutter was torpedoed by a German U-boat.

Vice Commandant Currier recalled the memory of Lt. Jack Rittichier, the heroic pilot of a U.S. Air Force rescue helicopter who was killed when his helicopter was shot down by enemy fire in Vietnam. The courageous aviator, Currier explained, had earned three Distinguished Flying Crosses for his courageous rescues of downed aviators. These were among the many examples, Currier concluded, "of the Coast Guard men and women who have made the ultimate sacrifice in service to our Nation."64

Admiral Papp and his predecessor, Commandant Thad Allen, frequently made the case for an expanded Coast Guard presence in the Arctic. In December 2012, it was announced that the Seattle, Washington, based Heavy Icebreaker *Polar Star* was reactivated after a four year, $57 million overhaul at the Vigor Industrial Shipyard. The *Polar Star* was scheduled for tests and trial runs in 2013. The 34-year-old icebreaker was said to be capable of cracking through a 20-foot wall of ice.

Washington State U.S. Senator Maria Cantwell and other lawmakers supported Admiral Papp's request for an increased presence in the Arctic

15. International Outreach and Arctic Expansion (2010–)

because frozen waterways were opening up for commercial and scientific exploitation and exploration,[65] and an increased U.S. domestic and military presence was necessary to respond to national and public safety considerations.

The international trips Admiral Papp took in 2012 revealed significant information and policy insights. United States Coast Guard missions and personnel were assessed, and the visits led to tactical information exchanges between the United States and the coast guards of host nations.

The commandant visited Guam, Singapore, Malta, and Bahrain. He returned from overseas on 1 December 2012 and had a revealing interview with *Navy Times* reporter Jacqueline Klimas. The reporter's perceptive questions and Papp's knowledge and honesty clearly chronicled the contributions of Coast Guard men and women.[66]

At the time of the interview, 379 Coast Guard personnel were serving overseas, 250 of them with Naval Patrol Forces in the Southwest Asia/Persian Gulf region. Coast Guard personnel were protecting oil infrastructure; patrolling waterways, rivers, and the expansive gulf maritime domain; and boarding vessels in support of U.S. Navy missions. Six Island Class Coast Guard patrol boats and their crews formed a strategic element of U.S. naval activities on the eve of the replacement of the smaller cutters with more advanced Fast Response Cutters.

Coast Guard units in Bahrain and Afghanistan inspected hazardous materials associated with weapons and vehicles before the equipment was shipped back to the United States. Other Coast Guard teams inspected shipping and port security operations in foreign ports "with a very small investment," Papp said, and "a high return because we are able to be the first line of defense" for cargoes scheduled to enter U.S. ports.[67]

Future federal budget cuts would affect personnel and assignments at home and abroad, as would the inevitable downsizing of U.S. missions, Papp explained. But he expected that new mission assignments would require the full utilization and geographic redistribution of Coast Guard personnel. Those changes, however, could postpone new recruitment, while not necessarily requiring present active duty personnel to be released from the service.[68]

The Coast Guard's responsibility and vigilance in monitoring and responding to Arctic oil exploration operations was tested in December 2012. Coast Guard inspections noted safety deficiencies on the Arctic drilling ship SS *Noble Discoverer*, the Noble Corporation vessel hired by Royal Dutch Shell Corporation.

The *Noble Discoverer* began its drilling mission off Alaska's Arctic shore in September 2012, and subsequently announced that the drilling rig had to be moved to avoid threatening drifting sea ice in the drilling area. Then the drilling vessel caught fire in the Alaskan port of Dutch Harbor in the Aleutian Islands. A backfiring engine ignited a blaze that the crew extinguished.

Noble Corporation reported that Coast Guard inspections discovered deficiencies in the ship's safety management and propulsion mechanisms. Royal Dutch Shell said other issues would be resolved during scheduled shipyard work in the state of Washington. Shell, Noble, and the Coast Guard would review the Alaskan drilling operations to better prepare the vessel and other entities for the 2013 petroleum drilling season, to comply with petroleum industry procedures and maritime laws.[69]

Maritime support issues plagued the Arctic oil drilling vessels through December of 2012 and into 2013, and challenged the seafaring skills of Coast Guard personnel. The USCGC *Alex Haley* was stationed 50 miles off of Kodiak Island to support the Royal Dutch Shell tug SS *Aiviq* and the unpowered mobile drilling vessel SS *Kulluk*. Weather and equipment issues interfered with Shell Oil's drilling into oil fields on the continental shelf in the Beaufort and Chukchi Seas. The tugboat engines broke down, but generators provided enough power to prevent uncontrolled drifting until the vessel was secured.

Coast Guard spokespersons informed the media that ongoing inspections were occurring, and Coast Guard and Shell Oil officials would make decisions about when and whether the *Aiviq* would be repaired on site at sea or assisted back to a shipyard for repairs and upgrades.[70]

Admiral Papp had often noted the essential and expanded role the Coast Guard must play in the Arctic, and the challenges the Arctic environment would pose to civilian shipping, corporations, Coast Guard missions and personnel. Commandant Papp's admonitions would come to pass, and Coast Guard crews measured up to early tests.

Troubles continued on 29 December 2012. U.S. Coast Guard helicopter crews were forced to evacuate crewmembers from the oil-drilling barge off the southern coast of Alaska as the *Kulluk* oil rig drifted toward shore in heavy seas and high winds with the danger of running aground. Rear Admiral Thomas Ostebo, the commander of the 17th Coast Guard District out of Juneau, Alaska, credited his helicopters and C-130 aircraft crews, and cutter crews for their professionalism in hazardous conditions.

The towing vessel SS *Aivig* and a second Shell Oil Company vessel, SS *Nanuq*, secured the drifting rig and headed for the nearest safe harbor, and eventually winter port in Seattle, Washington.[71] The SS *Kulluk* lost its towline in heavy seas and was guided ashore.

Heavy seas, high winds, and size of the vessels involved challenged

15. International Outreach and Arctic Expansion (2010–)   175

the crews in the Coast Guard rescue missions. Waves of 20 to 30 feet and winds of 30 to 40 knot plagued the Coast Guard cutter and aviation crews.

Coast Guard helicopters flew in from Coast Guard Air Station Kodiak to deliver engine components and technicians to the 360-foot SS *Aiviq*. The 280-foot Coast Guard icebreaker *Alex Haley* (WMEC-39) hooked a towline to the SS *Aiviq* that was towing the SS *Kulluk*. But heavy seas and high winds broke the *Haley* towline that then became tangled in one of the cutter propellers, forcing the icebreaker into port for repairs. The efforts of the *Haley* were credited with buying time for the deployment of other rescue assets.[72]

The rugged, magnificent, and extreme physical geography of Alaska poses enormous cultural topographic, maritime, weather and climate challenges for its Arctic and polar residents, and Coast Guard installations, assets, and personnel. The Coast Guard has patrolled the region since its U.S. Revenue Cutter presence in 1867 following the purchase of Alaska from Russia.

Given the challenging high latitude Arctic environment, the Coast Guard expanded its recruitment efforts in the urban, rural, and village Native American communities. Coast Guard recruiters, Air Station Kodiak spokeswoman Sara Francis said, would be looking to "the last [Alaskan] frontier for its next crop of service men and women," and seeking Native language speakers.[73]

Admiral Robert Papp's record of distinguished military service earned him honors and recognition from the Coast Guard, political leaders at home and abroad, and the other U.S. Armed Forces. In 2012, the *Navy Times* listed Commandant Papp as number 46 in its directory of the 100 most significant military leaders. The *Navy Times* referenced Papp's command history and the expanding Coast Guard role in the Arctic, and concluded that the Coast Guard contribution to national security was "vital."

The *Navy Times* endorsed the planned expansion of the Coast Guard in the Arctic, despite expected budget cuts, and cited Commandant Papp's mission priorities in difficult economic times. "So what we do," Papp said, "is train leaders who make decisions on what the highest priorities are on a day to day basis, and we attack those missions first. We use what is left over to do the lower-priority missions. And then, when disaster strikes, everything falls aside and we respond to that."

Admiral Robert J. Papp, Jr., and his commandant predecessors have carried out Coast Guard missions and responsibilities in exemplary fashion. Generally and historically speaking, the U.S Coast Guard commandants have earned the naval accolade "Well done."[74]

Epilogue: 2015 and Beyond

In the March 17, 2014, edition of *Navy Times,* Meghann Myers reported that Admiral Robert Papp was scheduled to retire as U.S. Coast Guard commandant in May after 39 years in the service. Admiral Papp heartily endorsed President Barack Obama's nomination of his successor, Vice Admiral Paul Zukunft.

The nomination of Zukunft to succeed Adm. Papp was announced by recently appointed Secretary of Homeland Security Jeh Johnson. At the time of the announcement, Vice Admiral Zukunft was serving as the Pacific Area and Defense Force West commander.

Zukunft graduated from the United States Coast Guard Academy at New London, Connecticut, in 1977, and subsequently commanded the U.S. Coast Guard cutters *Rush, Harriet Lane,* and *Cape Upright.*

After earning flag officer rank in 2006, Adm. Zukunft served as assistant commandant for marine safety and security, director of response policy, and commander of the Eleventh Coast Guard District, Alameda, California.

Admiral Zukunft earned the accolades of former Coast Guard Commandant Thad Allen, with whom he worked during the 2010 Deepwater Horizon oil spill in the Gulf of Mexico.

As Pacific Area commander, Adm. Zukunft administered Coast Guard operations from the Rocky Mountains, across the Gulf of Mexico, and transversing the oceans to the east coast maritime region of Africa. The waters off East Africa have been notorious for piracy activities. The U.S. Navy and U.S. Coast Guard conducted joint operations to suppress those activities, just as the sail/wind powered U.S. Revenue Marine cutters and crews had battled pirates off U.S. coasts in the early 19th century.

Meghann Myers reported that in his capacity as commander of

Defense Force West, Admiral Zukunft coordinated Coast Guard missions with the U.S. Defense Department and regional combat commanders.

Myers also covered the person nominated for the highest Coast Guard enlisted position: master chief petty officer of the Coast Guard. Command Master Chief Steven Cantrell was scheduled to assume the post in May of 2014, replacing Mike Leavitt, who served Commandant Robert Papp with distinction.

Command Master Chief Cantrell enlisted in the Coast Guard in 1983. Cantrell had previously served as enlisted petty officer in charge of Coast Guard stations at Harbor Beach, Michigan; Panama City Beach, Florida; Alexandria Bay, New York; and Wrightsville Beach, North Carolina.

Commands afloat as officer in charge of a variety of cutters honed Chief Cantrell's leadership and seafaring skills. Cantrell served on the cutters *Point Wells*, *Ridley*, *Point Camden*, *Rambler*, *Confidence*, and *Patoka*. He also served as command master chief to the vice commandant of the Coast Guard.

Command Master Chief Cantrell earned a master's degree in business administration (Grantham University), and several commendations, awards, and medals. His assignment immediately prior to his nomination as master chief petty officer, was as command master chief of the Atlantic Area.

The leadership history of the United States Coast Guard is the story of seemingly insurmountable administrative challenges, exemplary courage and creativity, command presence, and the ability to integrate domestic and national defense missions with a variety of public safety, law enforcement, other units of the U.S. Armed Forces. The Coast Guard has also conducted joint missions with—and even trained the law enforcement, search and rescue, and military agencies of—other nations.

Every historical period presented unique opportunities, new technology, and budget and personnel challenges to the Coast Guard. From its Revenue Marine stage in 1790 to the Revenue Cutter Service and U.S. Coast Guard eras, the service has had to respond to expanded domestic and national defense assignments at home and overseas in periods of technological and cultural change, and amid political and budget machinations.

The Coast Guard has been involved in every war and coordinated its missions with the other branches of the U.S. Armed Forces at home and overseas from 1790 to the present. It has performed its missions in heterogeneity of geographic realms and maritime domains, from mid-continental seasonal extremes to the tropics, and to Alaska and polar regions of the Arctic and Antarctic.

The United States Coast Guard has met a plethora of historic and contemporary challenges, alternating between expanded and reduced budgets; variable personnel, equipment and supplies; and evolving air, sea, and shore assets, and training requirements. The future will likely pose similarly unpredictable mission, technology, and fiscal requirements and surprises.

That U.S. Coast Guard leadership has invariably measured up to its assigned tasks ashore and afloat is testimony to its compelling service traditions, training, and pride. The history of Coast Guard leadership, from the earliest times of sailing cutters to steam vessels, and now to modern air and sea craft and national security cutters, appears to illustrate a paradigm of success and pragmatism that other civilian, governmental, and military institutions might benefit from emulating.

Although this book has emphasized male Coast Guard leaders, and particularly the commandants, one would be remiss not to credit and list several female leaders, in addition to those already cited in this book.

The sources for this information include oral conversations and interviews, email contacts, material from previous books on general Coast Guard history, and the service on the Great Lakes, in World War II, and national defense; and sources from the Office of the Coast Guard Historian in Washington, D.C.

MKC Tina Claflin is a Rhinelander, Wisconsin, native. One of the authors met her at the U.S. Navy Memorial in Washington, D.C., following a presentation. Chief Petty Officer Claflin was stationed at Arlington, Virginia, and served as the Women Afloat coordinator. MKC Claflin is a student of military leadership and the role and achievements of women in the service.

CPO Claflin served at sea in search and rescue and law enforcement missions, and was lead petty officer on the U.S. Coast Guard Academy training sailing barque USCGC *Eagle* (WIX-327).

On 20 May 2014, Machinery Technician Chief Claflin was honored by the Congressional Women's Caucus in a wreath laying ceremony at Arlington National Cemetery.

Yeoman Chief Jennifer Bell succeeded Claflin as the U.S. Coast Guard Women Afloat coordinator in the Personnel Services Division, Arlington, Virginia.

Lt. Cmdr. Holly Harrison, then a lieutenant, was in command of the USCGC *Aquidneck* (WPB-1309) in the North Arabian Gulf in 2003. As part of a U.S. Navy support unit in Operation Iraqi Freedom, Harrison commanded the 110-foot cutter on dangerous patrols in mined waters, and earned the Bronze Star for her and crewmember achievements. Subsequently in her distinguished career, Lt. Cmdr. Harrison served on other cutters, was a law enforcement instructor at Coast Guard training centers, and then assigned to U.S. Coast Guard Headquarters in the nation's capital.

Vice Admiral Vivien Crea (Ret., 2009) served as vice commandant of the Coast Guard under former Commandant Thad Allen (2006–2010). Prior to that, Crea was military aide to President Ronald Reagan and a distinguished Coast Guard aviator.

Vice Admiral Sally Brice-O'Hara (Ret.) was appointed vice commandant of the Coast Guard in 2010. Prior to that assignment, Brice-O'Hara had been commanding officer of Station Cape May (New Jersey), commander of Coast Guard Training Center Cape May, and the assistant director of admissions at the U.S. Coast Guard Academy in New London, Connecticut.

In 2013, Rear Admiral Cari B. Thomas was appointed commander of the 14th District, a Pacific maritime region stretching from Hawaii to Japan. Admiral Thomas's spouse, Cmdr. Gary M. Thomas (Ret.) was the last commander of the LORAN Support Unit, Cape May County, New Jersey (2012). After retirement, Cmdr. Thomas became the executive director of the Foundation for Coast Guard History.

In 2011, Coast Guard Commandant Admiral Robert J. Papp appointed Rear Admiral Sandra L. Stosz to the post of superintendent of the United States Coast Guard Academy. Prior to that appointment, Admiral Stosz had been the director of leadership and the Coast Guard Reserve, commanding officer of Training Center Cape May, and commander on the Great Lakes of the USCGC *Katmai Bay* (WTGB-101). In 2004 Adm. Stosz earned a master's degree in national security strategy from the National War College at the National Defense University in Washington, D.C.

The aforementioned women exemplify the many outstanding leaders in the Service.

The leaders of "Team Coast Guard" have measured up to and enhanced the legendary Coast Guard motto, "Semper Paratus." Indeed, "Always Ready."

Appendix: Commandants of the Coast Guard and Chiefs of the Revenue Marine Bureau

Chiefs of the Revenue Marine Bureau

1. 1843–1848 Capt. Alexander Fraser
2. 1848–1849 Capt. Richard Evans

In 1849 the Revenue Marine Bureau was dissolved, and the Revenue Marine came under the control of the Commissioner of U.S. Customs until the Revenue Marine Bureau was re-established in 1869.

3. 1869–1871 N. Broughton Devereux
4. 1871–1878 Sumner I. Kimball
5. 1878–1885 Ezra Clark
6. 1885–1889 Peter Bonnett

Commandants

7. 1889–1895 Capt. Leonard G. Shepard, U.S. Revenue Cutter Service, Chief, Revenue Marine Division
8. 1895–1905 Capt. Charles F. Shoemaker, USRCS, Chief, Revenue Marine Division
9. 1905–1911 Capt. Worth G. Ross, USRCS, Captain-Commandant. The office of Captain-Commandant was first created in 1908. Ross is therefore the first officer to hold that office and the official title of "Captain-Commandant." Yet Coast Guard historians have referred to Capt. Alexander Fraser (USRM) as "captain-commandant" and chief of the USRM (1843–1848), even though Fraser did not officially receive the captain-commandant title.
10. 1911–1919 Commodore Ellsworth P. Bertholf, Captain-Commandant; Chief, Division of the U.S. Revenue Cutter Service. In 1915 the USRCS became the United States Coast Guard.

11. 1919–1924 Rear Adm. William E. Reynolds, Captain Commandant, and then Rear Admiral-Commandant. Reappointed Commandant on 12 January 1923 with the rank of Rear Admiral, effective 2 October 1923. Adm. Reynolds was the first USCG officer to attain the rank of Rear Admiral.
12. 1924–1932 Rear Adm. Frederick C. Billard
13. 1932–1936 Rear Adm. Harry G. Hamlet
14. 1936–1946 Adm. Russell R. Waesche. Appointed Commandant as Rear Admiral, and full Admiral on 4 April 1945. The first USCG officer to hold ranks of Vice Admiral and Admiral.
15. 1946–1950 Adm. Joseph F. Farley
16. 1950–1954 Vice Adm. Merlin O'Neill
17. 1954–1962 Adm. Alfred C. Richmond. Appointed Commandant as Vice Admiral. Appointed Admiral on 1 June 1960 by act of 14 May 1960, Public Law 86–474, under which all USCG Commandants would thereafter automatically become Admirals.
18. 1962–1966 Adm. Edwin J. Roland
19. 1966–1970 Adm. Willard J. Smith
20. 1970–1974 Adm. Chester R. Bender
21. 1974–1978 Adm. Owen W. Siler
22. 1978–1982 Adm. John B. Hayes
23. 1982–1986 Adm. James S. Gracey
24. 1986–1990 Adm. Paul A. Yost, Jr.
25. 1990–1994 Adm. J. William Kime
26. 1994–1998 Adm. Robert E. Kramek
27. 1998–2002 Adm. James M. Loy
28. 2002–2006 Adm. Thomas H. Collins
29. 2006–2010 Adm. Thad W. Allen
30. 2010–2014 Adm. Robert J. Papp, Jr.
31. 2014– Adm. Paul Zukunft

Source: U.S. Department of Homeland Security/United States Coast Guard

Chapter Notes

Chapter 1

1. Thomas P. Ostrom, *The United States Coast Guard in World War II* (Jefferson, NC: McFarland, 2009), 1, 5, 9; *The United States Coast Guard in National Defense* (Jefferson, NC: McFarland, 2012), 1–6, 12.
2. "Commandants of the U.S. Coast Guard and Chiefs of the Revenue Marine Division," U.S. Department of Homeland Security, United States Coast Guard, http://www.uscg.mil/history/FAQS/comm.asp (accessed October 30, 2011).
3. "United States Revenue Cutter Service," Wikipedia, http://en.wikipedia.org/wiki/United_States_Revenue_Cutter_Service (accessed December 19, 2011).
4. Ibid.
5. "Eighteenth, Nineteenth and Early Twentieth Century Revenue Cutters: A Historic Image Gallery," U.S. Department of Homeland Security and the United States Coast Guard, 1, http://www.uscg.mil/history/webcutters/USRC_Photo_Index.asp.
6. Ibid., 5–7.
7. Ibid., 9, 10.
8. Ibid., 13.
9. "Founders of the U.S. Coast Guard: Creation of U.S. Revenue Marine, August 4, 1790," 2, Naval History Blog: U.S. Naval Institute, Naval History and Heritage Command, http://www.navalhistory.org/2011/08/04/founders_of-the-u-s-coast-guard.
10. Ibid., 2–3.
11. "Alexander Hamilton," United States History, 1–2, http://www.u-s-history.com/pages/h367.html.
12. Larry Schweikert and Michael Allen, *A Patriot's History of the United States: From Columbus's Great Discovery to the War on Terror* (New York: Penguin, 2004; Sentinel 2007), 123.
13. "United States Revenue Cutter Service," Wikipedia, The War of 1812, http://en.wikipedia.org/wiki/United-States-Revenue-Cutter-Service (accessed 10/30/11).
14. "Counter Piracy Operations," ibid.
15. "The Mexican-American War," ibid.
16. "The Civil War," ibid.
17. "The Spanish American War," ibid.
18. "Formation of the Coast Guard," ibid.

Chapter 2

1. Truman R. Strobridge, "Chronology of Aids to Navigation and the United States Lighthouse Service: 1716–1939," Public Affairs Division, United States Coast Guard, 1974, 1–35, U.S. Department of Homeland Security, United States Coast Guard, 1–35, http://www.uscg.mil/history/articles/h_USLHScrhon.asp (accessed January 28, 2012).
2. Ibid., 3–6.
3. Ibid., 6–19.
4. Ibid., 19–35.
5. Ibid.
6. Ibid., 19–34.
7. Ibid., 34.
8. Ibid., 34–35.
9. "The United States Lighthouse Service: Lighthouses, A Brief Administrative History," 1–8, http://www.michiganlights.com/lighthouseservice.htm (Revised: June 15, 2011; accessed January 28, 2012). The Michigan Lighthouse Conservancy is a nonprofit corporation that links to historical preservation groups. The conservancy records the history of the United States Life-Saving Service (USLSS) in Michigan, works to preserve life-saving stations located in the state, and credits the USLSS with saving thousands of

lives. The conservancy maintains an Endangered U.S. Life-Saving Station for Michigan and lists historic sites on Lake Michigan and Lake Superior.
 10. Ibid., 1.
 11. Ibid., 1–3.
 12. Ibid., 3–4.
 13. Ibid., 4–6.
 14. Ibid., 6–7.

Chapter 3

1. "Coast Guard Unit Duluth Honored," WDIO ABC Eyewitness News, Duluth, Minnesota, February 09, 2012, http://www.wdio.com/article/stories/S2490119.shtml?cat=11563 (accessed 2/10/12).
 2. "U.S. Life-Saving Service Heritage Association: Our Mission," http://uslifesavingservice.org/our-mission/ (accessed February 7, 2012). The association is a national nonprofit organization composed of dues paying members dedicated to writing the history of and preserving U.S. lifesaving, lifeboat, and lighthouse stations. It seeks to study the nation's maritime heritage and preserve the historic stations, boats, and equipment of the U.S. Coast Guard and its predecessor agencies. It publishes *Life Line* and *Wreck and Rescue*.
 3. "A Legacy: The United States Life-Saving Service," from "A History of the USLSS," on the website of the U.S. Life-Saving Service Heritage Association: "Informative History," by Dennis L. Noble, U.S. Life-Saving Service Heritage Association, "History of the USLSS," http://www.uslifesavingservice.org/history_of_the_uslss (accessed February 11, 2012). Dennis L. Noble, a retired Coast Guard senior chief, earned a Ph.D. in U.S. history from Purdue University. Noble is the author of several Coast Guard histories, including *That Others Might Live: The U.S. Life-Saving Service, 1878–1915* (Naval Institute Press, 1994).
 4. Ibid., 1.
 5. Ibid., 1–2.
 6. Ibid., 3–4.
 7. Ibid., 5–7.
 8. Ibid., 8.
 9. Thomas P. Ostrom, *The United States Coast Guard on the Great Lakes: A History* (Oakland, OR: Red Anvil/Elderberry Press, 2007), 27–29.
 10. Ibid., 30–33.
 11. Ibid. Author Tom Ostrom is indebted to Laura Jacobs, the curator of the Lake Superior Maritime Collections Archives in the Jim Dan Hill Library at the University of Wisconsin–Superior. UW–S staff member Al Miller, former journalist, maritime author, and public affairs department employee, was helpful with his guidance and expertise. Duluth Public Library reference librarian David Ouse and his colleagues directed the author to and through the valuable Coast Guard and Lake Superior collection of articles and photographs.
 12. Ibid., 27, 80–83, 87, 89–91.
 13. Ibid., 55.
 14. Ibid., 55–56.
 15. Ibid., 56.
 16. Ibid., 56–57.
 17. Ibid., 58.
 18. Ibid., 57.
 19. Ibid. Maritime writer and author Konnie LeMay is the editor of *Lake Superior Magazine*. LeMay's riveting description of the *Mataafa* tragedy is titled "For Those in Peril on the Sea." The article was published in *Lake Superior Magazine*, October-November 2005, 16–23.
 20. Dennis L. Noble, *That Others Might Live: The U.S. Life-Saving Service, 1878–1915* (Annapolis, MD: Naval Institute Press, 1994), 51.
 21. Ibid., 52–54.
 22. Ibid., 54.

Chapter 4

1. "Commandant of the Coast Guard," eNotes.com Reference, http://www.enotes.com/topic/Commandant_of_the_Coast_Guard (accessed October 30, 2011).
 2. "Captain-Commandant Alexander V. Fraser, USRCS," U.S. Department of Homeland Security and the United States Coast Guard, http://www.uscg.mil/history/people/FraserAlexander.asp (accessed October 30, 2011).
 3. Ibid.
 4. Ibid.
 5. Ibid.
 6. H.R. Kaplan and Lt. Cmdr. James F. Hunt, *This is the Coast Guard* (Cambridge, MD: Cornell Maritime Press, 1972), 13–18.
 7. Robert Erwin Johnson, *Guardians of the Sea: History of the United States Coast Guard, 1915 to the Present.* (Annapolis, MD: Naval Institute Press, 1987), 16.
 8. Howard V.L. Bloomfield, *The Compact History of the United States Coast Guard* (New York: Hawthorn Books, 1966), 39–45.
 9. Stephen H. Evans, *The United States Coast Guard, 1790–1915: A Definitive History* (Annapolis, MD: Naval Institute Press, 1949), 32–33.
 10. Ibid., 33–34. The evolution and chronology of the official designations of the

terms "U.S. Revenue Marine" and "U.S. Revenue Cutter Service" are disputed among maritime historians, but it is noteworthy that Lt. Fraser signed a letter of request for a cutter command dated March 8, 1838, as "Alex V. Fraser, U.S. Rev. Cutter Service" (Evans, p. 32).
11. Ibid., 36.
12. Ibid., 36–37.
13. Ibid., 64–75, 80.
14. Robert Erwin Johnson, *Guardians*, 16.
15. Ibid.
16. Evans, *A Definitive History*, 92–103.
17. Bloomfield, *Compact History*, 65–67.
18. "Sumner Increase Kimball," U.S. Department of Homeland Security and the United States Coast Guard, 1–3, http://www.uscg.mil/history/people/Sumner_Kimball.asp (accessed October 30, 2011).
19. Johnson, *Guardians*, 6–7.
20. Evans, *Definitive History*, 99–100.
21. Ibid., 102–103.
22. Ibid., 103–104.
23. "Capt. L.G. Shepard's Appointment by Secretary Windom," *The New York Times*, December 17, 1889.
24. Ibid.
25. Ibid.
26. "The Revenue Cutter Service: Mr. Sherman's Plan for Keeping It Under Control of the Treasury," Letter to the Editor, *The New York Times*, September 14, 1890.
27. Ibid.
28. "John G. Carlisle," NNDB (Notable Names Data Base), http://www.nndb.com/people/428/000209798/Bibliography/ (accessed January 21, 2012).
29. "Peter Bonnett's Ambition: Desire for a Place Has Led Him to Meddle with Mr. Carlisle's Affairs," *The New York Times*, June 10, 1894.

Chapter 5

1. "Leonard G. Sheppard, USRCS," U.S. Department of Homeland Security and United States Coast Guard, http://www.uscg.mil/history/people/LGShepardBio.asp (accessed October 30, 2011).
2. Stephen H. Evans, *The United States Coast Guard, 1790–1915: A Definitive History* (Annapolis, MD: United States Naval Institute, 1949), 152. The use of the names Revenue Marine and Revenue Cutter Service are chronologically troublesome and imprecise. Evans claims early legislation gave semi-official designations to the service. "Revenue Marine" was a popular phrase until the end of the 19th century. Evans contends that Congress first officially referred to the "Revenue Cutter Service" in 1863, a phrase in general use by 1890, until replaced, Evans concluded, by "Coast Guard" in 1915 (p. 7).
3. Ibid., 155–157.
4. Howard V.L. Bloomfield, *The Compact History of the United States Coast Guard* (New York: Hawthorn Books, 1966), 99.
5. Ibid., 100–101.
6. Truman R. Strobridge and Dennis L. Noble, *Alaska and the U.S. Revenue Cutter Service, 1867–1915* (Annapolis, MD: Naval Institute Press, 1999).
7. Ibid., 49–55.
8. Irving H. King, *The Coast Guard Expands, 1865–1915: New Roles, New Frontiers* (Annapolis, MD: Naval Institute Press, 1996), 72–81.
9. "Charles F. Shoemaker, USRCS," U.S. Department of Homeland Security and United States Coast Guard, http://www.uscg.mil/history/people/CFShoemakerBio.asp (accessed October 30, 2011).
10. Ibid.
11. Evans, *Coast Guard*, 158–159.
12. Ibid., 160–164.
13. Bloomfield, *Compact History*, 267.
14. Robert Erwin Johnson, *Guardians of the Sea: The United States Coast Guard, 1915 to the Present* (Annapolis, MD: U.S. Naval Institute, 1987), 15.
15. Strobridge and Noble, *Alaska and Revenue Cutter Service*, 114.
16. Ibid., 161–181.
17. King, *Coast Guard Expands*, 77–78.
18. Ibid., 80.
19. Evans, 184, 198–199.
20. "Worth G. Ross, USRCS," U.S. Department of Homeland Security and United States Coast Guard, http://www.uscg.mil/history/people/WGRossBio.asp (accessed October 30, 2011).
21. Strobride and Noble, *Alaska*, 109.
22. Ibid., 115.
23. King, *Coast Guard Expands*, 126, 131–132.
24. Ibid., 158–161.
25. Ibid., 223–225.

Chapter 6

1. "Ellsworth P. Bertholf, USRCS/USCG," U.S. Department of Homeland Security, and United States Coast Guard, http://www.uscg.mil/history/people/EPBertholfBio.asp (accessed October 10, 2011).
2. Ibid.
3. Ibid.
4. Ibid.
5. Steven H. Evans, *The United States Coast Guard, 1790–1915* (Annapolis, MD: United States Naval Institute, 1949), 134–139.

6. David Helvarg, *Rescue Warriors: The U.S. Coast Guard, America's Forgotten Heroes* (New York: Thomas Dunne Books, St. Martin's Press, 2009), 73.
7. Ibid., 73–74.
8. Ibid., 74–75.
9. Ibid., 256. U.S. Coast Guard Historian's Office.
10. C. Douglas Kroll, *A Coast Guardsman's History of the U.S. Coast Guard* (Annapolis, MD: Naval Institute Press, 2010), 4.
11. Ibid., 4–5.
12. Ibid., 55–57.
13. Irving H. King, *The Coast Guard Expands, 1865–1915* (Annapolis, MD: Naval Institute Press, 1996), 225.
14. Ibid., 240–241.
15. Ibid., 147–149.
16. Ibid., 149–150.
17. Ibid., 150–153.
18. Ibid., 153.
19. C. Douglas Kroll, *Commodore Ellsworth Bertholf: First Commandant of the Coast Guard* (Annapolis, MD: Naval Institute Press, 2002), 4–27.
20. Ibid., 28–32.
21. Ibid., 71–82.
22. Ibid., 82–88.
23. Ibid., 112–129.
24. Ibid., 128–135. Bertholf had been issued the temporary rank of commodore during the World War I Coast Guard–Navy partnership. But upon retirement, Bertholf was designated and compensated at his previous rank of captain-commandant (Kroll, p. 123).

Chapter 7

1. "William E. Reynolds, USCG," U.S. Department of Homeland Security and United States Coast Guard, http://www.uscg.mil/history/people/WReynoldsBio.asp (accessed October 30, 2011).
2. Alex R. Larzelere, *The Coast Guard in World War I* (Annapolis, MD: Naval Institute Press, 2003), 221.
3. Thomas P. Ostrom, *The United States Coast Guard and National Defense: A History from World War I to the Present* (Jefferson, NC: McFarland, 2012), 18.
4. Ibid., 198.
5. Truman R. Strobridge and Dennis Noble, *Alaska and the U.S. Revenue Cutter Service, 1867–1915* (Annapolis, MD: Naval Institute Press, 2009), 128.
6. Ibid., 168, 174.
7. Robert Erwin Johnson, *Guardians of the Sea: History of the United States Coast Guard, 1915 to the Present* (Annapolis, MD: Naval Institute Press, 1987), 63.

8. "Frederick Billard, USCG," U.S Department of Homeland Security and the United States Coast Guard, http://www.uscg.mil/history/people/FCBillardBio.asp (accessed October30, 2011).
9. Ibid.
10. Larzelere, *World War I*, 93, 123.
11. C. Douglas Kroll, *A Coast Guardsman's History of the U.S. Coast Guard* (Annapolis, MD: Naval Institute Press, 2010), 145.
12. Ibid., 143.
13. David Helvarg, *Rescue Warriors: The U.S. Coast Guard, America's Forgotten Heroes* (New York: Thomas Dunne Books, St. Martin's Press, 2009), 119–120.
14. H.R. Kaplan and Lt. Cmdr. H.R. Hunt, *This is the Coast Guard* (Cambridge, MD: Cornell Maritime Press, 1972), 49–55.
15. R.E. Johnson, *Guardians of the Sea*, 108–126.
16. "Harry Hamlet USCG," U.S. Department of Homeland Security and United States Coast Guard, http://www.uscg.mil/history/people/HGHamletBioasp (accessed October 30, 2011).
17. Ibid.
18. C. Douglas Kroll, *Coast Guardsman's History*, 151–152.
19. Ibid., 152–153.
20. R.E. Johnson, *Guardians of the Sea*, 127–128.
21. Ibid., 129–130.
22. Larzelere, *Coast Guard in World War I*, 106–110.
23. Ibid., 110.
24. Ibid., 230.

Chapter 8

1. Russell R. Waesche, Sr., U.S. Department of Homeland Security and United States Coast Guard, http://www.uscg.mil/history/people/RRWaescheSRBio.asp (accessed October 30, 2011).
2. Ibid.
3. Ibid.
4. Ibid.
5. Ibid.
6. David Helvarg, *Rescue Warriors: The U.S. Coast Guard, America's Forgotten Heroes* (New York: Thomas Dunne Books/St. Martin's Press, 2009), 178–179.
7. Ibid., 255–256.
8. Alex R. Larzelere, *The Coast Guard in World War I* (Annapolis, MD: Naval Institute Press, 2003), 231–232. An interesting perspective on Coast Guard duties on Atlantic merchant escort patrols in World War I was written by Cmdr. Stephen Surko, USN (Ret.): "At Sea in the Great War," in *Naval History,*

August 2012 (pp. 55–59). Cmdr. Surko based his article on the letters and photographs of his grandfather, Frederick R Foulkes (USCG), a petty officer on the USS *Manning* on the Atlantic Patrol. Foulkes photographed and described heavy seas, watches, berthing, galley food, abandon ship procedures, and his battle station on the cutter in a machine gun crew. Cmdr. Surko concluded the article with the revelation that his grandfather was called back to duty in World War II and served as a first mate on Liberty and Victory transport ships with the U.S. Merchant Marine.
   9. C. Douglas Kroll, *A Coast Guardsman's History of the U.S. Coast Guard* (Annapolis, MD: Naval Institute Press, 2010), 5–7.
   10. Ibid., 7–9.
   11. Ibid., 107–109.
   12. Robert Erwin Johnson, *Guardians of the Sea: History of the United States Coast Guard, 1915 to the Present* (Annapolis, MD: Naval Institute Press, 1987). Johnson chronicled his service in the World War II Coast Guard in his book *Bering Sea Escort: Life Aboard a Coast Guard Cutter in World War II* (Naval Institute Press, 1992).
   13. Ibid., 149–151.
   14. Ibid., 159–160.
   15. Ibid., 153–154.
   16. Ibid., 154.
   17. Ibid., 166–167.
   18. Ibid., 167.
   19. Ibid., 167–168.
   20. Ibid., 173–206.
   21. Ibid., 220–222.
   22. Ibid., 240–260.
   23. Ibid., 254–255.
   24. Thomas P. Ostrom, *The United States Coast Guard in World War II: A History of Domestic and Overseas Actions* (Jefferson, NC: McFarland, 2009), vii–viii.
   25. Ibid., 1.
   26. Ibid.
   27. Ibid., 62, 65.
   28. Thomas P. Ostrom, *The United States Coast Guard and National Defense: A History from World War I to the Present* (Jefferson, NC: McFarland, 2012), 198–199.
   29. Ibid., 2. Cmdr. Gary M. Thomas commanded the LORAN Support Unit in Wildwood, New Jersey, and was the commanding officer of the USCGR *Padre*. Cmdr. Thomas has also served as the executive director of the Foundation for Coast Guard history.
   30. Malcolm F. Willoughby, *The United States Coast Guard in World War II* (Annapolis, MD: Naval Institute Press, 1957/1989), vii.
   31. Ibid.
   32. Ibid., xi–xii.
   33. Ibid., ix.
   34. Ibid.
   35. "Rear Adm. Russell R. Waesche, Jr. USCG (Ret.)," Biographical Sketch, Public Affairs Division, U.S. Coast Guard Headquarters, Washington, D.C. (accessed January 2, 2013).

Chapter 9

   1. "John H. Farley, 1946–1949," U.S. Department of Homeland Security and United States Coast Guard, http://www.uscg.mil/history/people/JFFarleyBio.asp (accessed October 30, 2011).
   2. Ibid.
   3. Ibid.
   4. Ibid.
   5. C. Douglas Kroll, *A Coast Guardsmen's History of the U.S. Coast Guard* (Annapolis, MD: Naval Institute Press, 2010), 8.
   6. Robert Erwin Johnson, *Guardians of the Sea: History of the United States Coast Guard, 1915 to the Present* (Annapolis, MD: Naval Institute Press, 1987), 262–263.
   7. Ibid., 293–294.
   8. Ibid., 296.
   9. "Merlin O'Neill, USCG," U.S. Department of Homeland Security and United States Coast Guard, http://www.uscg.mil/history/people/MONeillBio.asp (accessed October 30, 2011).
   10. Ibid.
   11. Ibid.
   12. Ibid.
   13. Malcolm F. Willoughby, *The U.S. Coast Guard in World War II* (Annapolis, MD: Naval Institute Press, 1957, 1989), 208, 214, 223.
   14. Ibid., 268, 276.
   15. "Merlin O'Neill, USCG."
   16. Ibid.
   17. Ibid.
   18. Thomas P. Ostrom, *The United States Coast Guard and National Defense* (Jefferson, NC: McFarland, 2012), 36–41.
   19. "Merlin O'Neill, USCG."
   20. Ibid.
   21. Robert Erwin Johnson, *Guardians of the Sea*, 291–294.
   22. "Commandants of the U.S. Coast Guard: Alfred C. Richmond," U.S. Department of Homeland Security and U.S. Coast Guard, http://www.uscg.mil/history/people/ACRichmondBio.asp (accessed October 30, 2011).
   23. Ibid.
   24. Ibid.
   25. Ibid.
   26. Ibid.
   27. Ostrom, *The Coast Guard and National Defense*, 200.

28. Robert Erwin Johnson, *Bering Sea Escort: Life Aboard a Coast Guard Cutter in World War II* (Annapolis, MD: Naval Institute Press, 1992), 72–76, 81.
29. Willoughby, *The Coast Guard in World War II*, vii.
30. Ibid.
31. Ibid.
32. R.E. Johnson, *Guardians of the Sea*, 295–296.
33. Ibid., 328–330.
34. Ibid., 306–308.
35. Ibid., 319.

Chapter 10

1. "Edwin J. Roland, USCG," U.S. Department of Homeland Security and United States Coast Guard, http://www.uscg.mil/history/people/EJRolandBio.asp (accessed October 30, 2011).
2. Ibid.
3. Ibid.
4. Ibid.
5. Ibid.
6. David Helvarg, *"Rescue Warriors: The U.S. Coast Guard, America's Forgotten Heroes* (New York: Thomas Dunne Books, St. Martin's Press, 2009), 135–136.
7. Paul C. Scotti, *Coast Guard Action in Vietnam* (Central Point Oregon: Hellgate Press, 2000), 6.
8. Alex Larzelere, *The Coast Guard at War: Vietnam, 1965–1975* (Annapolis, MD: Naval Institute Press, 1997), 22, 72–73, 154–155, 193.
9. Thomas P. Ostrom, *The United States Coast Guard and National Defense: A History from World War I to the Present* (Jefferson, NC: McFarland, 2012), 200–201.
10. Robert Erwin Johnson, *Guardians of the Sea: History of the United States Coast Guard, 1915 to the Present* (Annapolis, MD: Naval Institute Press, 1987), 340–342.
11. "Willard J. Smith," U.S. Department of Homeland Security and United States Coast Guard, http://www.uscg.mil/history/people/WJSmithBio.asp (accessed October 30, 2011).
12. Ibid.
13. Ibid.
14. Ibid.
15. Larzelere, *The Coast Guard at War: Vietnam*, 124–125, 141–142, 244–245.
16. "Chester R. Bender, USCG," U.S. Department of Homeland Security and United States Coast Guard, http://www.uscg.mil/history/people/CRBenderBio.asp (accessed October 30, 2011).
17. Ibid.
18. Ibid.
19. R.E. Johnson, *Guardians of the Sea*, 345–346.
20. "Owen W. Siler, USCG," U.S. Department of Homeland Security and United States Coast Guard, http://www.uscg.mil/history/people/OWSilerBio.asp (accessed October 30, 2011).
21. Ibid.
22. Ibid.
23. Ibid.
24. Ibid.
25. Ibid.
26. "John B. Hayes, USCG," U.S. Department of Homeland Security and United States Coast Guard, http://www.uscg.mikl/history/people/JBHayesBio.asp (accessed October 30, 2011).
27. Ibid.
28. Michael Mansker, "Hayes, Adm. John Briggs, USCG (Ret.)," U.S. Coast Guard Oral History Program, *The Reminiscences of Admiral John Briggs Hayes*. Interview by Lt. (JG) Michael Mansker, USCG, 1985.
29. Ibid.

Chapter 11

1. "James S. Grace, USCG," U.S. Department of Homeland Security and United States Coast Guard, http://www.uscg.mil/history/people/JSGraceyBio.asp (accessed October 30, 2011).
2. Ibid.
3. Ibid.
4. Thomas P. Ostrom, *The United States Coast Guard and National Defense: A History from World War I to the Present* (Jefferson, NC: McFarland, 2012), 202.
5. Robert Erwin Johnson, *Guardians of the Sea: History of the United States Coast Guard, 1915 to the Present* (Annapolis, MD: Naval Institute Press, 1987), 355.
6. Ibid.
7. "Paul A. Yost, Jr., USCG," U.S. Department of Homeland Security and United States Coast Guard, http://www.uscg.mil/history/people/PAYostBio.asp (accessed October 30, 2011).
8. Malcolm F. Willoughby, *The U.S. Coast in World War II* (Annapolis, MD: Naval Institute Press, 1957/1989), v.
9. "Paul Yost, Jr., USCG."
10. Ibid.
11. Ibid.
12. David Helvarg, *Rescue Warriors: The U.S. Coast Guard, America's Forgotten Heroes* (New York: Thomas Dunne Books, St. Martin's Press, 2009), 136–137. The three future commandants who served in Southeast Asia during the Vietnam War were Paul

Yost, as mentioned above, Jim Loy, who did combat patrols on an 82-foot patrol boat and earned a Bronze Star, and Thad Allen, who commanded a LORAN Station in Thailand.
  13. Edward J. Marolda, *By Sea, Air, and Land: An Illustrated History of the U.S. Navy and the War in Southeast Asia* (Washington, D.C.: Naval Historical Center. 1994), 276–277.
  14. Alex Larzelere, *The Coast Guard at War: Vietnam, 1965–1975* (Annapolis, MD: Naval Institute Press, 1997), 105–107.
  15. Ibid., 68.
  16. Ostrom, *The United States Coast Guard and National Defense*, 204.
  17. "J. William Kime, USCG," U.S. Department of Homeland Security and United States Coast Guard, http://www.uscg.mil/history/people/JWKimeBio.asp (accessed October 30, 2011).
  18. Ibid.
  19. Ostrom, *The Coast Guard and National Defense*, 204.
  20. Helvarg, *Rescue Warriors*, 120.
  21. Ibid., 308.

Chapter 12

  1. "Robert E. Kramer, USCG," U.S. Department of Homeland Security and United States Coast Guard, http://www.uscg.mil/history/people/REKramekBio.asp (accessed October 30, 2011).
  2. Ibid.
  3. Ibid.
  4. Ibid.
  5. Ibid.
  6. David Helvarg, *Rescue Warriors: The U.S. Coast Guard, America's Forgotten Heroes* (New York: Thomas Dunne Books, St. Martin's Press, 2009), 322.
  7. Thomas P. Ostrom, *The U.S. Coast Guard on the Great Lakes: A History* (Oakland, OR: Red Anvil/Elderberry Press, 2007), 114–115.
  8. Thomas P. Ostrom, *The United States Coast Guard and National Defense: A History from World War I to the Present* (Jefferson, NC: McFarland, 2012), 204–205.
  9. "James M. Loy, USCG," U.S. Department of Homeland Security and United States Coast Guard, http://www.uscg.mil/history/CCG/Loy/jmloy_bio.asp (accessed October 30, 2011).
  10. Ibid.
  11. Ibid.
  12. Ibid.
  13. Thomas P. Ostrom, *The United States Coast Guard on the Great Lakes: A History* (Oakland, OR.: Red Anvil/Elderberry Press, 2007), 50–51, 60.
  14. Helving, *Rescue Warriors*, 137.
  15. Ibid., 79.
  16. Ibid., 259.
  17. Ibid.
  18. Ibid., 262–263.
  19. Ostrom, *The United States Coast Guard and National Defense*, 107–108.
  20. Ibid., 108.
  21. Ibid., 160–161.
  22. Ibid., 90.
  23. Donald T. Phillips and Adm. James M. Loy, *Character in Action: The U.S. Coast Guard on Leadership* (Annapolis, MD: Naval Institute Press, 2003), 160, 164–165.
  24. Ostrom, *The United States Coast Guard and National Defense*, 206.
  25. Phillips and Loy, *Character in Action*, 25, 33, 41, 57, 65, 91, 98, 111, 120, 139, 149.

Chapter 13

  1. "Admiral Thomas H. Collins, Commandant, U.S. Coast Guard," United States Coast Guard and Coast Guard Historian's Office (accessed 1 November 2012).
  2. "Attack on America: September 11, 2001 and the U.S. Coast Guard," United States Coast Guard and the Department of Homeland Security, U.S. Coast Guard Oral History Program, Operation Noble Eagle Documentation Project, Interviewee: Vice Admiral Thomas H. Collins, USCG Vice Commandant, Interviewer: Peter Capelotti, U.S. Coast Guard Reserves, 24 April 2002, pp. 1–14 (accessed 5 November 2012).
  3. Ibid.
  4. Ibid., 5.
  5. Ibid., 6–7.
  6. Ibid., 11.
  7. Ibid., 13–14.
  8. Ibid., 14.
  9. "Same Coast Guard, New Team," Admiral Thomas H. Collins, Coast Guard Birthday Celebration with Secretary Tom Ridge, James Creek Marina. August 6, 2003, U.S. Coast Guard and Department of Homeland Security (accessed 5 November 2012).
  10. Ibid.
  11. Thomas P. Ostrom, *The United States Coast Guard on the Great Lakes: A History* (Oakland, OR: Elderberry/Red Anvil Press, 2007), 51.
  12. Tom Beard, Jose Hanson, Paul C. Scotti (editors), *The Coast Guard* (Seattle, WA: Foundation for Coast Guard History, 2004), 29, 338.
  13. Ibid., 357.
  14. Ibid.
  15. Ibid., 356.
  16. Ibid.

17. "Admiral Thomas H. Collins," *Homeland Security Magazine*, http://www.govexec.com/magazine-homeland-security (accessed November 12, 2012).
18. "Admiral Thomas H. Collins, Commandant, U.S. Coast Guard," Address to the U.S. Commission on Ocean Policy, 22 November 2002, Department of Homeland Security and United States Coast Guard (accessed November 5, 2012).
19. Ibid.
20. Ibid.

Chapter 14

1. "Admiral Thad W. Allen, USCG (Ret.)," U.S. Department of Homeland Security and United States Coast Guard, http://www.uscg.mil/history/allen/AllenTWindex.asp (accessed October 30, 2011).
2. Ibid.
3. Ibid.
4. "Remarks by Admiral Thad Allen, Commandant U.S. Coast Guard, to the DHS Fellows, New York City," Monday January 28, U.S. Department of Homeland Security and United States Coast Guard, pp. 1–22, U.S. Coast Guard History Program, Transcript by Federal News Service, Washington, D.C. (accessed November 7, 2012).
5. Ibid., 1–3.
6. Ibid., 3.
7. Ibid., 4.
8. Ibid., 8.
9. Ibid., 11–13.
10. Ibid., 20–21.
11. Christopher Lagan, "Admiral Allen Delivers State of the Coast Guard Address," *Coast Guard Compass*, February 13, 2010, http://coastguard.dodlive.mil/2010/02/admiral-allen-delivers-state-of-the-coast-guard-address/ (accessed November 7, 2012).
12. Ibid.
13. Ibid.
14. Christopher Lagan, "Excerpts from Adm. Allen's Speech to the Surface Naval Association," *Coast Guard Compass*, January 14, 2010, http://coastguard.dodlive.mil/2010/01/video-excerpts-from-adm-allens-speech-to-the-surface-naval-association/ (accessed November 7, 2012).
15. Thomas P. Ostrom, *The United States Coast Guard on the Great Lakes: A History* (Oakland, OR: Red Anvil/Elderberry Press, 2007), 126.
16. Information on the background of Lt. Jim Dolbow was obtained from the websites of the U.S. Naval Institute, Amazon.com, and Institute of World Politics.
17. Ostrom, *The U.S. Coast Guard on the Great Lakes*, 166.
18. Ibid., 166–167.
19. Capt. Alex Larzelere, USCG (Ret.), *The Coast Guard at War: Vietnam, 1965–1975* (Annapolis, MD: Naval Institute Press, 1997), 275–279.
20. Ibid., 279.
21. Thomas P. Ostrom, *The United States Coast Guard and National Defense: A History from World War I to the Present* (Jefferson, NC: McFarland, 2012), 207.
22. David Helvarg, *Rescue Warriors: The U.S. Coast Guard, America's Forgotten Heroes* (New York: Thomas Dunne Books/St. Martin's Press), 2009.
23. Ibid., 321.
24. Ibid., 322.
25. Ibid., 323–325.
26. Ostrom, *The U.S. Coast Guard and National Defense*, 208–209.
27. Helvarg, *Rescue Warriors*, 249–256.
28. Ibid., 265.
29. Ibid., 250–251.
30. Ibid., 269–270.
31. Ibid., 250.
32. Ibid., 276–277.

Chapter 15

1. Candus Thomson, "The Interview: Adm. Sally Brice-O'Hara," *The Baltimore Sun*, April 30, 2012, http://articles.baltimoresun.com/2012-04-30/business/bs-bz-coast-guard-admiral-20120428_1_coast-guard-robert-papp-law-enforcement-boardings (accessed July 29, 2012).
2. "Admiral Robert J. Papp, Jr., Commandant, U.S. Coast Guard," U.S. Department of Homeland Security and U.S. Coast Guard (accessed February 25, 2011).
3. Thomas P. Ostrom, *The United States Coast Guard on the Great Lakes: A History* (Oakland, OR: Red Anvil-Elderberry Press, 2007), 137–139.
4. Ibid., 164.
5. Thomas P. Ostrom, *The United States Coast Guard and National Defense: A History from World War I to the Present* (Jefferson, NC: McFarland, 2012), 172.
6. Ibid., 184.
7. Ibid., 186.
8. Ibid., 224.
9. Glynn Smith, "Admiral Papp Reviews Mission of Patrol Forces Southwest Asia, *Coast Guard Compass*, Official Blog of the U.S. Coast Guard, November 18, 2011, http://coastguard.dodlive.mil/2011/11/adm-papp-reviews-mission-of-patrol-forces-southwest-asia/ (accessed July 29, 2012).

10. Glynn Smith, "North Pacific Coast Guard Forum 2010," *Coast Guard Compass*, September 16, 2010, http://coastguard.dodlive.mil/2010/09/north-pacific-coast-guard-forum-2010-2/ (accessed November 7, 2012).

11. Connie Braesch, "A Conversation with the Commandant," *Coast Guard Compass*, September 27, 2010, http://coastguard.dodlive.mil/2010/09/a-conversation-with-the-commandant/ (accessed November 7, 2012).

12. Connie Braesch, "Admiral Papp, Secretary Napolitano Honor Coast Guard Veterans," *Coast Guard Compass*, November 11, 2010, http://coastguard.dodlive.mil/2010/11/adm-papp-secretary-napolitano-honor-coast-guard-veterans/ (accessed November 7, 2012).

13. Christopher Lagan, "Adm. Papp Delivers State of the Coast Guard Address," *Coast Guard Compass*, February 10, 2011, http://coastguard.dodlive.mil/2011/02/adm-bob-papp-delivers-state-of-the-coast-guard-address/ (accessed November 7, 2011).

14. Glynn Smith, "Recapitalizing and Building Capacity: The National Security Cutters," *Coast Guard Compass*, February 22, 2011, http://coastguard.dodlive.mil/2011/02/recapitalizing-and-building-capacity-the-national-security-cutters/ (accessed November 7, 2012).

15. "Testimony of Admiral Robert J. Papp, Jr., Commandant, U.S. Coast Guard, Coast Guard Fiscal Year 2012 Budget Request Before the House Subcommittee on Coast Guard and Marine Transportation, March 2011," U.S. Department of Homeland Security and United States Coast Guard and Commandant United States Coast Guard (accessed November 7, 2012).

16. "Defending U.S. Economic Interests in the Changing Arctic: Is There a Strategy?" United States Senate Committee on Commerce, Science, and Transportation Subcommittee on Oceans, Atmosphere, Fisheries, and Coast Guard, July 27, 2011, Witness: Admiral Robert J. Papp, Jr., Commandant, U.S. Coast Guard (accessed November 7, 2012).

17. Ibid.
18. Ibid.
19. Ibid.

20. Glynn Smith, "Admiral Papp Focused on Counter-Piracy, Arctic at IMO Assembly," *Coast Guard Compass*, November 23, 2011, http://coastguard.dodlive.mil/2011/11/adm-papp-focused-on-counter-piracy-arctic-at-imo-assembly/ (accessed November 7, 2012).

21. Stephanie Young, "Honoring Our Profession: The Long Blue Line," *Coast Guard Compass*, January 6, 2012, http://coastguard.dodlive.mil/2012/01/honoring-our-profession-the-long-blue-line/ (accessed November 7, 2012).

22. Ibid.

23. Glynn Smith, "Adm. Papp Delivers Second State of the Coast Guard Address," *Coast Guard Compass*, February 23, 2012, http://coastguard.dodlive.mil/2012/02/adm-papp-delivers-second-state-of-the-coast-guard-address/ (accessed November 7, 2012).

24. Carl Nolte, "Coast Guard Commandant, 3 New Cutters in Alameda," *San Francisco Chronicle*, February 25, 2012, http://www.sfgate.com/bayarea/article/Coast-Guard-commandant-3-new-cutters-in-Alameda-3360326.php (accessed February 25, 2012).

25. Ibid.
26. Ibid.

27. Glynn Smith, "Dedicating a New Generation of Patrol Boat," *Coast Guard Compass*, March 2, 2012, http://coastguard.dodlive.mil/2012/03/dedicating-a-new-generation-patrol-boat/ (accessed November 7, 2012).

28. "Coast Guard Commandant Admiral Bob Papp's Remarks at the *Bernard C. Webber* Commissioning Ceremony," April 14, 2012, United States Department of Homeland Security and United States Coast Guard (accessed November 7, 2012).

29. Ibid.
30. Ibid.

31. "Testimony of Admiral Robert Papp, Commandant, U.S. Coast Guard on Accession to the 1982 Law of the Sea Convention Before the Senate Committee on Foreign Relations," June 14, 2012, U.S. Department of Homeland Security and United States Coast Guard and Commandant United States Coast Guard (accessed November 7, 2012).

32. Ibid.
33. Ibid.
34. Ibid.

35. "Written Testimony of U.S. Coast Guard Commandant Admiral Robert Papp, Jr. for a Senate Committee on Appropriations, Subcommittee on Homeland Security Field Hearing Titled 'U.S. Coast Guard Operations in Alaska,'" U.S. Coast Guard Air Station Kodiak, Kodiak, Alaska, August 6, 2012, U.S. Department of Homeland Security, http://www.dhs.gov/es/news/2012/08/06/written-testimony-us-coast-guard-commandant-admiral-robert-papp-jr-senate-committee (accessed November 7, 2012).

36. Ibid.
37. Ibid.

38. Dan Joling, Associated Press, "Admiral Confident in Coast Guard Arctic Readiness," *Alaska Journal of Commerce*, August 9, 2012, http://www.alaskajournal.com/Alaska-Jour

nal-of-Commerce/August-Issue-1–2012/Admiral-confident-in-Coast-Guard-Arctic-readiness/ (accessed August 9, 2012).

39. Robert J. Papp, Jr., "Proficiency: The Essence of Discipline," *Proceedings*, August 2012, 16–21.

40. Ibid.

41. Ibid., 17.

42. Ibid., 21.

43. "U.S. Coast Guard Member Killed in Crash off California Coast," Associated Press and Fox News, December 03, 2012, http://www.foxnews.com/us/2012/12/02/us-coast-guard-member-killed-in-crash-california-coast/ (accessed December 3, 2012).

44. "Coast Guard Commandant Admiral Bob Papp's Remarks at the Navy Memorial Fantail Breakfast," Navy Memorial, Washington, D.C., Wednesday August 29, 2012, Department of Homeland Security and United States Coast Guard (accessed November 7, 2012).

45. Ibid.

46. "Huntington Ingalls Industries," http://www.huntingtoningalls.com/ (accessed December 11, 2012).

47. "Ingalls Shipbuilding," http://shipbuildinghistory.com/history/shipyards/1major.htm (accessed December 11, 2012).

48. "Coast Guard Commandant Admiral Bob Papp's Remarks at the Keel Authentication Ceremony at Pascagoula, Mississippi, September 5, 2012," U.S. Department of Homeland Security and United States Coast Guard (accessed November 7, 2012).

49. "Seaman Apprentice William R. Flores, USCG," U.S. Department of Homeland Security and United States Coast Guard, http://www.uscg.mil/history/people/Flores.asp (accessed December 12, 2012).

50. "Coast Guard Commandant Admiral Bob Papp's Remarks at the *William Flores* Commissioning," St. Petersburg, Florida, November 3, 2012, U.S. Department of Homeland Security and United States Coast Guard (accessed November 7, 2012).

51. "Fast Response Cutter," Acquisition Directorate, United States Coast Guard, July 2012, http://www.uscg.mil/acquisition/sentinel/ (accessed December 12, 2012).

52. Ibid.

53. Commandant Papp's Remarks at the *Flores* Commissioning.

54. Ibid.

55. Cmdr. Glynn Smith, "Admiral Papp Addresses Surface Naval Community," *Coast Guard Compass*, January 13, 2012, http://coastguard.dodlive.mil/2012/01/adm-papp-addresses-surface-naval-community/ (accessed November 7, 2012).

56. Mickey McCarter, "Coast Guard Seeking Sources for Routine Repairs for Heavy Icebreaker, Set to Return to Duty," *Homeland Security Today*, December 10, 2012, http://www.hstoday.us/briefings/industry-news/single-article/coast-guard-proposes-long-awaited-rule-for-twic-readers/3ab28f831c1f42c2e43bae42dd1c8326.html (accessed December 11, 2012).

57. "U.S. Coast Guard Cutter *Polar Star* History," U.S. Department of Homeland Security and United States Coast Guard, http://www.uscg.mil/pacarea/cgcpolarstar/history.asp (accessed December 15, 2012).

58. Rick Wester, posted by Christopher Lagan, "Adm. Papp Visits International Partners in Malta," *Coast Guard Compass*, November 26, 2012, http://coastguard.dodlive.mil/2012/11/adm-papp-visits-international-partners-in-malta/ (accessed November 27, 2012).

59. "Commandant of U.S. Coast Guard Visits Singapore Under MPA Program," *Singapore News*, 26 November 2012, http://www.channelnewsasia.com/stories/singaporelocalnews/view/1239454/1/.html (accessed November 27, 2012).

60. Cmdr. Rick Wester, posted by Christopher Lagan, "Adm. Papp Spends Thanksgiving in Bahrain with Coast Guardsmen, Meets with U.S. and Bahraini Officials," *Coast Guard Compass*, November 27, 2012, http://coastguard.dodlive.mil/2012/11/adm-papp-spends-thanksgiving-in-bahrain-with-coast-guardsmen-meets-with-u-s-and-bahraini-officials/ (accessed November 27, 2012).

61. "Chief Boatswain's Mate Dies in Pursuit of Alleged Drug Boat," *Navy Times* and Associated Press, December 17, 2012, p. 28.

62. "Coast Guard Commandant Admiral Robert J. Papp's Remarks at the Memorial Service for BMCS Terrell Horne III," Coast Guard Base Los Angeles/Long Beach, California, 8 December 2012, U.S. Department of Homeland Security and United States Coast Guard (accessed December 14, 2012).

63. Ibid.

64. "Coast Guard Vice Commandant Vice Admiral John P. Currier's Remarks at the Veterans Day Coast Guard Wreath Laying Ceremony," Arlington National Cemetery, Arlington, Virginia, November 11, 2012, U.S. Department of Homeland Security and United States Coast Guard (accessed November 17, 2012).

65. "Coast Guard Reactivates Seattle-based Icebreaker," Tacoma *News Tribune* and Associated Press, December 15, 2012, http://www.thenewstribune.com/2012/12/15/2403568/coast-guard (accessed November 16, 2012).

Notes—Chapter 15

66. Jacqueline Klimas, "Papp Talks Overseas Manning," *Military/Navy Times*, December 24, 2012, p. 20.
67. Ibid.
68. Ibid.
69. Melodie Warner, "U.S. Coast Guard Notes Safety and Propulsion Deficiencies on Arctic-Bound Drillship," *gCaptain*, Germanischer Lloyd (GL), Dow Jones, December 27, 2012, http://gcaptain.com/coast-guard-notes-safety-propulsion/ (accessed December 28, 2012). *gCaptain* is a maritime and offshore news website.
70. Jill Burke, "Coast Guard Cutter Comes to Aid of Troubled Shell Ship, Drilling Rig," *Alaska Dispatch*, December 28, 2012, http://www.adn.com/article/coast-guard-cutter-comes-aid-troubled-shell-ship-drilling-rig (accessed December 29, 2012).
71. Kim Murphy, "Coast Guard Evacuates Crew of Troubled Oil Drilling Barge," *Los Angeles Times*, December 29, 2012, http://articles.latimes.com/2012/dec/29/nation/la-na-nn-shell-oil-drilling-20121229 (accessed December 29, 2012).
72. "Coast Guard Helps Disabled Ship, Barge." United Press International, December 30, 2012. http://www.upi.com/Top_News/US/2012/12/30/Coast-Guard-helps-disabled-ship-barge/UPI-34421356852863/ (accessed December 30, 2012).
73. Brianna Gibbs, "The USCG Wants You," KMXT 100.1 FM Public Radio, Kodiak Island, Alaska, December 26, 2012. http://www.kmxt.org/index2.php?option=com_content&do_pdf=1&id=4348 (accessed December 29, 2012).
74. "Admiral Robert Papp, Commandant, Coast Guard." *Navy Times*, December 24, 2012, p. 24.

Bibliography

Archival Sources

National Archives, Washington, D.C.: Documents of Admiral Russell R. Waesche, World War II Commandant, United States Coast Guard; and the commandant's son, Rear Adm. R.R. Waesche, Jr., Record Group Records of the United States Coast Guard, Entry 85, Office of the Commandant, Instructions and Notices, 1940–1979 (accessed January 16, 2013).

United States Coast Guard, Office of the Coast Guard Historian, Washington, D.C. Documents pertaining to Commandants Thomas H. Collins, Thad W. Allen, and Robert J. Papp, Jr. (accessed January 2, 2013).

Primary and Secondary Sources

"Admiral Robert Papp, Commandant, Coast Guard." *Navy Times*, December 24, 2012, p. 24.

"Admiral Thomas H. Collins, Commandant, U.S. Coast Guard." Address to the U.S. Commission on Ocean Policy, 22 November 2002. Department of Homeland Security and United States Coast Guard (accessed November 5, 2012).

"Alexander Hamilton." United States History. http://www.u-s-history.com/pages/h367.html.

"Allen, Admiral Thad W., Commandant, United States Coast Guard 2006–2010."

U.S. Department of Homeland Security and United States Coast Guard. http://www.uscg.mil/history/allen/AllenTWindex.asp (accessed October 30, 2011).

"Allen, Admiral Thad W., 23rd Commandant of the Coast Guard." U.S. Department of Homeland Security and United States Coast Guard (accessed November 8, 2012).

"Attack on America: September 11, 2001 and the U.S. Coast Guard." United States Coast Guard and U.S. Department of Homeland Security. U.S. Coast Guard Oral History Program: Operation Noble Eagle Documentation Project. Interview of Vice Admiral Thomas H. Collins, USCG, by Peter Capelotti, USCGR, on 24 April 2002 (accessed 2 November 2012).

Beard, Tom (editor-in-chief), Jose Hanson (managing editor), and Paul C. Scotti (graphics editor). *The Coast Guard*. Seattle, WA: Foundation for Coast Guard History/Westbrook, CT: Hugh Lauter Levin Associates, 2004.

"Bender, Chester R., USCG." U.S. Department of Homeland Security and United States Coast Guard. http://www.uscg.mil/history/people/CRBemderBop/asp (accessed October 30, 2011).

Bloomfield, Howard H.V. *The Compact History of the United States Coast Guard*. New York: Hawthorn Books, 1966.

Braesch, Connie. "Admiral Papp, Secretary Napolitano Honor Coast Guard Veterans." *Coast Guard Compass*, November 11, 2010. http://coastguard.

dodlive.mil/2010/11/adm-papp-secretary-napolitano-honor-coast-guard-veterans/ (accessed November 7, 2012).

———. "A Conversation with the Commandant." *Coast Guard Compass*, September 27, 2010. http://coastguard.dodlive.mil/2010/09/a-conversation-with-the-commandant/ (accessed November 7, 2012).

Burke, Jill. "Coast Guard Cutter Comes to Aid of Troubled Shell Ship, Drilling Rig." *Alaska Dispatch*, December 28, 2012. http://www.adn.com/article/coast-guard-cutter-comes-aid-troubled-shell-ship-drilling-rig (accessed December 29, 2012).

"Capt. L.G. Shepard's Appointment by Secretary Windom." *The New York Times*, December 17, 1889.

"Captain-Commandant Alexander V. Fraser (USRCS)." U.S. Department of Homeland Security, and the United States Coast Guard. http://www.uscg.mil/history/people/FraserAlexander.asp (accessed October 30, 2011).

"Charles F. Shoemaker, USRCS." U.S. Department of Homeland Security and United States Coast Guard. http://www.uscg.mil/history/people/CFShoemakerBio.asp (accessed October 30, 2011).

"Coast Guard Commandant Admiral Bob Papp's Remarks at the *Bernard C. Webber* Commissioning Ceremony." April 14, 2012. U.S. Department of Homeland Security and United States Coast Guard (accessed November 7, 2012).

"Coast Guard Commandant Admiral Papp's Remarks at the Keel Authentication Ceremony." Pascagoula, Mississippi, September 5, 2012. U.S. Department of Homeland Security and United States Coast Guard (accessed November 7, 2012).

"Coast Guard Commandant Admiral Robert J. Papp's Remarks at the Memorial Service for BMCS Terrell Horne III." Coast Guard Base Los Angeles/Long Beach, California. December 8, 2012. U.S. Department of Homeland Security and United States Coast Guard (accessed December 14, 2012).

"Coast Guard Commandant Admiral Bob Papp's Remarks at the Navy Memorial Fantail Breakfast." Navy Memorial, Washington, D.C., Wednesday, August 29, 2012. U.S. Department of Homeland Security and the United States Coast Guard (accessed November 7, 2012).

"Coast Guard Commandant Admiral Bob Papp's Remarks at the *William Flores* Commissioning." St. Petersburg, Florida, November 3, 2012. U.S. Department of Homeland Security and United States Coast Guard (accessed November 7, 2012).

"Coast Guard Helps Disabled Ship, Barge." United Press International, December 30, 2012. http://www.upi.com/Top_News/US/2012/12/30/Coast-Guard-helps-disabled-ship-barge/UPI-34421356852863/ (accessed December 30, 2012).

"Coast Guard Reactivates Seattle-based Icebreaker." Tacoma *News Tribune* and Associated Press, December 15, 2012. http://www.thenewstribune.com/2012/12/15/2403568/coast-guard (accessed November 16, 2012).

"Coast Guard Unit Duluth Honored." WDIO-TV (ABC) "Eye Witness News." Duluth, Minnesota, February 09, 2012. http://www.wdio.com/article/stories/S2490119.shtml?cat=11563 (accessed February 10, 2012).

"Coast Guard Vice Commandant Vice Admiral John P. Currier's Remarks at the Veterans Day Coast Guard Wreath Laying Ceremony." Arlington National Cemetery, Arlington, Virginia, November 11, 2012. U.S. Department of Homeland Security and United States Coast Guard (accessed November 17, 2012).

"Collins, Adm. Thomas H., Commandant, U.S. Coast Guard." United States Coast Guard and the Office of the Coast Guard Historian (accessed 1 November 2012).

"Commandant of the Coast Guard." eNotes.com Reference. http://www.enotes.com/topic/Commandant_of_the_Coast_Guard (accessed October 30, 2011).

"Commandant of U.S. Coast Guard Visits Singapore Under MPA Program." *Singapore News*, 26 November 2012. http://www.channelnewsasia.com/stories/singaporelocalnews/view/1239454/1/.html (accessed November 27, 2012).

"Defending U.S. Economic Interests in the Changing Arctic: Is There a Strategy?" United States Senate Committee on

Commerce, Science, and Transportation Subcommittee on Oceans, Atmosphere, Fisheries, and Coast Guard, July 27, 2011. Witness: Admiral Robert J. Papp, Jr., Commandant, U.S. Coast Guard (accessed November 7, 2012).

"Eighteenth, Nineteenth and Early Twentieth Century Revenue Cutters: A Historic Image Gallery." U.S. Department of Homeland Security and United States Coast Guard. http://www.uscg.mil/history/webcutters/USRC_Photo_Index.asp (accessed January 26, 2012).

"Ellsworth P. Bertholf, USRCS/USCG." U.S. Department of Homeland Security and United States Coast Guard. http://www.uscg.mil/history/people/EPBertholfBio.asp (accessed October 30, 2011).

Evans, Stephen H. *The United States Coast Guard, 1790–1815: A Definitive History*. Annapolis, MD: United States Naval Institute, 1949.

"Farley, John F." U.S. Department of Homeland Security and United States Coast Guard. http://www.uscg.mil/history/people/JFFarleyBio.asp (accessed October 30, 2011).

"Fast Response Cutter." Acquisition Directorate. United States Coast Guard, July 2012. http://www.uscg.mil/acquisition/sentinel/ (accessed December 12, 2012).

"Founders of the U.S. Coast Guard: Creation of the U.S. Revenue Marine, August 4, 1790." Naval History Blog: U.S. Naval Institute. Naval History and Heritage Command. http://www.navalhistory.org/2011/08/04/founders-of-the-u-s-coast-guard.

Gibbs, Brianna. "The USCG Wants You." KMXT 100.1 FM Public Radio, Kodiak Island, Alaska, December 26, 2012. http://www.kmxt.org/index2.php?option=com_content&do_pdf=1&id=4348 (accessed December 29, 2012).

"Gracey, James S." U.S. Department of Homeland Security and United States Coast Guard. http://www.uscg.mil/history/people/JSGraceyBio.asp (accessed October 30, 2011).

"Hamlet, Harry G., USCG." U.S. Department of Homeland Security and United States Coast Guard. http://www.uscg.mil/history/people/HGHamletBio.asp (accessed October 30, 2011).

"Hayes, John B., USCG." U.S. Department of Homeland Security and United States Coast Guard. http://www.uscg.mil/history/people/JBHayesBio.asp (accessed October 30, 2011).

Helvarg, David. *Rescue Warriors: The U.S. Coast Guard, America's Forgotten Heroes*. New York: Thomas Dunne Books, St. Martin's Press, 2009.

"Huntington Ingalls Industries." http://www.huntingtoningalls.com/ (accessed December 11, 2012).

"Ingalls Shipbuilding." http://shipbuildinghistory.com/history/shipyards/1major.htm (accessed December 11, 2012).

"John G. Carlisle." NNDB (Notable Names Data Base). http://www.nndb.com/people/428/000209798/Bibliography/ (accessed January 21, 2012).

Johnson, Robert Erwin. *Bering Sea Escort: Life Aboard a Coast Guard Cutter in World War II*. Annapolis, MD: Naval Institute Press, 1992.

———. *Guardians of the Sea: History of the United States Coast Guard, 1915 to the Present*. Annapolis, MD: Naval Institute Press, 1987.

Joling, Dan (Associated Press). "Admiral Confident in Coast Guard Arctic Readiness." *Alaska Journal of Commerce*, August 9, 2012. http://www.alaskajournal.com/Alaska-Journal-of-Commerce/August-Issue-1-2012/Admiral-confident-in-Coast-Guard-Arctic-readiness/ (accessed August 9, 2012).

Kaplan, H.R., and Lt. Cmdr. James F. Hunt. *This is the Coast Guard*. Annapolis, MD: Cornell Maritime Press, 1972.

"Kime, J. William, USCG." U.S. Department of Homeland Security and United States Coast Guard. http://www.uscg.mil/history/people/JWKimeBio.asp (accessed October 30, 2011).

King, Irving H. *The Coast Guard Expands, 1865–1915: New Roles, New Frontiers*. Annapolis, MD: Naval Institute Press, 1996.

Klimas, Jacqueline. "Papp Talks Overseas Manning." *Military/Navy Times*, December 24, 2012, p. 20.

"Kramek, Robert E., USCG." U.S. Department of Homeland Security and United States Coast Guard. http://www.uscg.mil/history/people/REKramekBio.asp (accessed October 30, 2011).

Kroll, C. Douglas. *A Coast Guardsman's History of the U.S. Coast Guard*. Annapolis, MD: Naval Institute Press, 2010.

———. *Commodore Ellsworth P. Bertholf: First Commandant of the Coast Guard*. Annapolis, MD: Naval Institute Press, 2002.

Lagan, Christopher. "Admiral Allen Delivers State of the Coast Guard Address." *Coast Guard Compass*, February 13, 2010. http://coastguard.dodlive.mil/2010/02/admiral-allen-delivers-state-of-the-coast-guard-address/ (accessed November 7, 20112).

———. "Admiral Bob Papp Delivers State of the Coast Guard Address." *Coast Guard Compass*, February 10, 2011. http://coastguard.dodlive.mil/2011/02/adm-bob-papp-delivers-state-of-the-coast-guard-address/ (accessed November 7, 2012).

———. "Excerpts from Adm. Allen's Speech to the Surface Naval Association." *Coast Guard Compass*, January 14, 2010. http://coastguard.dodlive.mil/2010/01/video-excerpts-from-adm-allens-speech-to-the-surface-naval-association/ (accessed November 7, 2012).

Larzelere, Alex R. *The Coast Guard at War: Vietnam, 1965–1975*. Annapolis, MD: Naval Institute Press, 1997.

———. *The Coast Guard in World War I: An Untold Story*. Annapolis, MD: Naval Institute Press, 2003.

LeMay, Konnie. "For Those in Peril on the Sea." *Lake Superior Magazine*, October-November, 2005, 16–23.

"Loy, James M., USCG." U.S. Department of Homeland Security and United States Coast Guard. http://www.uscg.mil/history/CCG/Loy/jmloy_bio.asp (accessed October 30, 2011).

Mansker, Michael. "Hayes, Adm. John Briggs, USCG (Ret.)" U.S. Coast Guard Oral History Program. Interview conducted by Michael Mansker, USCG, 1985.

Marolda, Edward J. *By Sea, Air, and Land: An Illustrated History of the U.S. Navy and the War in Southeast Asia*. Washington, D.C.: Naval Historical Center, 1994.

McCarter, Mickey. "Coast Guard Seeking Resources for Routine Repairs for Heavy Icebreaker, Set to Return to Duty." *Homeland Security Today*. December 10, 2012. http://www.hstoday.us/briefings/industry-news/single-article/coast-guard-proposes-long-awaited-rule-for-twic-readers/3ab28f831c1f42c2e43bae42dd1c8326.html (accessed December 11, 2012).

Murphy, Kim. "Coast Guard Evacuates Crew of Troubled Oil Drilling Barge." *Los Angeles Times*, December 29, 2012. http://articles.latimes.com/2012/dec/29/nation/la-na-nn-shell-oil-drilling-20121229 (accessed December 29, 2012).

Noble, Dennis L. *That Others Might Live: The U.S. Life-Saving Service, 1878–1915*. Annapolis, MD: Naval Institute Press, 1994.

Nolte, Carl. "Coast Guard Commandant, 3 New Cutters in Alameda." *San Francisco Chronicle*, February 25, 2012. http://www.sfgate.com/bayarea/article/Coast-Guard-commandant-3-new-cutters-in-Alameda-3360326.php (accessed February 25, 2012).

"O'Neill, Merlin, USCG." U.S. Department of Homeland Security and United States Coast Guard. http://www.uscg.mil/history/people/MONeillBio.asp (accessed October 30, 2011).

Ostrom, Thomas P. *The United States Coast Guard in National Defense: A History from World War I to the Present*. Jefferson, NC: McFarland, 2012.

———. *The United States Coast Guard in World War II: A History of Domestic and Overseas Actions*. Jefferson, NC: McFarland, 2009.

———. *The United States Coast Guard on the Great Lakes: A History*. Oakland, OR: Anvil/Elderberry Press, 2007.

Papp, Robert J., Jr. "Proficiency: The Essence of Discipline." *Proceedings*, August 2012, 16–21.

"Peter Bonnett's Ambition: Desire for a Place Has Led Him to Meddle with Mr. Carlisle's Affairs." *The New York Times*, June 10, 1894.

Phillips, Donald T., and Adm. James M. Loy. *Character in Action: The U.S. Coast Guard on Leadership*. Annapolis, MD: Naval Institute Press, 2003.

"Rear Adm. Russell R. Waesche, Jr., USCG (Ret.)." Biographical Sketch. Public

Affairs Division, U.S. Coast Guard Headquarters (accessed January 2, 2013).
"Remarks by Admiral Thad Allen, Commandant, U.S. Coast Guard, to DHS Fellows, New York City," January 28, 2008. U.S. Department of Homeland Security and United States Coast Guard. U.S. Coast Guard History Program. Transcript by Federal News Service, Washington, D.C. (accessed November 7, 2012).
"The Revenue Cutter Service: Mr. Sherman's Plan for Keeping It Under Control of the Treasury." Letter to the Editor, *The New York Times*, September 14, 1890.
"Reynolds, William E., USCG." U.S. Department of Homeland Security and the United States Coast Guard. http://www.uscg.mil/history/people/WEReynoldsBio.asp (accessed October 30, 2011).
"Richmond, Alfred C. (1954–1962)." U.S. Department of Homeland Security and the United States Coast Guard. http://www.uscg.mil/history/people/ACRichmondBio.asp (accessed October 30, 2011).
"Roland, Edwin J." U.S. Department of Homeland Security and the United States Coast Guard. http://www.uscg.mil/history/people/EJRolandBio.asp (accessed October 30, 2011).
"Ross, Worth G., USCG." U.S. Department of Homeland Security and the United States Coast Guard. http://www.uscg.mil/history/people/WGRossBio.asp (accessed October 30, 2011).
"Same Coast Guard, New Team." Admiral Thomas H. Collins, Coast Guard Birthday Celebration with Secretary Tom Ridge. James Creek Marina. August 6, 2003. United States Coast Guard and Department of Homeland Security (accessed 5 November 2012). Schweikert, Larry, and Michael Allen. *A Patriotic History of the United States: From Columbus's Great Discovery to the War on Terror*. New York: Sentinel, 2007.
Scotti, Paul C. *Coast Guard Action in Vietnam*. Central Point, OR: Hellgate Press, 2000.
"Seaman Apprentice William R. Flores, USCG." U.S. Department of Homeland Security and United States Coast Guard. http://www.uscg.mil/history/people/Flores.asp (accessed December 12, 2012).
"Shepard, Leonard G., USRCS." U.S. Department of Homeland Security and United States Coast Guard. http://www.uscg.mil/history/people/LGShepardBio.asp (accessed October 30, 2011).
"Siler, Owen W., USCG." U.S. Department of Homeland Security and United States Coast Guard. http://www.uscg.mil/history/people/OWSilerBio.asp (accessed October 30, 2011).
Smith, Glynn. "Admiral Papp Addresses Surface Naval Community." *Coast Guard Compass*, January 13, 2012. http://coastguard.dodlive.mil/2012/01/adm-papp-addresses-surface-naval-comunity/ (accessed November 2012).
———. "Adm. Papp Delivers Second State of the Coast Guard Address." *Coast Guard Compass*, February 23, 2012. http://coastguard.dodlive.mil/2012/02/adm-papp-delivers-second-state-of-the-coast-guard-address/ (accessed November 7, 2012).
———. "Adm. Papp Focused on Counter-Piracy, Arctic at IMO Assembly." *Coast Guard Compass*, November 23, 2011. http://coastguard.dodlive.mil/2011/11/adm-papp-focused-on-counter-piracy-arctic-at-imo-assembly/ (accessed November 7, 2012).
———. "Admiral Papp Reviews Mission of Patrol Forces Southwest Asia." *Coast Guard Compass*, November 18, 2011. http://coastguard.dodlive.mil/2011/11/adm-papp-reviews-mission-of-patrol-forces-southwest-asia/ (accessed July 29, 2012).
———. "Dedicating a New Generation Patrol Boat." *Coast Guard Compass*, March 2, 2012. http://coastguard.dodlive.mil/2012/03/dedicating-a-new-generation-patrol-boat/ (accessed November 7, 2012).
———. "North Pacific Coast Guard Forum 2010." *Coast Guard Compass*, September 16, 2010. http://coastguard.dodlive.mil/2010/09/north-pacific-coast-guard-forum-2010-2/ (accessed November 7, 2012).
———. "Recapitalizing and Building Capacity: The National Security Cutters." *Coast Guard Compass*, February

22, 2011. http://coastguard.dodlive.mil/ 2011/02/recapitalizing-and-building-capacity-the-national-security-cutters/ (accessed November 7, 2012).

"Smith, Willard J." U.S. Department of Homeland Security and United States Coast Guard. http://www.uscg.mil/history/people/WJSmithBio.asp (accessed October 30, 2011).

Strobridge, Truman R. "Chronology of Aids to Navigation and the United States Lighthouse Service." U.S. Coast Guard Public Affairs Division, 1974. U.S. Department of Homeland Security. United States Coast Guard. http://www.uscg.mil/history/articles/h_USLHSchron.asp.

Strobridge, Truman R., and Dennis L. Noble. *Alaska and the U.S. Revenue Cutter Service, 1867–1915*. Annapolis, MD: Naval Institute Press, 1999.

"Sumner Increase Kimball." U.S. Department of Homeland Security, and the United States Coast Guard. http://www.uscg.mil/history/people/Sumner_Kimball.asp (accessed October 30, 2011).

Surko, Stephen. "At Sea in the Great War." *Naval History*, August 2012, 54–59.

"Testimony of Admiral Robert Papp, Commandant, U.S. Coast Guard on Accession to the 1982 Law of the Sea Convention Before the Senate Committee on Foreign Relations." June 14, 2013. U.S. Department of Homeland Security and United States Coast Guard and Commandant United States Coast Guard (accessed November 7, 2012).

"Testimony of Admiral Robert J. Papp, Jr., Commandant of the U.S. Coast Guard. Coast Guard Fiscal Year 2012 Budget Request Before the House Subcommittee on Coast Guard and Marine Transportation, March 1, 2011." U.S. Department of Homeland Security and United States Coast Guard, and Commandant United States Coast Guard (accessed November 7, 2012).

"U.S. Coast Guard Member Killed in Crash off California Coast." Associated Press and Fox News, December 03, 2012. http://www.foxnews.com/us/2012/12/02/us-coast-guard-member-killed-in-crash-california-coast/ (accessed December 3, 2012).

"U.S. Coast Guard *Polar Star* History." U.S. Department of Homeland Security and United States Coast Guard. http://www.uscg.mil/pacarea/cgcpolarstar/history.asp (accessed December 15, 2012).

U.S. Life-Saving Service Heritage Association. "Our Mission." http://uslife-savingservice.org/our-mission/ (accessed February 7, 2012).

"United States Lighthouse Service: Lighthouses, A Brief Administrative History." June 15, 2011, 1–8. http://www.michiganlights.com/lighthouseservice.htm.

"United States Revenue Cutter Service." Wikipedia. http://en.wikipedia.org/wiki/United_States_Revenue_Cutter_Service (accessed December 19, 2011).

"Waesche, Russell R., Sr. (USCG)." U.S. Department of Homeland Security and United States Coast Guard. http://www.uscg.mil/history/people/RRWaescheSRBio.asp (accessed October 30, 2011).

"War of 1812." Wikipedia. http://en.wikipedia.org/wiki/United_States_Revenue_Cutter_Service (accessed October 30, 2011).

Warner, Melodie. "U.S. Coast Guard Notes Safety and Propulsion Deficiencies on Arctic-Bound Drillship." *gCaptain*. Germanischer Lloyd (GL). Dow Jones, December 27, 2012. http://gcaptain.com/coast-guard-notes-safety-propulsion/ (accessed December 28, 2012).

Wester, Rick. "Admiral Papp Spends Thanksgiving in Bahrain with Coast Guardsmen, Meets with U.S. and Bahraini Officials." *Coast Guard Compass*, November 27, 2012. http://coastguard.dodlive.mil/2012/11/adm-papp-spends-thanksgiving-in-bahrain-with-coast-guardsmen-meets-with-u-s-and-bahraini-officials/ (accessed November 27, 2012).

———. "Adm. Papp Visits International Partners in Malta." *Coast Guard Compass*, November 26, 2012. http://coastguard.dodlive.mil/2012/11/adm-papp-visits-international-partners-in-malta/ (accessed November 27, 2012).

Willoughby, Malcolm F. *The U.S. Coast Guard in World War II*. Annapolis, MD: Naval Institute Press, 1957/1989.

"Written Testimony of U.S. Coast Guard

Commandant Admiral Robert Papp, Jr. for a Senate Committee on Appropriations, Subcommittee on Homeland Security Field Hearing Titled 'Coast Guard Operations in Alaska.'" August 6, 2012, U.S. Coast Guard Air Station Kodiak, Kodiak, Alaska. U.S. Department of Homeland Security. http://www.dhs.gov/es/news/2012/08/06/written-testimony-us-coast-guard-commandant-admiral-robert-papp-jr-senate-committee (accessed November 7, 2012).

"Yost, Paul A., Jr. (USCG)." U.S. Department of Homeland Security and United States Coast Guard. http://uscg.mil/history/people/PAYostBio.asp (accessed October 30, 2011).

Young, Stephanie. "Honoring Our Profession: The Long Blue Line." *Coast Guard Compass*, January 6, 2012. http://coastguard.dodlive.mil/2012/01/honoring-our-profession-the-long-blue-line/ (accessed November 7, 2012).

Index

Numbers in **_bold italics_** indicate pages with photographs.

ABB Marine 141
Abercrombie-Winstanley 169
Academy *see* Coast Guard Academy
Act to Create the Coast Guard (1915) 15, 64, 65
Admiral Nimitz Foundation 135
Aerospace Rescue and Recovery 113
Aids to Navigation 17, 18, 19, 20, 21, **_22_**, 23, **_24_**, 25, 26–27, 109, 117, 124
Aiviq SS 174
Alameda, California 64, 115, 158, 161, 176
Alaska 18, 19, 46, 54, 59, 61, 63, 67, 72, 79, 104, 111, 115, 117, 119, 121, 123, 164, 165, 168, 174, 175; duties of USRM in Alaska 46; U.S. purchase of from Russia 46
Alaska and the U.S. Revenue Cutter Service 54
Alaskan Airline Flight 301 130
Aleutian Islands 165, 174
Allen, Clyde 146
Allen, Michael 13
Allen, Thad 144, **_145_**, 146–152, 172, 176, 179
American Bureau of Shipping 62, 70, 132
American Seaman SS 89
American Trader MV 124
Amphibious Training Unit 99
AMVER 105
Anchorage, Alaska 165
Antarctic regions 105, 150
Anti-submarine warfare patrols (ASW) 68, 69, 83, 93, 111
ANTS 25
Apostle Islands 34
Arabian Gulf Theater 170
Arctic Overland Relief Expedition 79
Arctic regions 72, 105, 150, 159, 160, 163, 164, 168–169, 172–173, 174
Arctic Research Commission (U.S.) 159

Arlington, Virginia 178
Arlington National Cemetery 62, 70, 80, 84, 155, 157, 172, 178
armament 89, 168
Armed Forces Industrial College 132
Armed Forces Staff College 111
Army and Navy Journal 53
Arundel Cove, Maryland 83
Ashland, Wisconsin 34
Atlantic Area Commander 122, 123, 132, 145, 150, 153
ATON 117; *see also* Aids to Navigation
Auxiliary *see* Coast Guard Auxiliary
aviation 19, 31, 32, 64, 69, 76, 77, 84, 90, 91, 93, 110–111, 113, 114, 115, 116, 118, 122, 142, 151, 154, 159, 164, 166, 171, 172, 175, 179

Baltimore, Maryland 57, 99, 103, 127
Barbers Point, Hawaii 114
Barr, Joseph 112
Barrow, Alaska 164
Bay City Shipyard 78
Bayfield, Wisconsin 34, 118
Beach Patrols 24, 30, 31, 91
Bell, Jennifer 178
Bender, Chester R. **_112_**, 113–114
"Bender's Blues" 114, 116
Bertholf, Ellsworth P. 40, 51, 53, 60, 61, **_62_**, 63–70, 73
Bertholf, Emilie Innes Sublett 70
Bering Sea Escort 104
Bering Sea Patrol 53, 61, 73, 78, 104, 158
Bethlehem Shipbuilding & Steel Corp. 78, 103
Bibb, A.B. 29
Billard, Frederick C. 73–74, **_75_**, 77–78
Bloomfield, Howard V.L. 43, 53

203

Index

Bolling AFB, D.C. 157
Bollinger Shipyards 151, 162, 168
Bonnett, Peter 8, 49, 50
Boston, Massachusetts 16, 25, 108
Boutwell, George *41*, 46, 47
Boylan, Malcolm 87
Brice-O'Hara, Sally 153, 179
British Petroleum Corporation 146
British Petroleum Oil Spill 144, 145, 146, 165
buoy tenders 118, 131, 141
Bureau of Marine Inspection 97
Burhoe, Scott 155
Bush, George W. 134, 141, 142, 145

Call, S.J. 61
Call Medical Clinic 65
Calumet SS 38
Canada 66, 76, 105, 122, 130, 133, 135, 154, 156, 164
Canadian Coast Guard 154
Canadian military and law enforcement agencies 133, 135, 154
Canadian Navy 105, 154
Cantrell, Steven 177
Cantwell, Maria 152, 172
Cape Cod, Massachusetts 163
Cape May, New Jersey 65, 153, 155, 179
Capelotti, Peter 138
Capricorn, SS 167
captain-commandant 8, 40, 52
Captain of the Port 69, 119, 123, 142, 154
Carden, Godfrey L 69
Caribbean interdiction 119, 122, 127, 130
Carlisle, John Griffin 50, 56, 57, 72
CG 36500 163
Character in Action: Coast Guard Leadership 135
Charleston, South Carolina 40, 137
Chase, Salmon P. 46
Cheboygan, Michigan 108
Chicago, Illinois 135, 154
Chief Petty Officer School (USCG) 166
Chief Petty Officers (CPOs) 166
Chronology of Lighthouse Service 16
Churchill, Winston 91
Civil War (U.S.) 10, 14, 45–46, 55, 57
Claflin, Tina 178
Clark, Ezra W. 8, 48, 49, 50
Clark, Vern 141
Cleveland, Grover 50
Cleveland, Ohio 108, 114, 136, 154
Coastal Communications Board 84
Coastal Confluence Zone 117
Coast Guard Academy 47, 55, 58, 72, 73, 78, 101, 104, 107, 114, 116, 118, 131, 153, 155, 157, 160, 178, 179
Coast Guard Air Station Kodiak 164
Coast Guard at War, Vietnam 149–150

Coast Guard Auxiliary 88, 98, 102, 133, 135, 148, 150, 155
Coast Guard Band 171
"Coast Guard Blue" 114
Coast Guard Expands (1865–1915) 55
Coast Guard Headquarters, Washington, D.C. 65, 70, 100, 131, 133, 137, 138, 141, 178
Coast Guard Hill 70
Coast Guard Historian 54, 178
Coast Guard in World War I 71, 81
Coast Guard in World War II 94, 98–99, 104, 123
Coast Guard Institute 82
Coast Guard Island 161
Coast Guard magazine 75
Coast Guard Memorial 155, 157, 172
Coast Guard Motto *see* Semper Paratus
Coast Guard on the Great Lakes 34
Coast Guard origins 15, 60, 61, 62
Coast Guard Reserve 87, 87, 88, 118, 133, 135, 138, 150, 155, 179; *see also* Coast Guard Women's Reserve
Coast Guard Role in Korean Conflict 100–101
Coast Guard Training Center, Cape May 153, 155, 179
Coast Guard Training Center, Petaluma 166
Coast Guard Women's Reserve 83, 86; *see also* Coast Guard Reserve; SPARS
Coast Guardsman's Manual 148
Cohen, William 134
Cold War 98, 100–102, 124, 130
Collins, John W. 55
Collins, Thomas H. 137, 138, *139*, 140–143
commandant 39, 149
Commission on Efficiency 64
Committee on Foreign Relations 163
Committee on Transportation and Oceans 159
Congressional Women's Caucus 178
contraband interdiction 117, 118
convoy escort 83
Coolidge, Calvin *22*, 77
Corpus Christi, Texas 115
COTP *see* Captains of the Port
Council on Foreign Relations 150
coxswains 93, 99
Crea, Vivien 150, 179
Creed of a Coast Guardsman 80
Cuba 130; *see also* Spanish-American War
Cuban migrations 108, 119, 132
Currier, John P. 153, 172
Curtis Bay, Maryland 58, 83
cutters 10

Daniels, Josephus 81
Dearborn, Michigan, 154

Deepwater Horizon oil spill 158, 165, 176; see also British Petroleum
Deepwater Project 132, 134, 137, 141, 144, 151, 152
Defender class boats 34
Defense Communications Board 97
Defense Force West commander 176
DeKort, Michael 151
Delaney, Sharp 12
Del Ray, California 166
Depression of 1929–1939 79
Desert Shield 128
Desert Storm 128
De Steiguer, Louis R. 81
Destroyer Deal 91
Destroyer escorts 89
Detroit, Michigan 68, 149, 154
Devereux, N. Broughton 8, 46
Dewey, George 12, 14, 45
DEWLINE 105
Dillon, Douglas 105
Dimick, Chester E. 58
Dispatch, HMS 14
Dolbow, Jim 148–149
Drug Enforcement Administration (DEA) 117, 119, 124
drug interdiction 52, 67, 117, 119, 128, 129, 158, 168
Duluth, Minnesota 26–27, 32–37, 76, 95, 154
Dutch Harbor, Alaska 174

Earhart, Amelia 90
Edmund Fitzgerald SS 33
Edwards, Richard S. 92
Eighth Coast Guard District 97, 107, 123, 132, 167
Eisenhower, Dwight D. 104, 105
El Paso, Texas 145
Eldridge, Frank 94
Eleventh Coast Guard District 115, 126, 176
Elizabeth City, North Carolina 113
Emery, C.E. 48
Environmental Protection Agency 118, 124, 147; see also pollution
Erickson, Frank 84
Espionage Act (1917) 69
Etheridge, Richard **30**, 37
Evans, Richard 40, 45
Evans, Stephen H. 8, 44, 48, 62–63
Evanston Life-Saving Station 37–38
Exclusive Economic Zone (EEZ) 163, 169
Exxon Valdez MV 124

Farley, James Francis 96–98, **99**
Faunce, John **10**, 29, 45, 46
Federal Emergency Management Agency (FEMA) 134

Fifth Coast Guard District 99, 122
First Coast Guard District 108
Fisheries Patrol and management 109, 116, 158, 164
Flores, William Ray 160–161, 162, 167, 168
Ford Island, Hawaii 84
Forgotten Service & War 100
Former Soviet republics 130
Forrestal, James 86, 97
Fort McNair 108, 129, 132
Fort Trumbull, Connecticut 58
Foulkes, Frederick R.
Foundation for Coast Guard History 94, 179
Fourteenth Coast Guard District 153, 179
Fowler, Henry W. 109
Francis, Sara 175
Fraser, Alexander V. 8, 15, 40–46, 47, 52
Fredericksburg, Texas, 135
Fresnel, Augustine 17, 21, 25

Gallatin, Albert 20
Galluzzo, John 27, 93
Galveston, Texas 110
Gamble, Aaron L. 66
Gatch, Thomas 83
General Engineering & Dry Dock Co. 78
Gertz, Bill 134
Glass, Carter 72, 73
Governors Island, New York 121, 129
GPS 91
Gracey, James S. 121–123, **125**, 141
Grant, Ulysses S. 47
Gray, Samuel F. 94
Great Depression see Depression
Great Lakes 11, 19, 32–37, 68, 75, 76, 78, 82, 83, 113–114, 118, 122, 131, 133, 135 - 136, 141, 149, 150, 153–154, 179
Greene, Wallace M. 109
Greenland 66, 90
Greenland Patrol 78, 90, 95
Grenada 122
Groton, Connecticut 111
Guadalcanal 93
Guam 111
Guardians of the Sea 88
Gulf of Mexico 165, 176
Gulf Wars 127

Haas, Nelson 67
Hagee, Michael 135
Haitian earthquake 148
Haitian migration 119, 129, 130, 132
Hall, Norman B. 69
Hamilton, Alexander 7, **9**, 12, 13, 20, 167
Hamlet, Harry G. **76**, 79–81, 82–83, 87
Hamlet, Oscar C. 53, 79
Harding, Lawrence 91
Harrison, Holly 178–179

Hawaii 97; *see also* Fourteenth Coast Guard District; Honolulu; Pearl Harbor
Hayes, John B. *116*, 118–120
Healy, Michael A. 54, 55, 57, 72
Helvarg, David 63, 64, 128, 150, 151, 152
Henderson MV 37
Higgins boats 93
Hill, John 67
Hill Library, UW-S 34
Historical Section (USCG) 94, 104
Homeland Security Act (2003) 147
Honolulu, Hawaii 137
Hoover, Herbert 79
Horne, Terrell 166, 171–172
Hornsby, Thomas 12
Houston, David 72
Houston Ship Canal 130
Howland Island 90
Hull, James, 133
Humble, Richard 37
Hunt, James F. 42
Huntington Ingalls Industries 166–167
Hurricane Katrina 144, 145, 148, 149, 152
Hydrographic Office NYC 66

Ice Patrol *see* International Ice Patrol
icebergs 66
Icebreakers 83, 105, 116, 117–118, 126, 141, 150, 159, 169
immigration interdiction 67, 119
Industrial College of U.S. Armed Forces 126
Influence of Sea Power 63
Ingalls Shipbuilding 166
Inland Seas 32, 82, 112, 141
Integrated Deepwater System Project 142; *see also* Deepwater Project
Interagency Task Force on USCG Roles and Missions (1999) 142
International Conference on Sea Safety 62
International Conference on Tanker Safety & Pollution 127
International Ice Patrol 62, 64, 66, 78
International Maritime Law Institute 170
International Maritime Organization (IMO) 126, 159, 160, 163, 170
international sovereignty claims 159
International Whaling Conference 98, 103
Inuit natives 61, 63
Iraq *see* Operation Iraqi Freedom
Island Class cutters 151, 162

Jackson, Andrew 40
James, Joshua 29
Japan Coast Guard 156
Jarvis, David H. 61, 63
Jeannette, SS 71, 72
Jefferson, Thomas 13
Johnson, Jeh 176

Johnson, Lyndon B. 109, 114
Johnson, Robert Erwin 42–43, 46, 74, 80, 88, 89, 92, 102, 104, 109–110
Johnston, Charles E. 66
Joint Chiefs of Staff 149
Jupiter Class cutters 131

Kaplan, H.R. 42
Keel Authentication ceremony 167
Keeper Class cutters 131, 132
keepers 131
Key West, FLA 118
Kimball, Sumner I. 8, 26, 27, *28*, 29, 30, 32, 46–48, 50, 64
Kime, J. William 121, 126, *127*, 128, 141
King, Ernest J. 92
King, Erving H 55, 65, 67
King, H.D. 23–24
Kings Point, New York 104
Klimas, Jacqueline 173
Kodiak, Alaska, 164, 175
Korean War 98, 100–101, 102
Krajeski, Thomas 170
Kramek, Robert E. 129, *130*, 131–132, 141
Kroll, C. Douglas 64, 70, 76, 85
Kulluk SS 174

Labrador, HMCS 105
Lake Class cutters 78
landing craft 92
Langdon, Brandon 171
Larzelere, Alex 71, 74, 81, 84, 149
Latin American interdiction 128, 130
law enforcement 117, 118
Law of the Sea Convention 123, 159, 163, 164
League of Coast Guard Women 78
Lee, Frederick 14
Leavitt, Michael P. 157, 170, 177
Legacy: U.S. Life-Saving Service 27
Legend Class Cutters 151–152
LeMay, Konnie 36
Lend-Lease Act 91
Lieberman, Joseph 139
Life Saving Service *see* United States Life Saving Service
Lighthouse Board 45
Lighthouse conferences 103
Lighthouse Establishment 17, 21
Lighthouse Service *see* United States Lighthouse Service
Lightship No. 117 19
lightships 17, 84
Lincoln, Abraham 14, 46
Little Brewster Island Lighthouse 17
LNBs 25
Lockheed Martin Corp. 151
Lockport, Louisiana 162, 168
Long Beach, California 115, 126, 171

Long Island Sound 137
LORAN 25, 92, 94, 101, 105, 109, 111, 117–118, 120, 121, 126, 145, 149–150, 154, 179
Los Angeles, California 166, 171
Loy, James M. 129, *131*, 132–136, 138, 141, 142
LST 120
Lusitania RMS 96
Lyle guns 30

M&S Henderson 37
MacVeagh, Franklin 64
Mahan, Alfred Thayer 63
Malta Maritime Squadron 169–170
Manitowoc Marine Group 141
Mansker, Michael 119, 120
Mariel Boat Lift 119
Marine Corps *see* United States Marine Corps
Marine Hospital Service 31, 59
Marine Inspection Office 99
Marine Safety and Security Teams 143
Marinette Marine Corporation 131, 141
Maritime and Port Authority 170
Maritime Defense Zone Atlantic 123
Maritime Defense Zone Pacific 126
Maritime Domain 131, 138
Maritime Service Training Station 103
Market Time Patrols 109, 113
Marquette Maritime Museum 27
Massachusetts Humane Society 28
Mataafa SS 36–37
Matsumae, Japan 118, 120
McAdoo, William G. 66
McConnell, John P. 113
McDonald, John D. 81
McKenzie, Donald 35, 36
McKinley, William 63
McLane, Louis 8, 44
Meade, George 45
Melli, Joseph 170
Mellon, Andrew 78
Merchant Marine Inspection Office 103
Merchant Marine Technical Naval Engineering 126
merchant ship safety conference 108
Mexican-American War 14
Miami, Florida 116, 127, 162
Michigan Lighthouse Conservancy 20
Middle East 133, 170; *see also* Persian Gulf
migration-immigration *see* interdiction
Military Leadership Award 132
Milwaukee, Wisconsin 154
Mineta, Norman 132
minorities (ethnic, gender) 30, 37, 91, 116, 118, 150
MLB 36527 34
Monahan, Nancy 137
Moore, Tiffany 170

Morgan, J.P. 64
Morgenthau, Henry 80, 88
Morrison, James J. 55, 57
motto (USCG) *see* Semper Paratus
Munro, Douglas A. *86*, 93
Muriel Boat Lift 119
Muscat, Geoffrey 170
Myers, Meghann 176

Nalty, Bernard C. 12
Nantucket Lightship *24*
Nantucket Shoals, Massachusetts 19
Napolitano, Janet 146, 155, 157, 165
narcotics *see* drug interdiction
national defense 118, 122, 126, 134–135, 141, 163
National Defense University 129, 179
National Distress System 142
National Drug Control Policy 126
National Fleet Agreement 141
National Graduate School of Systems Management 150
National Guard 148
National Incident Commander 146
National Museum of the Pacific War 135
National School of Systems Management 150
National Security Cutters 84, 151, 158, 167
National War College 108, 116, 179
Native American communities 175
natural disasters 89–90, 124, 144, 148
Naval Academy 55, 67
Naval Air Systems Command 152
Naval Forces Central Command 156
Naval Institute Press 94, 123, 135
Naval Patrol Forces 173
Naval Sea Systems Comman 152
Naval War College 61, 63, 68, 79, 118, 124, 129, 153
NAVGUARD 139
Navy Patrol Squadron VP-44 111
Navy School of Aviation 69
Navy Times 151, 171, 173, 175, 176
NCOs 120
Neutrality Patrol 90
New Haven, Connecticut 137
New London, Connecticut 47, 78, 89176, 179
New Orleans, Louisiana 93, 97, 123
New York City 21, 66, 69, 103, 112, 121, 123, 129, 133, 136, 138
New York Times 49, 50, 70, 151
Newcomb, Frank 15
Newell, William A. 28
Newman MV 37
Newport, Rhode Island 63, 79, 124
Nimitz, Chester W. 94–95; *see also* Admirial Nimitz Foundation; Hagee; National Museum of the Pacific War

Nine-Eleven ("9/11[qm]") 147, 148, 154; *see also* September 9, 2011
Ninth Coast Guard District 109, 112, 133, 135–136, *141, 153; see also* Great Lakes
Nitze, Paul H. 112
Nixon, Richard M. 114, 116
Noble, Dennis L. 26, 27, 32, 37, 54, 72
Noble Corporation 173–174
Noble Discoverer SS 173
Nolte, Carl 161–162
Noonan, Fred 90
Norfolk, Virginia 46, 69, 111
North Arabian Gulf 178
North Pacific CG Forum 156
Northern Route 159
Northrop Grumman Corp. 84, 151
Notice to Mariners 21
"Nullification Crisis" 41

Obama, Barack 146
Ocean Station cutters 90, 116
oceanographic exploration 150, 164, 169
Office of Acquisition 137
Office of the Coast Guard Historian 178; *see also* Coast Guard Historian
oil pollution 103, 117, 130, 144–145, 146, 164, 173–174
Oil Protection Act (1990) 124
oil tankers and barges 116, 124
Olson, Justin 27
One-Eighties ("180's") 131
O'Neill, Merlin 98, 99, *100*, 101–102
Operation Able Manner 130
Operation Arctic Shield 164
Operation BALTOPS 130
Operation Enduring Freedom 140
Operation Frontier Shield 130
Operation Gulf Shield 130
Operation Iraqi Freedom 140, 156, 178
Operation Liberty Shield 140
Operation Noble Eagle Project 138
Operation Trade Winds 130
Operation Unitas 130
Oral History Program 119, 138
Ostebo, Thomas 174
Overland Expedition (1897–1898) 61, 62–63, 65

Pacific Area Commander 122, 176
Panga vessel 171
Papp, Robert J., Jr. 146, 153–159, *160*, 161–176, 177, 179
Pascagoula, Mississippi 84, 151, 166, 167
Patrol Forces Southwest Asia 156, 170
Patton, Vince 167
Pea Island Life-Saving Station *30*, 37
Pearl Harbor, Hawaii 19, 97, 84, 160
Pelletier, LeRoy 57
Pendleton, SS 163

Pensacola, Florida 69, 110, 113, 115
Pentagon 133, 138, 139; *see also* United States Department of Defense
Perry, Oliver H. 11
Persian Gulf 124, 128, 156, 173, 178
Petaluma, California 166
Peters, Fred C. 12
Philadelphia, Pennsylvania 69
Philadelphia Navy Yard 82, 98, 102
Philippines 109, 113
Phillips, Donald T. 135, 136
piracy 14, 156, 160, 176
Pleasanton, Stephen 20–21
Pluta, Paul 167
Polar Class icebreakers 117, 159
Polar Code 160
Polar regions 11, 46, 73, 78, 79, 117, 144, 159, 164, 168–169
pollution control 114, 116
port security 62, 69, 100, 109, 118, 119, 135, 140, 142, 163
Port Security 98, 116
port security units (PSUs) 140
Portland, Maine 121
Pratt, William V. 79
Price, Scott T. 100–101
Proceedings 12, 140
Prohibition 72, 73, 75, 76, 83
Purdue University 85
Putnam, George R. 21, *22*

Quasi-War with France 8, 9

Reagan, Ronald 179
Record, SS 36
Reed-Hill, Ellis 94
Report of Vessels on Ice Patrol (1913) 66
Reserves *see* Coast Guard Reserve
Rescue 21 System 143
Rescue Warriors 150
Revenue Marine 7–15; headquarters 48
Revolutionary War 7
Reynolds, William E. 71–73, *74*
RHI 171
Rhinelander, Wisconsin 178
Richmond, Alfred C. 94, *101*, 102 -106
Ridge, Tom *140*, 147
Rittichier, Jack 172
Roland, Edwin J. 104, 107–109, *110*, 112
Roosevelt, Franklin D. 20, 79, 83, 91, 93
Roosevelt, Theodore 56
Ross, W. J. 73
Ross, Worth G. 40, *42*, 58–59
Royal Canadian Mounted Police 154
Royal Canadian Navy *see* Canadian Navy
Royal Dutch Shell Corporation 173, 174
Royal National Lifeboat Institution 35
rum runners 75
Rum War 76, 77

Index

Rumsfeld, Donald 152
Rush-Bagot Agreement (1817) 154
Russia 61, 71, 156, 164, 175
Russian Federation 130

Safety at Sea Conference (1912)
Sailors, Marines, and Airmen Club 132
St. Louis, Missouri 116, 121
St. Petersburg, Florida 113, 137, 167
Salerno, Brian 160
Sam Flint, MV 36
San Diego, California 113
San Francisco, California 114, 124
San Francisco Chronicle 161
SAR 21
Sault Ste. Marie, Michigan 19, 69
School of Instruction 47, 53, 56, 58, 59, 82
Schweikart, Larry 13
Science and Technology Directorate 159
Sea Float 125
Search and Rescue (SAR) Stations 118
Seattle, Washington 111, 123, 169, 172
Second Coast Guard District 116
Secret Service 135
Secretary Class cutters 89
Semmes, Raphael 45
"Semper Paratus" 75, 94, 179
Sentinel Class FRCs 151, 162, 167–168
September 11, 2001, terrorist attacks 126, 138, 145, 152, 154
Seventeenth Coast Guard District 115, 119, 123, 164
Seventh Coast Guard District 127, 128
Shanksville, Pennsylvania 133, 138
Shell Oil Company 165, 174
Shepard, Leonard G. 40, 48–49, 51, 52, **53**, 54, 55
Sherman, John 49–50
ship inspection 116
ship monitoring and boarding 122–123
Shoemaker, Charles F. 37, 51, **55–58**
SHORAN 24
Siberia 72
Sibert, Stewart 166, 171
Siler, Owen W. 114, **115**, 116–118
Singapore Maritime Port Authority 170
Sixty ("60") Minutes 151
slavery 9
Smith, Edward H. "Iceberg" 90
Smith, Willard J. 110, **111**, 112–113, 114
South Korea 156
sovereignty claims and interests 159, 163, 169
Soviet Union 109, 127; *see also* former Soviet republics; Russia; Russian Federation; USSR
space shuttle support missions 122
Spanish-American War 12, 15, 58
Spanish Civil War 107

SPARS 86, 88
Speedwell, HMS 14
Spencer, John C. **40**, 41, 43, 44, 45
Split Rock Lighthouse 34
Squadron One (Vietnam) 108, 109, 118
Stanton, Edwin M. 46
State of the Coast Guard Addresses 148, 155, 157, 161
Steamboat Inspection Service 28, 35
Stone, Elmer F. 69
Stonehouse, Frederick 27, 32
"storm warriors" 30
Stosz, Sandra L. 155, 179
Stratton, Dorothy 83, 85–86, **87**, 97; *see also* SPARS
Strike Teams 117, 143
Strobridge, Truman R. 12, 16, 18, 20, 54, 72
Superior, Wisconsin 34, 76, 154
surf boats 30
Surface Naval Association 148
Surface Navy Association 168
Suzuki, Hisayasu 156
Swift Boats 125

Taft, William H. 22, **63**, 64
tanker safety and pollution 127
Team Coast Guard 88, 136, 165, 179
terrorist attacks *see* September 11, 2001; War on Terror
Thin Blue Line 172
Third Coast Guard District 103, 123
Thirteenth Coast Guard District 111
Thomas, Cari 179
Thomas, Gary M. 93–94, 179
Thompson, Warner K. 90
Three-Seventy-Eights (378s) 158
Three-Twenty-Sevens (327s) 89, 90
Titanic SS 64
Todd Shipyards 108
Tolman, George R. 33
Transportation Security Administration (TSA) 132, 135
Traverse City, Michigan 111, 113
Travis, William 14
Treasury Class cutters 89
Treasury Department *see* United States Department of Treasury
Trevitt, C.S. 48
tribal governments 164
Truman, Harry 93, 100
Turner, Richmond K. 99
Tuttle, Francis 63
TWA Flight 800 130
Twelfth Coast Guard District 114

United Airlines Flight 93 138
United Dry Dock Yard 78
United States: Air Force 92, 113; Armed

Index

Forces 77, 81, 83, 85, 89, 113, 124, 126, 148, 175, 177; Army 17, 18, 21, 45, 74, 83, 109, 121, 124, 140, 148; Border Patrol 77, 134–135; Coast Guard *see* Coast Guard; Department of Commerce 16, 18, 59, 146; Department of Customs 17, 45, 77, 117, 119, 124, 134, 140, 154; Department of Defense (DOD) 112 105, 117, 124, 158, 162, 177; Department of Homeland Security (DHS) 8, 126, 132, 133, 134–135, 140, 141, 142, 146, 147, 150, 157,158, 162, 171; Department of Immigration 59, 134, 140, 154; Department of Interior 146; Department of State 123, 169; Department of Transportation (DOT) 8, 109–110, 117, 122, 126, 141; Department of Treasury 7, 8, 20; Department of War 19, 72; Life-Saving Service 15, 26–38, 69; Lighthouse Service 15, 16–25, 69, 83; Marine Corps 7, 69, 78, 93, 99, 109, 135, 148, 166; Marshal Service 59; Merchant Marine 78, 88–89, 91, 98, 101, 103, 104, 127; Navigation and Steamboat Inspection Service 15, 93; Navy 7, 8, 14, 17, 45, 62–70, 71–73, 77–85, 90, 92–93, 99, 103, 105, 108–109, 113, 115, 119, 123–125, 133–134, 138–139, 141, 148, 152, 156, 164, 166, 168, 170, 173, 176, 178; Public Health Service 17, 18, 59, 65, 67, 105; Revenue Cutter Service Academy 83; Revenue Marine (Cutter) Service 7–15, 175, 176; Revenue School of Instruction 82; Secret Service 76

U.S. Coast Guard Academy *see* Coast Guard Academy
USCGAUX *see* Coast Guard Auxiliary
U.S. Coast Guard Destroyer Force 79
U.S. Coast Guard Headquarters 70, 84; *see also* Coast Guard Headquarters
U.S. Coast Guard in World War II 94, 98
U.S. Coast Guard Museum 114
U.S. Coast Guard Training Center 65
U.S. Coast Guard Cutters (USCGC): ; *Acushnet* 77; *Alex Haley* 174, 175; *Algonquin* 78; *American Sailor* 103; *Androscoggin* 98, 145; *Aquidneck* 170, 178; *Ariadne* 118; *Barataria* 121; *Bernard C. Webber*; *Bertholf* NSC 64, 65, 152, 158, *161*, 164, 165, 167; *Bibb* 89, 113; *Blackthorn* 161, 167; *Bothwell* 82; *Boutwell* 126; *Bramble* 105; *Campbell* 89, 103, 112; *Cape Morgan* 137; *Cape Upright* 176; *Casco* 126; *Cassin* 98; *Cayuga* 78, 107; *Champlain* 78; *Chelan* 78; *Citris* 145; *Comanche* 78; *Confidence* 177; *Corwin* 71; *Courier* 101; *Duane* 89; *Eagle* (WIX-327) 112, 153, 178; *Eastwind* 105; *Escanaba* 78, 107; *Flores* FRC 162, 167–168; *Forward* 153; *Gallatin* 118, 145; *Gresham* 96, 98; *Haida* 43 88, 98, 102, 103, 104; *Halibut* 166, 171; *Hamilton* CGC/NSC 89, 158, 167; *Harriet Lane* 176; *Healy* 57, 168, 169; *Herndon* 98, 102; *Ida Lewis* 132; *Ingham* 89; *Itasca* 78, 90; *Jarvis* 65; *Katmai Bay* 179; *Kimbal* 89l; *Mackinac* 74; *Mackinaw* 108, 111, 141; *Mariposa*, 121; *McCall* 97; *Mendota* 78, 113; *Midgett* 129, 132; *Modoc* 97; *Mohave* 79, 95, 96, 98, 102; *Mohawk* 78, 96, 168; *Monoghan* 98; *Morgenthau* 118; *Morrill* 96; *Nemesis* 107; *Northland* 89, 90; *Northwind* 105; *Onondaga* 74, 78, 96; *Ossippee* 69, 113; *Papaw* 153; *Patoka* 177; *Point Camden* 177; *Point Lomas* 132; *Point Wells* 177; *Polar Sea* 169; *Polar Star* 117, 169, 172; *Ponchartrain* 78, 97, 102; *Rambler* 177; *Red Beech* 153; *Reliance* 108; *Resolute* 124; *Ridley* 177; *Rush* 176; *Sagebrush* 118; *Saranac* 78, 110; *Scaly* 96; *Sebago* 78; *Seminole* 96; *Seneca* 96, 155, 172; *Shaw* 102, 107; *Shoshone* 78; *Snohomish* 82; *Spar* 105; *Spencer* 89; *Storis* 105; *Stratton* NSC 87, 152, 167; *Tahoe* 78; *Tahoma* 78, 80; *Tampa* 69, 155, 172; *Taney* 89, 108, 115, 160; *Valiant* 132; *Vigilant* 118, 137; *Waesche* NSC 84, 152, 158, 167, 168; *Wainwright* 102; *Walnut* 168; *Webber* 162; *Wilkes* 97, 107; *William R. Flores* FRC; *Yamacraw* 96; *Yeaton* 89
U.S. Commission on Ocean Policy 142
U.S. Fleet Patrol Force 96
U.S. Life-Saving Service Heritage Association 27, 93
U.S. Lighthouse Board 21
U.S. Merchant Marine Academy 104
U.S. Naval Academy *see* Naval Academy
U.S. Naval Institute 12, 149
U.S. Naval War College *see* Naval War College
U.S. Navy Memorial 178
U.S. Navy School of Aviation 69
U.S. Navy Ships (USS): *Aphrodite* 73, 74, 75; *Bayfield* 115; *Beale* 82, 83; *Constellation* 67; *Ericsson* 98; *Galena* 14; *Harvard* 58; *James* 79, 81; *Leonard Wood* 98–99; *Hunter Liggett* 115; *Leonard Wood* 98; *Marietta* 79, 81; *Monitor* 14; *Peacock* 14; *Tucker* 82; *Vance* 108; *Winslow* 15
U.S. News and World Report 155
U.S. Revenue Cutters (USRC): *Alabama* 14; *Alert* 40; *Algonquin* 56, 69; *Barry* 11, 13; *Bear* 11, 54, 61, 63, 68, 72, 79, 80; *Bering Strait* 114; *Bothwell* 82; *Chase* 49, 53, 58, 59, 67, 73, 79; *Corwin* 71, 72, 73; *Dobbin* 47; *E.A. Stevens* 14; *Eagle* 14; *Ewing* 40; *Fessenden* 11, 35; *Grant* 11; *Gresham* 56; *Harriet Lane* 10, 14, 42;

Hudson 15, 56; *Itasca* 58, 69; *James Madison* 13; *Jefferson* 13; *Lawrence* 42, 44, 45; *Levi Woodbury* 61, 67; *Lewis Cass* 55, 57; *Louisiana* 14; *Manning* 56, 58, 69; *Massachusetts* 9, 10; *McClane* 71; *McCulloch* 11, 15, 56; *Miami* 14, 45–46, 66; *Morrill* 68; *Onondaga* 56, 68; *Ossippe* 113; *Pamlico* 82; *Perry* 59; *Pickering* 9, 10; *Rush* 49; *Seminole* 11; *Seneca* 66, 69, 70; *Seward* 56; *Snohomish* 82; *Surveyor* 14; *Tampa* 69, 70; *Thetis* 59; *Washington* 56; *Windom* 53; *Winona* 11, 59; *Woodbury* 58, 61, 67; *Yamacraw* 69
USSR 124
University of Wisconsin-Superior 34

Van Boskerck, Francis S. 75
Vessels on Ice Patrol (1913)
Veterans Day commemorations 157, 172
Viele, Egbert L. 46
Vietnam War 108, 109, 112, 113, 118, 123, 124–125, 132, 133, 140, 145, 149–150, 172
Vigor Industrial Shipyard 172
Volpe, John "W" 113, 114
Volstead, Andrew J. 76

"W" 78
Waesche, Russell R. 61, 69, 82–84, **85**, 86–95, 97, 104, 106
Waesche, Russell R., Jr. 95
Wagner, Robert F. 108
Wake Island 126
War Department 19
War of 1812–1815 8, 11, 13
War on Terror 129, 133–136, 141, 147
War Shipping Administration 103
Ward, Norvell G. 109
Washington, George 7, 20, 167
Washington, D.C. 47, 65, 70, 131, 133, 137, 138, 139, 141, 178, 179; *see also* Coast Guard Headquarters

Washington (D.C.) Navy Yard 112
WAVES 85
weather patrol 116
Webber, Bernie 162–163
Webster, W. Russ 1–2
Weeden, Gary 170
Western Area Command 176
Whiting, William Fairchild **22**
Willoughby, Malcolm F. 94, 98–99, 104, 105, 123
Wilson, Woodrow 15, 60, 62, 64, 65, 66, 68, 70, 72, 84, 172
Windom, William 49, 52, 53
Women Afloat coordinator 178
women in the Coast Guard 157, 178–179; *see also* minorities; SPARS; specific names
Women Leadership Symposium (USCGA) 157
Women's Coast Guard Reserve 86
Woods, John, 36
World War I 8, 62, 68, 74, 79, 81, 84, 96, 155, 157, 172
World War I Memorial (USCG) 155, 157, 157
World War II 8, 11, 20, 24, 83–86, 88–95, 98, 103, 104, 108, 111, 113, 115, 146, 160
WPBs 109
Wrangle Island 72

Xuereb, Martin G. 170

Year of the Chief 166
Yost, Paul A., Jr. 121, 123–125, **126**, 128, 141
Young, Lam Yi 170

Zukunft, Paul 176, 177
Zumwalt, Elmo 113

www.ingramcontent.com/pod-product-compliance
Ingram Content Group UK Ltd.
Pitfield, Milton Keynes, MK11 3LW, UK
UKHW041958140426
5217IPUK00015B/855